Did She or Didn't She?

Also by Mart Martin

The Voyeur's Guide to Men and Women in the Movies

Did She or Didn't She?

Behind the Bedroom Doors of 201 Famous Women

MART MARTIN

A CITADEL PRESS BOOK
Published by Carol Publishing Group

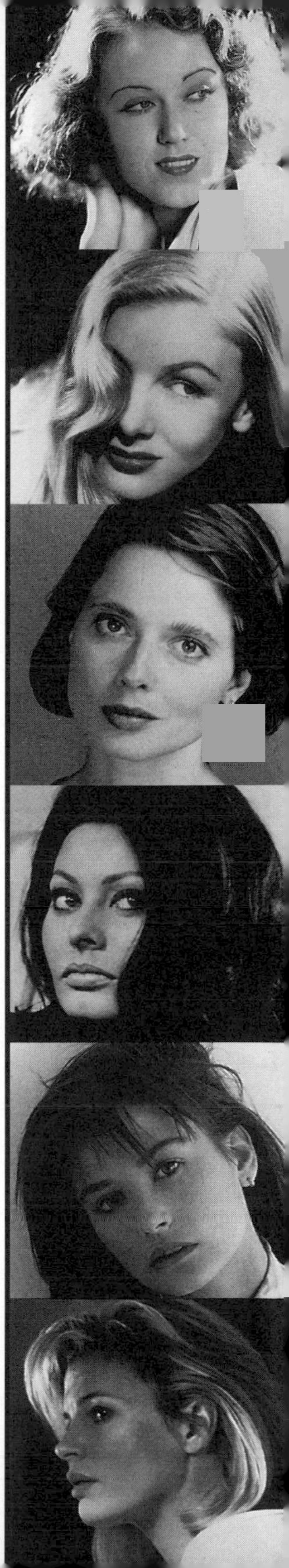

To the staff of the Reserve Desk and
Inter-Library Loan Department
of the
San Francisco Public Library.

Our public libraries and those who staff them
are truly national treasures.

A Citadel Press Book
Published by Carol Publishing Group
Citadel Press is a registered trademark of Carol Communications, Inc.

For editorial, sales and distribution, and queries regarding rights and permissions, write to Carol Publishing Group, 120 Enterprise Avenue, Secaucus, N.J. 07094

In Canada: Canadian Manda Group, One Atlantic Avenue, Suite 105, Toronto, Ontario M6K 3E7

Carol Publishing Group books are available at special discounts for bulk purchases, sales promotions, fund-raising, or educational purposes. Special editions can also be created to specifications.

Manufactured in the United States of America
10 9 8 7 6 5 4 3 2

Library of Congress Cataloging-in-Publication Data

Martin, Mart.
Did she or didn't she?: behind the bedroom doors of 201 famous women / Mart Martin.
p. cm.
"A Citadel Press book."
ISBN 0-8065-1669-0 (pbk.)
1. Actresses—United States—Biography. 2. Actresses—United States—Sexual behavior. 3. Celebrities—United States—Biography. 4. Celebrities—United States—Sexual behavior.
PN2285.M348 1995
791.43'028'092273—dc20
[B] 95-19918
CIP

Contents

Hollywood is no place for a woman to find a husband, especially her own.—Denise Darcel, actress

Preface

Did she or didn't she? Frankly, I don't know for certain—and it seems highly unlikely that anyone will ever know what's fact and what's fantasy about these women. What we do have to assist in our peeking is what they have told on themselves, along with what others have gossiped about them in various autobiographies, biographies, and reams of reminiscences.

Did she or didn't she . . . have a string of lovers and multiple marriages? A thirties drama queen summed up the frustration that women in the public eye must feel sometimes when she snapped, *"I'm not a star. I'm a woman!"*

Did she or didn't she . . . have a reputation among those who knew her that was vastly different from the public's perception of her? Many of these women did. For example, even though one woman wore ladylike white gloves and ended her life as a respected princess she was "like a cold dish with a man until you got her pants down, then she'd explode." Or so one of her many lovers tattled.

Did she or didn't she . . . make use of the infamous casting couch as she ascended to fame? Admittedly, some of these women made appearances there. One legend who did said, "Well, it sure as hell beat the hard cold floor." A sexpot from the fifties was even blunter. According to her, "The casting couch did exist and I did occasionally find myself on it. Many of us who made a career out of the movies did. Many, many more than want to admit it."

Did she or didn't she . . . always tell the truth about her love life? Hollywood gossip columnist Sheilah Graham, who knew many of these women quite well, said, "It has amused me to see how these ladies remember their pasts when interviewed on television—either too many men in their lives or too few—mostly the latter." Maybe director Alfred Hitchcock was being more honest that we realize when he told us,

"All love scenes started on the set are continued in the dressing room after the day's shooting is done."

My original intention when I began peeking around bedrooms was to concentrate solely on women from the cinema. Then, various other women began appearing with more and more frequency among the original cast of characters. It seemed as if they were almost demanding to be included. Especially since some of them had given so much—to so many—in order to reach their high station in life. All these women are public figures, most are performers, which has caused me to reach a conclusion about them. Their ultimate sexual consummation seems to be not between the sheets of a bed but on the sheets of the newsprint they've generated. Richard Porier in *The Performing Self* stated it most aptly when he said, "for artists, sometimes performing their art isn't enough, so they turn their lives into an artistic performance."

Did she or didn't she? We can only rely on the names, quoted remarks, facts, and information on these pages to help us try to decide. These came from innumerable books and journals—especially biographical and autobiographical works—anecdotal volumes dealing with specific individuals and films in general, articles, reviews, and interviews published in newspapers and magazines. The bibliography lists all this material for those interested in delving further into the lives of specific individuals.

Now, before turning this page to peek behind some interesting bedroom doors and wonder who we might find there, it would be wise to remember screenwriter Wilson Mizner's words about romantic involvements: "Some of the greatest love affairs I've known involved one actor or actress, unassisted."

Acknowledgments

I appreciate Mitch Rose, my agent, who believes in me when I set down a new path. It's always enjoyable working with an editor like Bruce Shostak, an expert at keeping a good idea from falling by that pathside. Copy editor Steve Boldt assisted me where I stumbled on the path. And there are simply too many others to thank personally who made certain that everything stayed on the chosen path. My special gratitude goes to Mary Ann Narvaez and Ed Hamilton, for making our daily time together so pleasant.

Did She or Didn't She?

June Allyson 1917–

✦ She Said

I always wanted to be a movie star. I thought it meant being famous and having breakfast in bed. I didn't know you had to be up at four A.M.

When people ask me what the hardest thing was for me in acting, I would say, "Singing a song." I could not read music, so I had to memorize everything.

✦ They Said

She isn't pretty. She certainly isn't sexy. She sings fairly well. She doesn't dance all that well, either. But she's got something. —Studio executive

She's got a voice like Jimmy Durante's. —Dick Powell, actor and husband

✦ First Sexual Experience

Unknown.

✦ Husbands

Dick Powell, actor-director (costar in *The Reformer and the Redhead,* '50)
Glenn Maxwell, barbershop owner
Dr. David Ashrow, surgeon

✦ Did You Know?

Hedda Hopper, to Allyson's extreme annoyance, asked during an interview if her breasts were real. Allyson merely replied, "Yes, ma'am."

Betsy Blair, who was in the chorus of *Panama Hattie* on Broadway with her, has said that Allyson developed a clever way of drawing attention to herself during the play's run. Blair claimed that on the nights Allyson knew someone important was in the audience, she would trip or fall down as the chorus exited. Allyson always got noticed and even drew a round of applause from the audience when she stood up again.

Lovers, Flings, or Just Friends?

- John F. Kennedy, U.S. president
- Alan Ladd, actor (costar in *The McConnell Story,* '55)
- Peter Lawford, actor (costar in *Good News,* '47)
- Dean Martin, singer-actor
- Jon Peterson, antique dealer
- David Rose, conductor-composer
- Jimmy Stewart, actor (costar in *The Glenn Miller Story,* '54)

Ursula Andress 1936–

✦ She Said

It seemed easy. All I had to do was run through the film with nothing on. —Referring to her exposure in *Dr. No* ('62)

I don't think that such a thing will make you a success. And if this is what success is based upon, no thank you! —Commenting in 1963 on why she wouldn't do a nude scene in a film

If the role demands it, then naturally I will remove my clothes. —Changing her mind by the late 1960s about doing a nude scene

I tell my conservative women friends who bother me about my youthful lover to "fuck off" or go get them one of their own. —Defending her relationship with younger lover Harry Hamlin, back when they were an item

✦ They Said

Ursula Andress. The name has always sounded like a spoonerism to me. —John Simon, critic

Ursula's emergence from the sea in Dr. No *is still unsurpassed in cinematic sexiness.* —*The Washington Post*

She's a bloody sex symbol and all that, and yet she's one of the nicest people you'll ever meet. —Peter O'Toole, who costarred with her in *What's New, Pussycat?* ('65)

✦ First Sexual Experience

Unknown.

✦ Husbands

John Derek, director-actor, spouse of sexually alluring women

✦ Did You Know?

Sophie's Choice author William Styron says he always "pictured Ursula Andress as Sophie: a wild lioness, a tangled mane of emotion." Meryl Streep, a far, far different type of actress from Andress, ended up playing the part and won an Oscar for it.

Lovers, Flings, or Just Friends?

- Jean-Paul Belmondo, French actor
- Marlon Brando, actor
- Sean Connery, actor (costar in *Dr. No,* '62)
- James Dean, actor
- John DeLorean, automaker
- Fausto Fagone, twenty-year-old Italian student
- Daniel Gelin, French actor
- Harry Hamlin, actor (costar in *Clash of the Titans,* '81)
- Dennis Hopper, actor
- Marcello Mastroianni, actor (costar in *The Tenth Victim,* '65)
- Ryan O'Neal, actor
- Peter O'Toole, actor (costar in *What's New, Pussycat?,* '65)
- Fabio Testi, Italian actor

Julie Andrews 1935–

Lovers, Flings, or Just Friends?

John Calley, cinema executive
Mike Nichols, director

✦ She Said

The four-letter words are flying, every other actress bares her bosom in one picture or another, the stories are becoming more and more trashy or totally far-out, and women have a worse and worse deal of it. I just want to make sure that if I go back to the screen, I don't make a fool of myself. I'm prepared to wait a few years until something right comes along. —Her reasons for almost ceasing to appear in films during the late 1970s

I'm an actress and the part called for it. I've always had a rather nice body, but people who had only seen my movies assumed I was either sexless or puritanical. —Explaining why she showed her boobs in husband Blake Edwards's satire *S.O.B.* ('81)

✦ They Said

She has sex appeal with dignity. Her sex appeal is subtle but glowing. —Bill Walsh, who worked with Andrews on *Mary Poppins* ('64)

She's got quite a cross to bear. I'd hate to be Mary Poppins. —Blake Edwards

The last of the really great dames. —Paul Newman, costar of *Torn Curtain* ('66)

✦ First Sexual Experience

Unknown, but probably her first husband, Tony Walton.

✦ Husbands

Tony Walton, British set and costume designer
Blake Edwards, director (directed her in *S.O.B.*, '81)

✦ Did You Know?

Andrews's romance with Blake Edwards began when she heard that he'd made the offhand remark that she was "so sweet she probably has violets between her legs." Highly amused at his comment, she sent him a bunch of violets and a note. Soon thereafter they began keeping company.

Lovers, Flings, or Just Friends?

- Lou Adler, music producer
- Peter Brown, actor
- Eddie Fisher, singer-actor
- Steve McQueen, actor (costar in *The Cincinnati Kid,* '65)
- Elvis Presley, singer-actor (costar in *Viva Las Vegas,* '64)
- Burt Sugarman, businessman

Ann-Margret 1941–

✦She Said

When a man tells me I'm sexy, it's the biggest compliment he can possibly pay me.

A man who is honest with himself wants a woman to be soft and feminine, careful of what she's saying, and to talk like a man.

Look at those silly films I did in Hollywood. They didn't exactly inspire me to have faith in my talent.

✦They Said

She was a lady. Everybody's wet dream. —Steve McQueen, actor and costar in *The Cincinnati Kid* ('65)

I'm the only person in this room who doesn't want to fuck you. —Maureen Stapleton, actress, at a screening of *Bye Bye Birdie* ('63) for an almost entirely male audience

Ann-Margret comes through dirty *no matter what she plays. She does most of her acting inside her mouth. She gleams with built-in innuendo. Men seem to have direct-action responses to Ann-Margret. They want to give her what she seems to be asking for.* —Pauline Kael, film critic

✦First Sexual Experience

Unknown.

✦Husbands

Roger Smith, actor-manager

✦Did You Know?

In a town obsessed with status symbols, particularly automobiles and lavish transportation, Ann-Margret once had one of the ritziest: a 14K-gold golf cart.

Elvis Presley once had a round, pink bed specially made for Ann-Margret.

Elizabeth Ashley 1939–

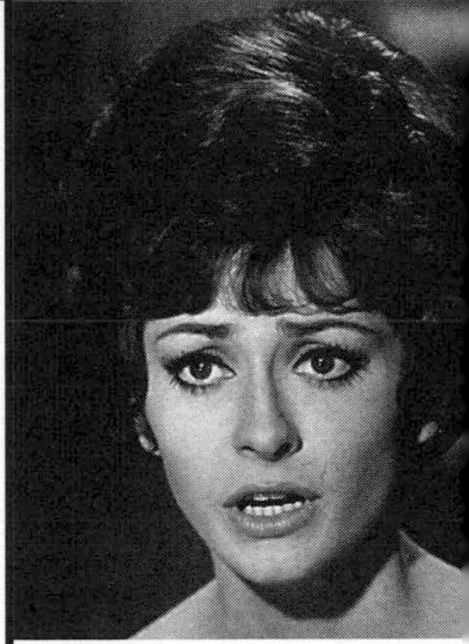

✦ She Said

My sexuality has always been very erratic. There are times when I couldn't be less interested in it and other times when I'm hardly interested in anything else.

I smoked a lot of dope. I made it with a lot of guys. I tried every way I could think of to act just as bad and outrageous as I could. —Referring to a "wild" period of her life in New York City

✦ They Said

Kid, you're as good-lookin' as Audrey Hepburn. Neither one of you has any tits. But you're a lot tougher and meaner and dirtier. —Marty Rackin, head of production at Paramount

✦ First Sexual Experience

Unknown.

✦ Husbands

James Farentino, actor
George Peppard, actor (costar in *The Third Day,* '65)
George Peppard, actor
James McCarthy, actor

✦ Did You Know?

Ashley had sex during the middle of the afternoon with novelist Tom McGuane in a Milford, Connecticut, movie house where *The Sting* ('73) was playing. He found the situation extremely amusing and said if the tabloids had known about it, they would have headlined, POPCORN, PUSSY AND POT! STAR BLOWS SCRIBE AT MILFORD MATINEE!

Lovers, Flings, or Just Friends?

Albert Finney, actor
Tom McGuane, novelist-screenwriter
Tom Nardini, actor

Lovers, Flings, or Just Friends?

- Jimmy Ash, actor
- John Barrymore Sr., actor (costar in *Beau Brummell,* '24)
- Russell Bradbury, studio executive
- Ronald Colman, actor
- Clark Gable, actor
- Ferris Hall, actor
- John Huston, director (directed her in *The Maltese Falcon,* '41)
- George S. Kaufman, playwright
- John Monk Saunders, screenwriter
- Bill Winslow, studio publicity executive

Mary Astor 1906–1987

✦ She Said

It was wonderful to fuck the sweet afternoon away. . . . I don't know where George [Kaufman] got his staying power! He must have cum three times in an hour! —Comment from Astor's notorious diary, which her second husband used against her in a divorce trial

Sexually, I was out of control, I was drinking too much. I found myself late in the evening thinking someone terribly attractive and wondering the next morning, "Why, why?"

✦ They Said

You are so goddamned beautiful you make me feel faint. —John Barrymore Sr., whispering in Astor's ear before shooting a scene

You may say I *did not keep a diary.* —George S. Kaufman, playwright

✦ First Sexual Experience

Lost her virginity to actor John Barrymore Sr. when she was only seventeen and he was in his forties.

✦ Husbands

Kenneth Hawkes, producer and brother of director Howard Hawks
Dr. Franklyn Thorpe, physician
Manuel "Mike" De Campo, Mexican socialite-playboy
Sgt. Thomas Gordon Wheelock, U.S. military

✦ Did You Know?

And what eventually happened to Astor's notorious diary after the divorce trial ended? It was impounded by the court and kept locked away until 1952, when it was burned, still unread by the general public and press.

Lauren Bacall 1924–

✦ She Said

I was a commodity, a piece of meat. —On how she thought Hollywood viewed her when she first arrived

I never believed marriage was a lasting institution. . . . I thought that to be married for five years was to be married forever.

✦ They Said

You can't jump every time he calls. He'll have no respect for you. —Bacall's mother telling the nineteen-year-old actress how to handle the forty-ish Humphrey Bogart

✦ First Sexual Experience

Probably lost her virginity to first husband Bogart, since she's said, "Nice Jewish girls stayed virgins until they were married." If she wasn't a nice Jewish girl, then maybe first love Kirk Douglas was the recipient.

✦ Husbands

Humphrey Bogart, actor (costar in *To Have and Have Not,* '44)
Jason Robards Jr., actor

✦ Did You Know?

Bacall was a friend and strong supporter of Democratic presidential candidate Adlai Stevenson. Marlene Dietrich once appeared on the set of Bacall's film *How to Marry a Millionaire* ('53) to tell her that Stevenson, with whom Dietrich was having one of her "mini-affairs," hadn't called her lately and that she couldn't understand why. She requested that if Bacall saw or heard from Stevenson, to please ask him to call. Bacall relayed the message, but wondered if Stevenson's feelings for Dietrich were beginning to wane.

Bacall was "engaged" to singer Frank Sinatra, which was supposed to be a well-kept secret. Somehow word got out, which appears to have annoyed "Ole Blue Eyes," and he speedily dumped the actress. Her opinion on how he acted in the situation: "He behaved like a complete shit."

Lovers, Flings, or Just Friends?

- Len Cariou, actor
- Kirk Douglas, actor (costar in *Young Man With a Horn,* '50)
- Harry Guardino, actor
- Basil Hoskins, actor
- Frank Sinatra, singer-actor
- Henry Stewart, businessman
- Peter Stone, playwright
- Emmanuel Ungaro, couturier

Lovers, Flings, or Just Friends?

Prince Carlo Borromeo, Italian nobleman

Ben Gazzara, actor

Robert Mitchum, actor (costar in *Mister Moses*, '65)

Franco Nero, actor

Carroll Baker 1931–

✦ She Said

The ability to act is of no importance to the jackals who run this industry.

It was a terrible stigma being a sex goddess. In the end it led to a nervous breakdown.

Frankly, I don't know how I survived the Hollywood rat race as long as I did without going completely nuts.

✦ They Said

Carroll Baker couldn't be sexy if she was spread-eagled naked on the cover of Life *magazine.* —Raquel Welch

More bomb than bombshell. —Judith Crist, film critic

✦ First Sexual Experience

Lost her virginity to Louie Ritter when he attacked her in a train compartment while traveling to Los Angeles. He later married her.

✦ Husbands

Louie Ritter, hotel owner
Jack Garfein, director
Donald Burton, actor

✦ Did You Know?

Baker has claimed that when she and Marilyn Monroe auditioned at the same time for Lee Strasberg's Actors Studio in New York, she overheard playwright Paddy Chayefsky, one of the judges, comment after he first saw Marilyn, "Oh, boy, would I like to fuck that."

Josephine Baker 1906–1975

✦ She Said

I'm not immoral, I'm only natural.

If I'm going to be a success, I must be scandalous. I must amuse people.

The whores of the streets of Paris are wearing my jewels. —Bemoaning the fact that she had been forced to sell her jewels

✦ They Said

She was looking for the perfect penis and she was looking hard. —Anonymous Austrian actor reflecting on her sojourn in Berlin and the lines of men he saw outside her dressing room

She is the Nefertiti of now. —Pablo Picasso, artist

She was a tiger lily out of a scum pond. —Nathan B. Young, judge, who knew of her childhood

✦ First Sexual Experience

Probably lost her virginity to her first husband, since she married him when she was thirteen.

✦ Husbands

Willie Wells, foundry worker
William Howard Baker, Pullman porter
Jean Lion, millionaire sugar broker
Jo Bouillon, orchestra leader

✦ Did You Know?

During her period with the Folies-Bergère in Paris, Baker would spend an hour each day scrubbing herself all over with lemons in an attempt to make herself "whiter."

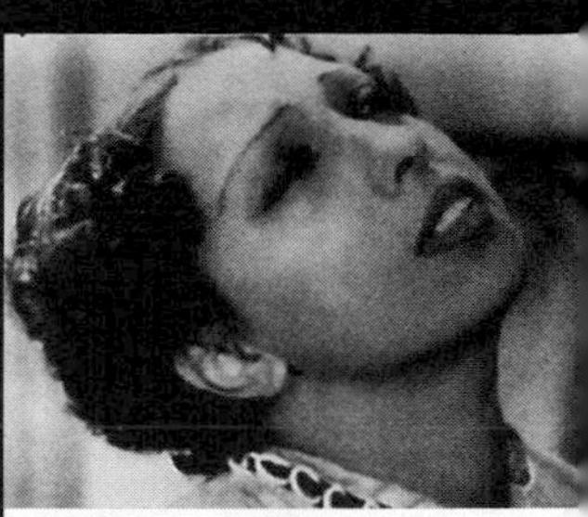

Lovers, Flings, or Just Friends?

- Ahmed ben Bachir, court chamberlain to the caliph of Spanish Morocco
- George Balanchine, choreographer
- "Bricktop," Parisian cafe/nightclub owner-singer
- Alexander Calder, sculptor
- Maurice Chevalier, singer-actor
- Colette, author
- Paul Colin, painter
- Ralph Cooper, producer of amateur nights at Harlem's Apollo Theatre
- Gaston Doumergue, president of France
- El Glaouni, the pasha of Marrakesh, Morocco
- Duke Ellington, composer-musician
- Gustav, crown prince of Sweden (and later King Gustav VI Adolf)
- Ernest Hemingway, author
- Libby Holman, singer
- Claude Hopkins, bandleader
- Le Corbusier, French architect
- Maharajah of Kapurthala, Indian nobleman
- Benito Mussolini, Italian dictator
- Juan Perón, Argentinian dictator and husband of ex-film-star Evita
- Pablo Picasso, artist
- Jacques Pills, French singer and later the first Mr. Edith Piaf
- Luigi Pirandello, Italian playwright
- Max Reinhardt, director
- George Simenon (George Sim), author and creator of The Saint
- Clara Smith, singer
- *and,* as Josephine phrased it, "thousands of lovers," both male and female

Lovers, Flings, or Just Friends?

S. N. Behrman, author-screenwriter

Milton Berle, comedian

Pandro S. Berman, RKO producer

Harry P. Cohn, head of Columbia Pictures

Broderick Crawford, actor

Johnny DeVita, hometown boy

Pat DiCiccio (DiCicco), playboy (and the first Mr. Thelma Todd and the first Mr. Gloria Vanderbilt)

Brian Donlevy, actor

Paul Douglas, actor

Henry Fonda, actor (costar in *Yours, Mine and Ours,* '68)

Roger Furse, photographer

Mack Grey, bodyguard-companion to George Raft

Alexander Hall, director

Fred Kohlmar, casting director

Peter Lawford, actor

Russell Markert, choreographer (whose dance troupe later transformed into the Rockettes)

Gene Markey, screenwriter-producer

Robert Mitchum, actor

George Raft, actor

Bennie Rubin, RKO talent scout

George Sanders, actor (costar in *Lured,* '47)

Franchot Tone, actor (costar in *Her Husband's Affairs,* '47)

Orson Welles, actor-director

and probably some "beaus" around Jamestown, New York, where Lucy was referred to by some as the town "hussy."

Lucille Ball 1911–1989

✦ She Said

Love? I was always *falling in love!*

My name is Lucille Ball. If lost, return me to my master—Desi. —Inscription on a bracelet Lucy wore for a while in the late 1940s

✦ They Said

Lucille wasn't the kind of girl you took home to meet mother. —Monroe Greenthal, press agent

She looked like a two-dollar whore who had been badly beaten by her pimp. She had a black eye, her hair was hanging down in her face, and her skin-tight dress was coming apart at the seams. —Desi Arnaz, remembering his first glimpse of Lucy

I never knew Lucille to be the sort of girl who would throw herself at men, but if someone propositioned her and she was genuinely attracted to him, he had a good chance of getting somewhere. —Kay Vaughan, friend

✦ First Sexual Experience

Possibly lost her virginity to Johnny DeVita, a local hoodlum in Jamestown, New York, whom she dated when she was fourteen and he was twenty-one.

✦ Husbands

Desi Arnaz III, actor and bandleader

Gary Morton, actor-entertainer

✦ Did You Know?

Broderick Crawford was rumored to have given Lucy a black eye when she broke off their engagement and refused to return the ring.

In late 1944, tired of Desi's womanizing, Lucy filed for divorce. He called the night before their hearing and invited her out to dinner. They ended up spending the night together, and Desi was amazed the next morning when Lucy jumped out of bed, worried that she'd be late for the court appointment. She attended the hearing, then proceeded to return to Desi for an afternoon and another night of lovemaking. The following day they announced the divorce was off, because under California law if a couple had sex during the one-year waiting period, the divorce was invalid. Lucy and Desi remained married another seventeen years.

Tallulah Bankhead 1902–1968

✦ She Said

I don't know what *I am, dahling. I've tried several varieties of sex. The conventional position makes me claustrophobic, and all the others give me either a stiff neck or lockjaw.*

My father warned me about men and booze, but he never mentioned a word *about women and cocaine.*

Cocaine isn't habit-forming. I should know—I've been using it for years.

✦ They Said

I suppose you could say Tallulah was a tramp in the elegant sense. —Tennessee Williams, playwright, whose play *The Milk Train Doesn't Stop Here Anymore* starred the actress

Tallulah burns her candle at all ends. —Cecil Beaton, costume-scenic designer

A day away from Tallulah is like a month in the country. —Howard Dietz, lyricist

A parrot around Tallulah must feel as frustrated as a kleptomaniac in a piano store. —Fred Allen, humorist

✦ First Sexual Experience

Was seduced at age sixteen by Hope Williamson, a nineteen-year-old aspiring actress. She later said that she lost her "technical" (presumably meaning to a male) to Lord Alington when she was appearing on the stage in London.

✦ Husbands

John Emery, actor

✦ Did You Know?

Arriving at one Hollywood party, Tallulah spotted Errol Flynn. She rushed over, bellowing, "Errol dahling," fell to her knees, and buried her face in his crotch. As she was leaving, she encountered Lillian Gish, who expressed her pleasure at seeing Tallulah again, commenting on how well both of them were still doing after all the years that had passed. Tallulah, not to be outdone, said, "Dear Lillian, and here we are, still surviving after all these years, you with your face lifted and your vagina dropped, and me with my vagina lifted and my face dropped."

Lovers, Flings, or Just Friends?

Cleveland Amory, writer
John Barrymore Sr., actor
Robert Benchley, humorist
Gladys Bentley, singer
Leonard Bernstein, conductor-composer
Marlon Brando, actor
Yul Brynner, actor
Winston Churchill, British statesman
Gary Cooper, actor (costar in *The Devil and the Deep,* '32)
Katharine Cornell, actress
Helmut Dantine, actor
Douglas Fairbanks Jr., actor
Dave Garroway, TV personality
Billie Holliday, singer
Libby Holman, singer
Patsy Kelly, actress
William Langford, actor
Beatrice "Bea" Lillie, comedienne
Fredric March, actor (costar in *My Sin,* '31)
Hattie McDaniel, actress (and Scarlett O'Hara's "Mammy")
Burgess Meredith, actor
Robert Montgomery, actor (costar in *Faithless,* '32)
Edward R. Murrow, journalist
Johnny Ray, singer
Robert Ryan, actor
Lilyan Tashman, actress
Laurette Taylor, actress
Sybil Thorndyke, actress
Walter Wanger, producer
Johnny Weissmuller, actor
John Hay "Jock" Whitney, socialite-businessman
plus lots of other men and women

Lovers, Flings, or Just Friends?

Milton Berle, comedian-actor

Theda Bara 1890–1955

✦She Said

I'm going to continue doing vampires as long as people sin. For I believe that humanity needs the moral lesson and it needs it in repeatedly larger doses. —Remarking about how long she would continue to play her famous role as a "vamp"

To understand those grand days with the world of movies so new and all, we have to remember that people believed what they saw on the screen. Nobody had then destroyed their illusion. They thought the stars of the screen were the way they saw them. Nobody had knocked down any of their idols. Now—they know—it's all just make-believe.

✦They Said

She is pretty bad, but not enough to be remembered always. —Alexander Woollcott, critic

So, for years they thought Theda Bara was the wickedest woman in the world. Yet, as far as I know, there was never one word of gossip about Theda Bara of any kind, anytime, anywhere. —Adela Rogers St. Johns, author

✦First Sexual Experience

Unknown.

✦Husbands

Charles Brabin, director (directed her in *La Belle Russe,* '19)

✦Did You Know?

Bara once touched a hat in a New York City department store; after she left, a mob of women broke windows and left merchandise strewn all over the floor because they were all trying to get to the hat and touch it in order to acquire some of her "power" over men.

Among the clauses in a three-year contract that Bara signed in 1916 were those that said she must (a) be heavily veiled while in public, (b) could only go out at night, and (c) must close the curtains on her limousine.

Brigitte Bardot 1934–

✦ She Said

I have always adored beautiful young men. Just because I grow older my taste doesn't change. So if I can still have them, why not?

I prefer to be naked in the sun. —Perhaps why she quit appearing in films where she was famed for shedding her clothes

. . . now spending my time trying to erase the Bardot legend. —Describing her life since she quit appearing in films

✦ They Said

She took to lovemaking with extraordinary intensity. Sometimes she held up a mirror so she could see me making love to her. —Roger Vadim, tattling as only an ex-spouse can

All I can say is that when I'm trying to play serious love scenes with her, she's positioning her bottom for the best angle shots. —Stephen Boyd

Seeing her dance, a saint would be tempted. —Simone de Beauvoir, French author–social critic

✦ First Sexual Experience

Lost her virginity to Roger Vadim, who met and pursued her when she was only fifteen.

✦ Husbands

Roger Vadim, French director (directed her in *. . . And God Created Woman,* '56)
Jacques Charrier, French actor
Gunther Sachs, German millionaire playboy
Bernard d'Ormale, French politician

✦ Did You Know?

Bardot has attempted suicide at least four times—the first when she was fifteen. Her methods have ranged from taking an overdose of sleeping pills to walking into the ocean to drown.

Bardot's family were such devout Catholics, and moralists, that they forced Roger Vadim to spend his wedding night on the family's living room sofa. He and Brigitte had only held the civil ceremony, with the religious ceremony scheduled for the next day; in her family's eyes, the couple wasn't "properly" married yet.

Lovers, Flings, or Just Friends?

Gilbert Bécaud, singer
Jean-Paul Belmondo, actor
Stephen Boyd, actor (costar in *Les Bijoutiers du Claire de Lune,* '58)
Miroslav Brozek, actor-sculptor
Alain Carre, secretary-companion
Henri-Georges Clouzot, director
Sean Connery, actor (costar in *Shalako,* '68)
Olivier Despax, French television star
Sacha Distel, French singer
Jicky Dussart, photographer
Michel Engels, publisher
Sami Frey, actor (costar in *La Vérité,* '61)
Serge Gainsbourg, French songwriter
Patrick Gilles, young lover (costar in *Les Femmes,* '69)
François Giuletti, bartender
Jean-Noel Grinda, tennis player
Mick Jagger, singer-actor
Louis Jourdan, actor (costar in *La Mariée est trop belle,* '56)
Christian Kalt, bartender–tattling author–lover
Louis Malle, director
Luigi Rizzi, Italian nightclub owner
Gustavo Rojo, Spanish actor
Michael Sarne, singer-actor-director (costar in *A Coeur joie,* '67)
Laurent Terzieff, French actor (costar in *A Coeur joie,* '67)
Jean-Louis Trintignant, French actor (costar in *. . . And God Created Woman,* '56)
Raf Vallone, Italian actor

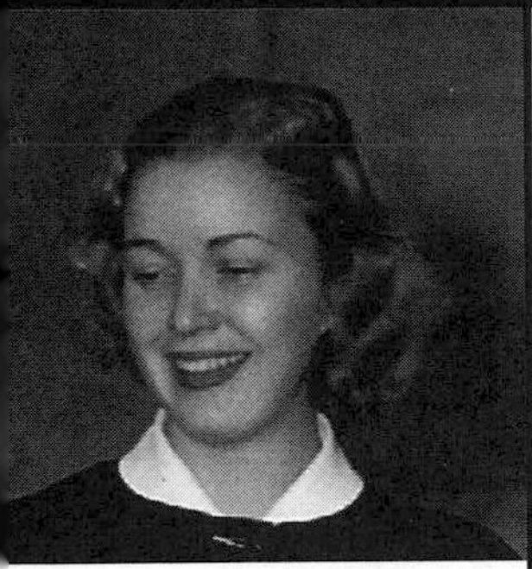

Lovers, Flings, or Just Friends?

Eddie Albert, actor (costar in *Eagle Squadron,* '42)
George Brent, actor
Rory Calhoun, actor
Fred de Cordova, producer
Brian Donlevy, actor (costar in *Nightmare,* '42)
Anthony Drexel Duke, society heir
Leif Erickson, actor
Tom Farrell, drinking buddy
Henry Fonda, actor
Alan Hale Jr., actor
Jon Hall, actor (costar in *Eagle Squadron,* '42)
Van Heflin, actor
Jack "Lash" LaRue, actor
Sinclair Lewis, author-playwright
Victor Mature, actor
John McNeill, a "pickup" trick
Don Porter, actor
Baron Eric Rothschild, society heir
Robert Stack, actor (costar in *Eagle Squadron,* '42)
Glenn Stensel, actor
Jimmy Stewart, actor

Diana Barrymore 1921–1960

✦She Said

I was married, but I loved to flirt. I couldn't help it. It belonged to the excitement of being alive.

I don't mind being punched. Noel Coward said women should be struck regularly like a gong, and he's right. Women are no damn good.

✦They Said

Let those machines get hold of you and they'll ruin you. Look what they did to your father. —Blanche Oelrichs Thomas (aka Michael Stranger, poetess), her mother, warning her about making films

She was very oversexed, that girl . . . couldn't get enough. If I needed her for a shot, she could always be found in one of the men's dressing rooms. —Arthur Lubin, who directed her first film, *Eagle Squadron* ('42)

Diana is a horse's arse, quite a pretty one, but still a horse's arse. —John F. Barrymore, her father

You simply must not drink like that. You know how your father drinks—it might be inherited. —Cobina Wright Sr., society hostess

✦First Sexual Experience

Probably lost her virginity to Anthony Drexel Duke, a socialite heir to the Duke tobacco fortune and related to three of society's "biggest" family names—the Biddles, the Dukes, and the Drexels. Diana was briefly engaged to him.

✦Husbands

Bramwell Fletcher, actor
John Howard, tennis pro
Robert Wilcox, actor

✦Did You Know?

Diana once became obsessed with marrying homosexual playwright Tennessee Williams, spending a couple of years scheming with two of his best female friends to lure him into marriage with her. Tennessee didn't take Diana's bait.

Barrymore was once scrambling eggs when, strange as it seems, she managed to fall into the skillet and ended up with second-degree burns on her buttocks.

Kim Basinger 1954–

✦ She Said

These are the fields where I learned oral sex. —Describing the small town she bought—Braselton, Georgia—near where she grew up.

There are many things to do other than intercourse. And they're so much more sensual and fun, as nasty and powerful. And I adored every one of them.

Women are cynical about being used as sex objects. Which is a shame, because it's fun to use your sexuality.

✦ They Said

Just looking at her makes me want to screw her. —Menachem Golan, producer

Kim is so perfect—face, features, and figure—that she looks like someone made not by nature but by an artist. —Nestor Almendros, cinematographer

✦ First Sexual Experience

Unknown.

✦ Husbands

Ron Britton, makeup artist
Alec Baldwin, actor (costar in *The Marrying Man,* '91)

✦ Did You Know?

There's a rumor that before her marriage Basinger "tried" out all of her male costars, then rated their performance in her diary.

Lovers, Flings, or Just Friends?

Jeff Bridges, actor (costar in *Nadine,* '87)

Sean Connery, actor (costar in *Never Say Never Again,* '83)

Richard Gere, actor (costar in *No Mercy,* '86)

Michael Keaton, actor (costar in *Batman,* '89)

Jon Peters, hairdresser-producer

Prince, singer-actor

Robert Redford, actor (costar in *The Natural,* '84)

Burt Reynolds, actor (costar in *The Man Who Loved Women,* '83)

Dale Robinette, model

Mickey Rourke, actor (costar in *9 1/2 Weeks,* '86)

Phil Walsh, fitness trainer

Lovers, Flings, or Just Friends?

Russell Birdwell, agent

Yul Brynner, actor (costar in *The Ten Commandments,* '56)

Peter Lawford, actor

Joseph L. Mankiewicz, screenwriter-director (directed her in *All About Eve,* '50)

George Montgomery, actor

Gregory Ratoff, director

John Shelton, actor

Anne Baxter 1923–1985

✦ She Said

A marriage is happier when a man is more or less the sun and the woman's in the shadow, and what actress wants to be in the shadows?

The minute any woman has any brains in Hollywood, it's supposed to cancel them sexually. They didn't know how to sell them if they can't sell them sexually.

✦ They Said

In Hollywood, Miss Baxter is known for three things—driving ambition, unlimited energy, and a completely honest, if occasionally withering, tongue. —John Gold, British critic

She was a very small woman. —Gene Foote, actor

✦ First Sexual Experience

Unknown.

✦ Husbands

John Hodiak, actor (costar in *Homecoming,* '48)
Randolph Galt, Australian rancher
David Klee, banker

✦ Did You Know?

Baxter was fired from the stage production of *The Philadelphia Story* (which also starred Katharine Hepburn) during its pre-Broadway tryouts in 1939.

Baxter's best screen moment was when she played Eve in *All About Eve* ('50). While many people are aware that her costar Bette Davis was a last-minute replacement for an injured Claudette Colbert, few realize that Baxter herself was also a replacement. Her role (as the scheming wanna-be actress Eve) was originally scheduled for Jeanne Crain, but she became pregnant and had to drop out.

Constance Bennett 1904–1965

✦ She Said

Hollywood's gossipmongers have gleefully reported me as being in the arms of first one, then another. Anyone who habitually reads the fan magazines and newspaper chatter-columns might well conclude that I am a female Casanova, and that I cry my loves from the house-tops.

No! Five years from now, when I am married and have a family, I don't want pictures of me in underwear staring at me from the Police Gazette. —Refusing to pose for cheesecake photos in Hollywood

✦ They Said

She was crazy about money and sex. —Irene Mayer Selznick, daughter of MGM's Louis B. and wife of producer David O. Selznick

She had a reputation around Hollywood for attracting other girls' men, though on purpose or not, I don't know. —Adela Rogers St. Johns, author

Her face was her talent, and when it dropped, so did her career, right out of sight! —Bette Davis

✦ First Sexual Experience

Probably lost her virginity to first husband Chester Moorhead, whom she married when she was seventeen.

✦ Husbands

Chester Moorhead, student
Philip Morgan Plant, heir to a steamship company
James Henri Le Bailly de la Falaise, Marquis de la Coudraye (and the third Mr. Gloria Swanson)
Gilbert Roland, actor (costar in *Our Betters,* '33)
Brig. Gen. John Theron Coulter, U.S. Army

✦ Did You Know?

Constance Bennett was well-known for her business acumen and loved to accumulate money. Her father, actor Richard Bennett, was once asked why she persisted in working so hard while placing a high emphasis on her money. Doesn't she realize she can't take it with her? they posed. He replied about his headstrong daughter, "If she can't take it with her, she won't go."

Lovers, Flings, or Just Friends?

Joel McCrea, actor (and costar in *Born to Love,* '31)
David O. Selznick, producer

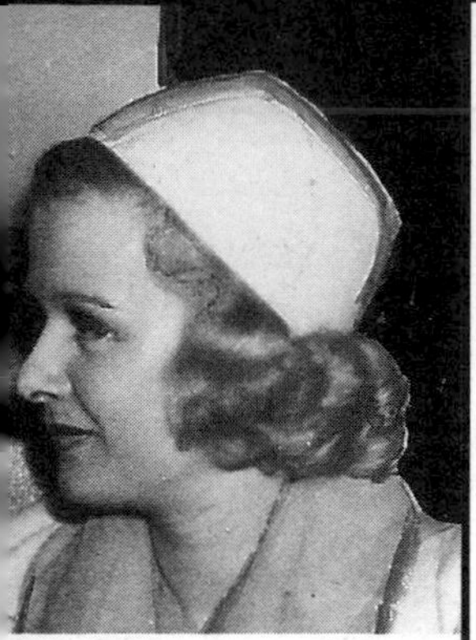

Lovers, Flings, or Just Friends?

- John Considine Jr., Feature Film Co. executive
- Donald Cook, actor
- Bing Crosby, singer-actor (costar in *Mississippi,* '35)
- Lord Dudley, British aristocrat
- John Emery, actor
- Charles Feldman, agent
- Errol Flynn, actor
- Jennings Lang, agent
- John McClain, theater critic
- George Jean Nathan, critic
- Myron Selznick, her agent and brother of producer David O.
- Jack Thompson, entertainer
- Spencer Tracy, actor (costar in *She Wanted a Millionaire,* '32)

Joan Bennett 1910–1990

✦She Said

I suppose it there was a such a thing as a conventional Bennett, I was it. —Referring to the well-publicized antics of her mother, father, and two sisters, all of whom had multiple marriages and love affairs

Because I happen to be an actress, I see no reason to forfeit every claim to plain old garden-variety intelligence and common sense.

✦They Said

She seemed to be the quintessence of a movie star. Everything about her shone—her burnished head, her jewels, her famous smile, her lovely long legs, and the highly publicized fact that she pulled down thirty thousand bucks a week. —David Niven, actor

✦First Sexual Experience

Probably lost her virginity to John (Jack) Fox, shortly before she married him when she was sixteen years old.

✦Husbands

John (Jack) Marion Fox, businessman
Gene Markey, screenwriter (who was also the third Mr. Myrna Loy and the second Mr. Hedy Lamarr)
Walter Wanger, producer
David Wilde, author-publisher

✦Did You Know?

On December 13, 1951, Bennett's husband, producer Walter Wanger, shot her lover (and agent) Jennings Lang. Wanger had discovered the affair sometime earlier and threatened that he would "take care" of any man who attempted to break up his marriage. He ended up being sentenced to four months in prison for the assault. Lang lost something more as a result of the encounter: a testicle.

Candice Bergen 1946–

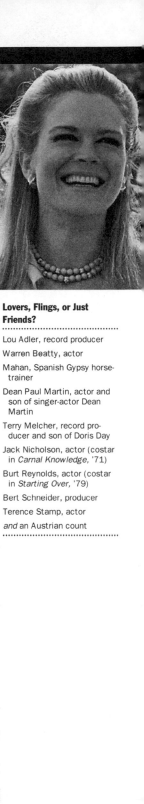

✦ She Said

Most men are such jerks about beautiful women, it's hard not to despise them.

I always thought actress *was synonymous with* fool.

Hollywood is like Picasso's bedroom.

✦ They Said

She's a really pretty girl with appalling taste in men. There's something spinsterish about her. —Truman Capote, writer and social gadfly

I don't think of her as a porcelain creature. I think of her in blue jeans and pigtails. —Frances Bergen, her mother

✦ First Sexual Experience

Unknown.

✦ Husbands

Louis Malle, French director

✦ Did You Know?

Bergen hated to try to explain to her foreign friends that her father was a ventriloquist (*i.e.*, that he made his living "talking" to wooden dummies on the radio, so she'd just say he was in real estate.

Lovers, Flings, or Just Friends?

- Lou Adler, record producer
- Warren Beatty, actor
- Mahan, Spanish Gypsy horse-trainer
- Dean Paul Martin, actor and son of singer-actor Dean Martin
- Terry Melcher, record producer and son of Doris Day
- Jack Nicholson, actor (costar in *Carnal Knowledge,* '71)
- Burt Reynolds, actor (costar in *Starting Over,* '79)
- Bert Schneider, producer
- Terence Stamp, actor
- *and* an Austrian count

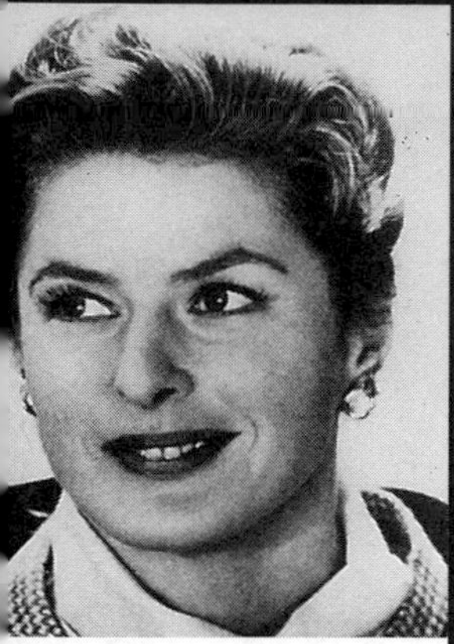

Lovers, Flings, or Just Friends?

- Larry Adler, musician
- Robert Anderson, playwright
- Charles Bernheim, American-based French businessman
- Yul Brynner, actor (costar in *Anastasia,* '56)
- Lt. Gen. Simon Bolivar Buckner Jr., U.S. military
- Robert Capa, photographer
- Gary Cooper, actor (costar in *Saratoga Trunk,* '45)
- Joseph Cotten, actor (costar in *Gaslight,* '44)
- Bing Crosby, actor (costar in *The Bells of St. Mary's,* '45)
- Victor Fleming, director (directed her in *Dr. Jekyll and Mr. Hyde,* '41)
- Leslie Howard, actor (costar in *Intermezzo,* '39)
- Burgess Meredith, actor
- Gregory Peck, actor (costar in *Spellbound,* '45)
- Anthony Quinn, actor (costar in *The Visit,* '64)
- David O. Selznick, producer
- Omar Sharif, actor (costar in *The Yellow Rolls-Royce,* '64)
- Spencer Tracy, actor (costar in *Dr. Jekyll and Mr. Hyde,* '41)
- *plus* many other actors and directors

Ingrid Bergman 1915–1982

✦She Said

Even if the whole world should fall upon me, I don't care. This is my child and I want it. —Commenting on her pregnancy carrying the "love child" of Italian director Roberto Rossellini

With everyone being naked in films today, I wouldn't want to act if I had to start now.

✦They Said

She had a certain aspect of her that was almost masculine. She was so professional. When studio people would pinch her ass or something, she'd give them a dry smile as if they were men in a locker room. —Christopher Isherwood, screenwriter on *Rage in Heaven* ('41)

Ingrid told me often that she couldn't work well unless she was in love with either the leading man or the director. —Peter Lindstrom, her first husband

She'd do it with doorknobs." —Alfred Hitchcock, director, who directed her in several films

Ingrid wasn't interested in sex all that much. She did it like a polite girl. —Larry Adler, musician who had an affair with her

But she doesn't do the things a whore does. —Roberto Rossellini, who got her pregnant and destroyed her first marriage, annoyed that Bergman wouldn't fellate him

✦First Sexual Experience

Probably lost her virginity to her first husband, since he appears to have been the first man with whom she ever had a real date.

✦Husbands

Petter (Peter) Lindstrom, Swedish doctor
Roberto Rossellini, Italian director (directed her in *Stromboli,* '50)
Lars Schmidt, Swedish theatrical producer

✦Did You Know?

During the making of *Goodbye Again* ('61), Bergman attempted to seduce costar Anthony Perkins, who was homosexual during that period, by inviting him to her dressing room to rehearse a kissing scene. He went, but insisted on standing near the door, which he kept open.

Jacqueline Bisset 1944–

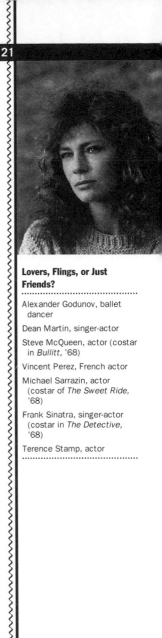

✦ She Said

Marriage seems to be a word which finishes a relationship. It doesn't start it. I think people should stop talking about your living together and start living themselves.

I'm fascinated by a man with a twinkle in his eye.

✦ They Said

One of the greatest bodies I've ever worked with. —Edith Head, costume designer

She has one of the most gorgeous faces in the world—those eyes! But she has black, straggly, thin hair. And she loves it that way. —Ross Hunter, producer

You happen to be a rather pretty girl, but it has nothing to do with you *and it won't last anyway, so go out and develop yourself as a person.* —Bisset's father, giving her some advice early in life

✦ First Sexual Experience

Unknown.

✦ Husbands

Victor Drai, jeans manufacturer–producer

✦ Did You Know?

Roman Polanski, who was arrested for sexual relations with a minor female after he'd taken "erotic" photographs of her at Jack Nicholson's house, planned at first to use Bisset's home for the photo shoot. He decided that the light was "wrong" at her house that day, so he went over to Nicholson's, where all his troubles began.

Lovers, Flings, or Just Friends?

- Alexander Godunov, ballet dancer
- Dean Martin, singer-actor
- Steve McQueen, actor (costar in *Bullitt,* '68)
- Vincent Perez, French actor
- Michael Sarrazin, actor (costar of *The Sweet Ride,* '68)
- Frank Sinatra, singer-actor (costar in *The Detective,* '68)
- Terence Stamp, actor

Lovers, Flings, or Just Friends?

Bing Crosby, singer-actor

Charles Feldman, agent-producer

Hal Hayes, millionaire architect

Lewis Warner, son of Harry Warner, one of the brothers in Warner Bros. studios

Joan Blondell 1909–1979

✦She Said

Picture people aren't like stage people. . . . They can't laugh at themselves as we vaudeville folks used to do.

I'd be a far bigger star today if I'd concentrated on my career.

I always had one leg on the movie set and one leg at home.

✦They Said

For me the sexiest woman on the screen ever was Joan Blondell. —George C. Scott, actor

We must put brassieres *on Joan Blondell and make her cover up her breasts or we are going to have these pictures stopped in a lot of places. I believe in showing their forms, but, for Lord's sake, don't let those* bulbs *stick out.* —Jack L. Warner, studio head, in a memo to Hal Wallis, producer

Joan Blondell always a little drunk. —F. Scott Fitzgerald, writer, in one of his notebooks

✦First Sexual Experience

Possibly lost her virginity in Dallas, Texas, in her late teens when she was assaulted and possibly raped by an Oklahoma millionaire who was giving her a ride home.

✦Husbands

George Barnes, cameraman
Dick Powell, actor-director
Michael Todd, producer (who was also the third Mr. Elizabeth Taylor)

✦Did You Know?

When she was married to actor Dick Powell, and they were both under contract to Warners Bros. studios, many people around the lot referred to the duo as Big Tits and Dopey.

During her marriage to Todd, Blondell frequently suffered from his legendary violent temper—he broke her arm on one occasion during a fight.

Claire Bloom 1931–

✦She Said

I like to work in Hollywood, but I don't like to live there. I'm too young to die.

The problem of fading beauty in a woman is one of the most powerful themes not only of drama, but of life itself.

✦They Said

She could not be more beautiful without upsetting the balance of nature. —Walter Kerr, drama critic

She is not a nice Nelly and she has no inhibitions. —George Cukor, director

✦First Sexual Experience

Unknown.

✦Husbands

Rod Steiger, actor (costar in *Three Into Two Won't Go,* '69)
Hilliard Elkins, producer
Philip Roth, author (who wrote *Portnoy's Complaint*)

✦Did You Know?

While Bloom was filming *Limelight* ('52) with Charlie Chaplin, Buster Keaton, also in the film, did an unusual thing. After days of being on the set and maintaining a silent, noncommunicative stance toward Bloom, he suddenly approached her. He withdrew a postcard from his pocket, which showed a large, elaborate mansion. He carefully explained in a soft, friendly voice that the house had once been his Hollywood home. Then, he returned the postcard to his pocket and never again spoke to her on the set.

Lovers, Flings, or Just Friends?

Richard Burton, actor (costar in *Look Back in Anger,* '58)

Sydney Chaplin, actor and son of Charlie

Laurence Olivier, actor (costar in *Richard III,* '55)

Lovers, Flings, or Just Friends?

- Richard Arlen, actor (costar in *Wings,* '27)
- Paul Bern, producer and later the second Mr. Jean Harlow
- Eddie Cantor, actor
- Gary Cooper, actor (walk-on bit in *It,* '27)
- Jimmy Dundee, stuntman
- Charles Farrell, actor
- Victor Fleming, director (directed her in *Mantrap,* '26)
- John Gilbert, actor
- Lawrence Gray, actor (costar in *Kid Boots,* '26)
- Jessie Hibbs, football player
- Arthur Jacobson, cameraman
- Sam Jaffe, producer
- Bela Lugosi, actor (who kept a nude photo of her in his house for years afterward)
- Hy Manners, football star–minor actor
- Fredric March, actor (costar in *The Wild Party,* '29)
- Tom Mix, silent western star
- William Earl Pearson, physician
- Harry Richman, singer-actor
- John Rinehardt, film technician
- Charles "Buddy" Rogers, actor (costar in *Wings,* '27)
- Gilbert Roland, actor (costar in *The Plastic Age,* '25)
- "Slapsie" Maxie Rosenbloom, boxer-actor
- Robert Savage, socialite
- B. P. Schulberg, producer
- Eddie Sutherland, director (directed her in *The Saturday Night Kid,* '29)
- John Wayne, actor
- William Wellman, director
- *plus* many, many other men from all professions

Clara Bow 1905–1965

✦ She Said

Being a sex symbol is a heavy load to carry, especially when one is very tired, hurt, and bewildered.

The more I see of men, the more I like dogs.

I'm a curiosity in Hollywood. I'm a big freak because I'm myself.

✦ They Said

She came from Brooklyn. *She looked cheap. Men wanted to screw her.* —Sam Jaffe, a producer who did

Her social persona was taboo, and it was rather silly, because God knows Mary Pickford and Marion Davies certainly had plenty to hide. It's just that they hid it and Clara didn't. —Lina Basquette, actress and friend

She tried to be vivacious, she tried to be fascinating, she tried to be clever, and she just worked her body and mind and soul to death. —Charles "Buddy" Rogers, costar and lover

✦ First Sexual Experience

Lost her virginity to her father, Robert Bow, when she was sixteen. Clara's mother had been confined with mental problems, leaving Clara to keep house and cook for her father. He was plagued with mental troubles also and confused his daughter for his wife.

✦ Husbands

Rex Bell, cowboy star–politician (costar in *True to the Navy,* '30)

✦ Did You Know?

Clara awoke one evening to find her mother holding a butcher knife at her throat, saying, "You're going to hell. I'll see you dead before you become an actress." Bow escaped, but was plagued by insomnia for the rest of her life.

Clara Bow frequently menstruated twice a month.

Hollywood's best joke about Clara's sexual promiscuity: Clara Bow laid everything but the linoleum.

Fanny Brice 1891—1951

✦ She Said

I never liked the men I loved, and I never loved the men I liked.

If I tried, I got everything in my life I ever wanted. But with men, the harder I tried, the harder I flopped.

Men always fall for frigid women because they put on the best show.

✦ They Said

She had this extraordinary smile, so that if you were in the audience, you knew the smile was directed at you and you only and that she had never smiled at anyone before. George Cukor, director

The woman is a publicity hog. W. C. Fields, costar in several editions of the Ziegfeld Follies

✦ First Sexual Experience

Probably lost her virginity to her first husband, the barber she married when she was only fifteen, although she falsely claimed the marriage was never consummated. Tales vary, but one or the other left after three days, effectively ending the marriage. They weren t formally divorced until years later.

✦ Husbands

Frank White, barber
Jules Nicky Arnstein, aka Nick Arnold, shady character
Billy Rose, theatrical producer

✦ Did You Know?

Fanny once got into a hard-hitting, knock-down, drag-out backstage fight with fellow stage actress Lillian Lorraine over Fanny s continued involvement with Fred Gresheimer, to whom Lorraine was married. Fanny won the fight, then proceeded to drag Lorraine, by her hair, cavewoman fashion, out onto the stage. The crowd went wild and gave Brice a standing ovation.

Lovers, Flings, or Just Friends?

John Conte, singer-actor (who left Alice Faye for her, then moved on from Brice to marry Marilyn Maxwell)

Fred Gresheimer, wealthy playboy

Lovers, Flings, or Just Friends?

A. C. Blumenthal, financier
Humphrey Bogart, actor
Bill Burns, publicist
Charlie Chaplin, actor
Gustav Diessl, German actor (costar in *Pandora's Box*, '28)
Greta Garbo, actress
Edmund Goulding, director
Dr. Richard Hoffman, psychiatrist
Buster Keaton, comedian-actor
Pepi Lederer, Marion Davies's lesbian niece
John Lock, stockbroker
George Preston Marshall, owner of the Washington Redskins
Townsend Martin, screenwriter
"Prince" David Mdivani, pseudo-Georgian prince and one of the "marrying Mdivani" brothers
G. W. Pabst, director (directed her in *Diary of a Lost Girl*, '29)
William Paley, later head of CBS
Harvey Parry, her double in *Beggars of Life* ('28)
Jack "Mr. Syphilis" Pickford, brother of actress Mary
Addison "Jack" Randall, cowboy star
Fritz Rasp, German actor (costar in *Diary of a Lost Girl*, '29)
Karl von Bieck, German financier
Walter Wanger, producer

Louise Brooks 1906–1985

✦ She Said

The best lovers I ever had were homosexuals.

From the age of fifteen I was pursued by lesbians and I was attracted to them, but not sexually.

Love is a publicity stunt, and making love—after the first curious raptures—is only another petulant way to pass the time waiting for the studio to call.

The best-read idiot in the world. —Describing herself

✦ They Said

Louise Brooks is the only woman who had the ability to transfigure no matter what film into a masterpiece. —Ado Kyrou, French film critic

The nastiest gal I've ever seen. It was known all over how bad she was. —Ethylene Clair, silent-film star

You're a lousy actress and your eyes are too close together. —Richard "Dick" Arlen, actor

✦ First Sexual Experience

Unknown for certain, but possibly lost her virginity to Bill Burns, publicist.

✦ Husbands

Edward Sutherland, director
Deering Davis, playboy

✦ Did You Know?

Brooks said that actress Constance Bennett, with whom she was good friends, taught her how to "enter a nightclub with my evening wrap clutched high at my shoulders and my head thrown back with an expression of one approaching a smoldering dump."

Brooks posed for the model of Dixie Dugan, the long-running cartoon strip.

Brooks's nickname among her cohorts was Hellcat. She said they gave it to her because she often made the remark, "I like to drink and fuck," around them so frequently.

Maria Callas 1923–1977

✦ She Said

I work: therefore I am. What do you do if you do not work?

Love is a single thing. You love, you worship, you honor; they go together.

I never attempted to be a film star in any way, shape, or form. I resisted it with all my might.

✦ They Said

If any heroine—Greek or otherwise—became the tragic plaything of the gods, it was Maria Callas. —Taki Theodoracopulos, society writer

She was a fat, clumsily dressed woman, a refugee, a gypsy, when I met her. —Giovanni Batista Meneghini, her manager and spouse

Callas is the first nostril-flarer since Susan Hayward. —Rex Reed, film critic, detailing her strong points in her first film, *Medea* ('70)

✦ First Sexual Experience

Probably lost her virginity to Meneghini, possibly shortly before they were married, since she was overweight and basically unattractive when they first met.

✦ Husbands

Giovanni Batista Meneghini, brick manufacturer

✦ Did You Know?

Callas rejected two film roles (Elizabeth Taylor's role in *Boom!* '68, and the role—Sarah—that Ava Gardner played in *The Bible,* '66) before making her film debut in Pasolini's *Medea* ('70).

Marlene Dietrich, who thrived on performing *hausfrau* chores for those she admired, once spent an inordinate number of hours boiling down eight pounds of pure beef to make a quart of the purest beef broth for Callas. The diva took a sip, then asked Dietrich, "It's very good. Tell me, what brand of cubes do you use?"

Lovers, Flings, or Just Friends?

Guiseppe di Stefano, tenor

Evangelias Mangliveras, baritone

Aristotle Onassis, Greek shipping tycoon (whose child she aborted)

Luchino Viscounti, director

Lovers, Flings, or Just Friends?

Charles Feldman, producer

William Holden, actor (costar in *The 7th Dawn*, '64)

Capucine 1933–1990

✦ She Said

I hated my real name [Germaine]. *In France it's as common as Gladys.*

"I used to think I needed a man to define myself. No more."

✦ They Said

If you were more of a woman, I would be more of a man. Kissing you is like kissing the side of a beer bottle. —Laurence Harvey, being characteristically waspish during the filming of *Walk on the Wild Side* ('62)

I worked with her, but when we met and shook hands, she acted as if she was nobility and I was being introduced into the royal presence. —Anne Baxter, who also costarred with her in *Walk on the Wild Side*

✦ First Sexual Experience

Unknown.

✦ Husbands

Capucine never married.

✦ Did You Know?

What does *capucine* mean? It's French for "nasturtium," and much more exotic than her real name.

For years the rumor floated around the movie industry that Capucine was actually a transsexual. That rumor was made somehow ironic when, near the end of her life, she began admitting her lesbianism.

When she committed suicide, Capucine chose a method far removed from the overdose of barbiturates that most actresses choose: she jumped out of the window of her eighth-floor penthouse in Lausanne, Switzerland.

Judy Carne 1939–

✦ She Said

When I talked about my relationship with another woman, I was the first *celebrity who talked about her* lesbian *experiences.*

And now, folks, it's Sawk it to me time! —Judy's most famous line from television

✦ They Said

We don't need this kind of publicity and neither do you. —A group of Screen Gems TV executives chastising Judy over her lesbian relationship with her friend Ashley

✦ First Sexual Experience

Lost her virginity to an older man she met in a theater where she was working.

✦ Husbands

Burt Reynolds, actor
Robert Bergmann, TV commercial producer

✦ Did You Know?

Bob Guccione of *Penthouse* offered Carne $50,000 to pose in photos with another woman, which he would personally shoot and run in his magazine. Carne declined, saying, "If I appear in *Penthouse* with my head buried in a huge set of tits, I can kiss my acting career goodbye."

Lovers, Flings, or Just Friends?

- Ashley, lesbian friend
- Warren Beatty, actor
- Lana Cantrell, Australian singer
- Peter Deuel, actor (costar in television's *Love on a Rooftop*)
- Dean Goodhill, photographer
- Glen Mason, British singer
- Steve McQueen, actor
- Stirling Moss, British race-car champion
- Anthony Newley, actor-singer
- Vidal Sassoon, hair magnate

Lovers, Flings, or Just Friends?

- Warren Beatty, actor (costar in *Promise Her Anything,* '66)
- Richard Johnson, British actor
- Roger Vincent, Australian lawyer

Leslie Caron 1931–

✦ She Said

I hate musicals. I had toe shoes on from eight-thirty in the morning until six every night. I was constantly in agony.

I don't think Hollywood is an appropriate place for a woman of forty.

I got what I have now through knowing the right time to tell terrible people when to go to hell.

I haven't the slightest idea of what the public thinks of me and I don't care.

✦ They Said

She is tiresome, argumentative, stubborn, delays activity of the film. She has to have everything clear in her brain before she proceeds; otherwise, she is incapable. —Cecil Beaton, photographer-designer, who worked with Caron on *Gigi* ('58)

✦ First Sexual Experience

Unknown.

✦ Husbands

George Hormel II, meatpacking heir
Peter Hall, British theatrical director
Michael Laughlin, producer

✦ Did You Know?

In addition to her famed dancing with Gene Kelly, Caron has danced onstage with both Rudolf Nureyev and Mikhail Baryshnikov.

Caron was one of the many bedroom conquests of Warren Beatty, in an affair that caused her marriage to Peter Hall to fall apart. Describing Warren after their time together ended, she said, "He tends to maul you."

Gabrielle "Coco" Chanel 1883–1971

✦ She Said

A woman is closest to being naked when she is well-dressed.

A fashion that does not reach the streets is not a fashion.

A woman must smell of woman and not like a rose.

The life one leads does not amount to much, but the life one dreams, that's the great thing, because it will continue after one is dead.

✦ They Said

She made a lady look like a lady. Hollywood wants a lady to look like two ladies. —*The New Yorker,* reflecting on why Chanel's designs for Hollywood films were unappreciated

From this century, in France, three names will remain: de Gaulle, Picasso, and Chanel. —André Malraux, French cultural minister and author

She had power. She knew what she was doing and she took nothing from anybody. Not even me. Usually, I don't like that type, but I liked her. I don't know why. —Samuel Goldwyn, who brought Chanel to Hollywood to design costumes for his films

✦ First Sexual Experience

Probably lost her virginity to Etienne Balsan, a French soldier and her first strong love.

✦ Husbands

Chanel remained mademoiselle her entire life, although she did turn down the chance to become the Duchess of Westminster when she declined the British Duke's offer of marriage.

✦ Did You Know?

What did Chanel think of Hollywood? She called it "the Mont-Saint-Michel of tit and tail."

Author Jacqueline Susann, who also had a fling with Ethel Merman, claimed that Chanel made sexual advances to her, but that she rejected them.

During her sixty-five years as a fashion designer Chanel never once used the color green.

Lovers, Flings, or Just Friends?

- Etienne Balsan, French soldier
- Henri Bernstein, writer
- Arthur Capel, English gentlman–sportsman
- Hugh Richard Arthur Grosvenor, Duke of Westminster, British aristocrat
- Paul Iribe, artist (and former set designer for Cecil B. DeMille)
- Grand Duke Dmitri Pavlovich, cousin of Czar Nicholas II and one of Rasputin's assassins
- Pablo Picasso, artist
- Pierre Reverdy, French poet
- Misia Sert, wife of painter José-Maria Sert and patroness of artists Bonnard, Vuillard, and Renoir
- Igor Stravinsky, composer
- Luchino Visconti, director
- Hans Gunther von Dincklage, German *Abwehr* agent
- Harrison Williams, socialite

Lovers, Flings, or Just Friends?

Warren Beatty, actor (when she was sixteen, or so she told *Playboy*)

Rob Camilletti, actor–bagel baker

Marc Connally, exotic dancer

Tom Cruise, actor

Joshua Donen, talent agent

Les Dudek, rock musician

Ron Duguay, hockey player (NY Rangers)

David Geffen, record mogul

John Heard, actor

Bill Hudson, producer

Val Kilmer, actor

John Loeffler, composer-singer

Richie Sambora, rock musician (lead guitar, Bon Jovi)

Gene Simmons, rock band KISS's bass player–singer (who's claimed that he's slept with more than two thousand women)

Eric Stoltz, actor (costar in *Mask*, '85)

and one of her mother's thirty-five-year-old boyfriends when she was fourteen and a half

Cher 1946–

✦ She Said

I believe in face-lifts and nips and tucks. You know, if I wanted to put tits on my back, they're mine.

The truth is, I don't enjoy kissing people I don't know. —Mentioning the difficulties she's had starring with some people, for instance Nicolas Cage in *Moonstruck* ('87)

My rule of thumb, and it's never failed me, is that if a man is a good kisser, he's a good fuck.

Someday I'm going to write a book that's going to make everybody crazy.

✦ They Said

Anyone who could be a personality and wear those clothes and who is also a serious actress has to be schizophrenic. —Peter Yates, director

Cher is solid [plastic] *proof that six thousand fingernails and six hundred thousand costume changes can do wonders for a flat singer.* —James Spina, *Women's Wear Daily*

There is absolutely no BS about her. —John Patrick Shanley, who wrote her Oscar-winning role in *Moonstruck* ('87)

✦ First Sexual Experience

Lost her virginity at age fourteen to an older guy, a little Italian who lived next door, about whom she has said, "His brain was in his crotch."

✦ Husbands

Salvator (Sonny) Philip Bono, singer

Gregory LeNoire (Greg) Allman, rock musician (she filed for divorce after nine days, but reconsidered)

✦ Did You Know?

Real name: Cherilyn LaPiere Sarkisian

The last time they made love, Marc Connally said Cher straddled him and fed him whipped cream and strawberries from parts of her body.

Julie Christie 1940–

✦ She Said

Marriage—it's like signing your life away.

I don't think men see any lusty sexiness in me. The appealing thing is an air of abandonment. Men don't want any responsibility, and neither do I.

I'm not a myth or legend, just somebody who works in films. I don't do anything public. I try to live a private life when I'm not working.

✦ They Said

Julie doesn't like being a movie star. All she wants is to act. If she had her way, she'd like a nice role in a film that doesn't require a lot of recognition. —Robert Altman, who directed her in *McCabe and Mrs. Miller* ('71)

She's almost pathologically honest. —Warren Beatty, actor, costar, and former lover

✦ First Sexual Experience

Unknown.

✦ Husbands

Christie has thus far remained unmarried, or if she has ever married, she's kept it extremely secret.

✦ Did You Know?

During her period as an acting student in London, Christie has described herself as "a vagrant," saying she "used to go around to friends' houses carrying my own mattress."

Lovers, Flings, or Just Friends?

- Warren Beatty, actor (costar in *McCabe and Mrs. Miller,* '71)
- Don Bessant, British art teacher
- Duncan Campbell, news editor
- Alan Dobie, actor and the first Mr. Rachel Roberts
- Brian Eno, rock musician–producer
- Omar Sharif, actor (costar in *Doctor Zhivago,* '65)
- Terence Stamp, actor

Lovers, Flings, or Just Friends?

Len Cariou, actor
Woody Harrelson, actor-singer
William Hurt, actor
John Starke, producer
Kevin Kline, actor

Glenn Close 1947–

✦ She Said

"I have never wanted to be a man. I feel sorry for them."

I'm a very competitive person, but I don't believe in competing with individual people because it's destructive.

I've had two failed marriages. I don't know if it's a good state for me.

✦ They Said

I have a thing for her. She really titillates me. —Michael Douglas, costar in *Fatal Attraction* ('87), where he showed how titillated he could be by Glenn

✦ First Sexual Experience

Unknown.

✦ Husbands

Cabot Wade, rock guitarist
James Marsalis, venture capitalist
Stephen Beers, carpenter

✦ Did You Know?

At the female boarding school she attended, Close organized an acting troupe called The Fingernails—the Group with Polish.

Claudette Colbert 1903–

✦ She Said

I could dish dirt, perhaps, about some of the people encountered along the way, but I think dirt-dishing is negative.

Some people like me. Some people don't. You can never get everyone to like you, and why knock oneself out trying?

A wife shouldn't bore a husband with her petty ills. He never knew what picture I was in from one year to the next. —Remarking on her long-lasting, thirty-five-year second marriage

✦ They Said

I always felt she handled herself remarkably well—every inch the lady, with remarkable sense and control. —Mitchell Leisen, director

God, they had her in the sack with every halfway good-looking man she ever acted with. —Preston Sturges, director, on Hollywood rumors

✦ First Sexual Experience

Unknown.

✦ Husbands

Norman Foster, actor (who later married Loretta Young's sister, actress Sally Blane)

Dr. Joel Pressman, physician

✦ Did You Know?

Colbert, thinking she had a flaw on the right side of her face, always demanded that she be photographed in films only on the left side of her face. Around the sets, the right side of her face was dubbed "the dark side of the moon," because no one ever saw it.

During her marriage to Foster, she and Foster maintained separate residences and lived apart, "to keep our love alive," as she phrased it.

Lovers, Flings, or Just Friends?

Maurice Chevalier, singer-actor (costar in *The Big Pond,* '30)

Gary Cooper, actor (costar in *His Woman,* '31)

Leslie Howard, actor

Fred MacMurray, actor (costar in *Gilded Lily,* '35)

Preston Sturges, director (directed her in *The Palm Beach Story,* '42)

Joan Collins 1933–

✦ She Said

When I get to be forty years old, and even fifty, it won't bother me because I'll avoid those low-cut dresses with the old baggy flesh hanging around. I'll wear high necks and long sleeves. —Remark from a 1962 interview, when she was twenty-nine. She obviously changed her mind about her mode of dress when she actually reached her forties and fifties.

To me, I've got a great body. Sometimes it looks terrific, and if it's photographed right, it can look absolutely great.

✦ They Said

I picked her up on my yacht in Miami. She was so boring, I put her ashore in Palm Beach. —Ramfis Trujillo, Dominican playboy

Joan Collins displays her breasts on Dynasty *as if bra-cup size was a measure of personal magnificence.* —*Vogue* magazine

She always lived her life like a man. If she saw a guy she wanted to go to bed with, she went after him, and that was unacceptable behavior at the time. —Jackie Collins, sister and author

✦ First Sexual Experience

Lost her virginity to Maxwell Reed, her first husband, who drugged her unconscious on one of their first dates. She claimed to have revived just as he was "trying to push a strange, soft object in my mouth."

✦ Husbands

Maxwell Reed, British actor
Anthony Newley, British actor
Ron Kass, record company executive
Peter Holm, businessman

✦ Did You Know?

Collins's first husband, Maxwell Reed, tried to convince her to go to bed with a fat, old Arab sheik, who had offered Reed £10,000 sterling for the privilege of enjoying one night of her charms. She adamantly refused and soon sought a divorce from the ungallant Reed.

Lovers, Flings, or Just Friends?

- Warren Beatty, actor
- Harry Belafonte, singer-actor (costar in *Island in the Sun,* '57)
- Marlon Brando, actor
- Sydney Chaplin, actor and son of Charlie
- George Englund, producer
- Robert Evans, producer
- Jon-Erik Hexum, actor (costar in *The Making of a Male Model,* '83)
- Nicky Hilton, hotel-chain heir and the first Mr. Elizabeth Taylor
- Dennis Hopper, actor
- David Janssen, actor
- Arthur Loew Jr., cinema-chain heir (and grandson of Adolph Zukor, head of Paramount Studios)
- Ryan O'Neal, actor
- Terence Stamp, British actor
- Peter Therodoracopolis, businessman
- Gabriele Tinti, actor (costar in *Esther and the King,* '60)
- Robert Wagner, actor (costar in *Stopover Tokyo,* '57)

Joan Crawford 1904–1977

✦ She Said

Well, it sure as hell beat the hard, cold floor. —Replying to a query on whether or not she had ever been on the proverbial Hollywood "casting couch"

If ever there was a time in my life when I might have become a lesbian, that was it. —Describing being introduced to Garbo at a dinner party and looking closely into the Swede's face

✦ They Said

She's slept with every male star at MGM except Lassie. —Bette Davis, sniping at Joan's sexual excesses

To be Joan Crawford's boyfriend a man must be a combination of bull and butler. —William "Billy" Haines, actor-decorator and close friend of Crawford's

That terrible, vulgar woman with the pop eyes beats her children . . . . But what do you expect from that class—a cheap tap dancer. —Marlene Dietrich, who wasn't the greatest mother in the world either

✦ First Sexual Experience

Lost her virginity to a boy from Northeast High School during a nighttime tryst in a Kansas City public park.

✦ Husbands

James Welton, saxophone player
Douglas Fairbanks Jr., actor
Franchot Tone, actor (she said he was a "ten-inch cocksman who compelled women to pay homage to his shaft")
Phillip Terry, minor actor
Alfred Steele, head of Pepsi-Cola

✦ Did You Know?

While she was a starving chorus girl in New York City, Joan appeared in at least two porno films *(Velvet Lips, The Casting Couch).* Both she and MGM denied it, but they attempted to buy up all copies of the films (and stills) in the 1930s when blackmailed for a rumored $100,000. They obviously didn't succeed in obtaining everything, as stills from the films have been featured in at least two books.

Pseudoprudish Joan believed in using silly euphemisms for certain sexual things. For instance, she called having sex "they went to heaven" and referred to women's breasts as "ninny pies."

Lovers, Flings, or Just Friends?

- Dorothy Arzner, director
- Jean-Pierre Aumont, French actor
- Greg Bautzer, lawyer and Hollywood "escort"
- Yul Brynner, actor
- Jeff Chandler, actor
- Steve Cochran, actor (costar in *The Damned Don't Cry,* '50)
- Jackie Cooper, ex-cinemoppet (whom Joan seduced when he was seventeen)
- Kirk Douglas, actor (she liked his armpits, which were clean-shaven for his role in *Champion,* '49)
- Richard Egan, actor (costar in *The Damned Don't Cry,* '50)
- Henry Fonda, actor (costar in *Daisy Kenyon,* '47)
- Glenn Ford, actor
- Clark Gable, actor (costar in *Dancing Lady,* '33)
- John Garfield, actor (costar in *Humoresque,* '46)
- Jackie Gleason, actor
- Cary Grant, actor
- Van Heflin, actor
- Rock Hudson
- John F. Kennedy, U.S. president
- Joseph L. Mankiewicz, director-producer
- Tony Martin, singer
- Jack Oakie, actor
- Tyrone Power, actor
- Robert Preston, actor
- Nicholas Ray, director
- Martha Raye, comedienne-actress
- Barbara Stanwyck, actress
- Robert Sterling, actor
- Spencer Tracy, actor
- John Wayne, actor
- Johnny Weissmuller, actor

Lovers, Flings, or Just Friends?

John F. Kennedy, U.S. president

Red Skelton, actor (costar of *A Southern Yankee,* '48)

Arlene Dahl 1924–

✦ She Said

In one of my films I played a nymphomaniac, a dipsomaniac, and a kleptomaniac—which is not terribly ladylike, even by Hollywood standards.

The reason I don't make films today is that in the old days actresses used to play *parts—now they* reveal *them.*

✦ They Said

The only two natural beauties in Hollywood who could step in front of a camera without one spot of makeup are Liz Taylor and Arlene Dahl. —Louella Parsons, Hollywood columnist

Being married to Arlene Dahl was very nice at nighttime. But in the daytime, it was like being married to Elizabeth Arden. —Fernando Lamas

✦ First Sexual Experience

Unknown.

✦ Husbands

Lex Barker, actor (who was also the fourth Mr. Lana Turner)

Fernando Lamas, actor and costar of *The Diamond Queen* ('53) (who was also the 3rd Mr. Esther Williams)

Christian R. Holmes, oil tycoon

Alexis Lichine, businessman

Rounseville W. Schaum, industrialist–television executive

Marc Rosen, perfume executive

✦ Did You Know?

Fernando Lamas once said that in all the years of their marriage he never once saw Dahl minus her makeup. Rumor had it that she arose before him each morning to put it on before he'd see her.

Dorothy Dandridge 1923–1965

✦ She Said

Some people kill themselves with drink or hurl themselves in front of a train. I hurled myself in front of another white man. —Speaking of her disastrous romantic relationships with white men

If it is possible for a human being to be like a haunted house, maybe that would be me.

✦ They Said

Never forget, with the white man you will never be equal. —Sukarno, president of Indonesia, cautioning Dandridge about her life

Color was the major tragedy in Dottie's life. Dottie hated being black, and If Dottie had two choices, she would pick the one that hurt her the most. She was the supreme masochist. —Geri Branton, a close friend of Dandridge's

She was our Marilyn. —Lena Horne

✦ First Sexual Experience

Dandridge lost her virginity at age sixteen, when she was thrown on a bed and assaulted by a friend of her mother's, Eloise Matthews, who used the excuse that she was checking to see if Dandridge was still a virgin. Her first sexual encounter with a man came on her wedding night with Harold Nicholas.

✦ Husbands

Harold Nicholas, dancer (of the dancing Nicholas Brothers)
Jack Denison, nightclub owner

✦ Did You Know?

When Dandridge was about to give birth to her only child, a daughter, she delayed the trip to the hospital for several hours. She claimed later that she had waited because her husband was out drinking, although he's denied it. The delay meant the birth had to be assisted with forceps, resulting in severe brain damage to the child. As a result the daughter never spoke and was mentally retarded.

Lovers, Flings, or Just Friends?

- Harding Allbrite, actor
- Harry Belafonte, singer
- Peter Lawford, actor
- Juan Alvarez de Costigliana Freye Vivaldez Marinez, Brazilian millionaire
- Gerald Mayer, director and nephew of MGM mogul Louis B.
- Phil Moore, coach-accompanist
- Otto Preminger, director (directed her in *Carmen Jones,* '54)
- Michael Rennie, actor

Lovers, Flings, or Just Friends?

- Giuseppe Amato, Italian producer
- Donald "Red" Barry, actor
- Milton Berle, comedian-actor
- Kirk Douglas, actor (costar in *The Walls of Jericho,* '48)
- Howard Hughes, aviator–cinema mogul
- Philip Kalavos, doctor
- Joseph Mankiewicz, writer-director (directed her in *A Letter to Three Wives,* '49)
- Vic Orsatti, agent
- Rudolph Sieber, chicken farmer (aka Mr. Marlene Dietrich)
- Darryl F. Zanuck, studio head

Linda Darnell 1921–1965

✦ She Said

They chose me to play the Virgin Mary in Song of Bernadette *('43) because I was the only real virgin in Hollywood at the time.*

I've had all of the good things any woman could ever desire, and most of the bad things no woman wants.

I've got more balls than most men do! If there's anything I hate, it's a weak man.

✦ They Said

There were two things Linda could never manage—her mother and her money. —A close friend who was familiar with Darnell's ongoing problems in both areas

A sweeter girl never lived. —Henry Hathaway, who directed her in *Brigham Young—Frontiersman* ('40)

✦ First Sexual Experience

Unknown, although she may have lost her virginity to her first husband, J. Peverell Marley, whom Linda married when she was nineteen and he was forty-two.

✦ Husbands

J. Peverell Marley, studio cameraman
Philip Liebmann, brewery head
Merle Roy Robertson, airline pilot

✦ Did You Know?

For the men who wanted to get into Linda's pants and succeeded, the visit wasn't always that memorable. At least to Linda. One director who bedded her said, "I don't even think she knew who was on top of her." Another Hollywood star had a far different fetish about Linda. He wasn't eager to get into her pants, he wanted *all* her clothes. Dan Dailey, homosexual, but married, loved to wear women's clothes, both at home and out in public. He had a particular penchant for Darnell's gowns, and used to make midnight raids on the wardrobe department at the studio to snitch them.

Marion Davies 1897–1961

✦ She Said

Somebody told me I should put a pebble in my mouth to cure my stuttering. Well, I tried it, and during a scene I swallowed the pebble. That was the end of that.

I was no Sarah Bernhardt. I was no great actress.

When I'm entertaining at home, no one can tell me to get out. —Revealing why she liked to act as one of Hollywood's most popular hostesses

✦ They Said

Upon my honor,

I swear I saw a Madonna,

Standing alone in a niche,

Above the door,

Of a glamorous whore,

Of a prominent son of a bitch —Nasty rhyme most often attributed to Dorothy Parker. Davies had a Madonna mounted in a niche over the door of her "bungalow" at the MGM lot.

Marion was a woman with a heart bigger than herself, and a great sense of humor. —Close personal friend

✦ First Sexual Experience

Unknown.

✦ Husbands

Capt. Horace Brown, Maritime Service

✦ Did You Know?

Davies was well-known for her rowdy sense of humor, which included gags, elaborate pranks, and saying outrageous things to the most unlikely people. She once asked halo-haired genius Albert Einstein, "Al, why don't you get a haircut?" Among her most notable pranks was one she pulled on President Calvin Coolidge. When the teetotaler president came to visit, Marion slipped him a glass of Tokay wine, assuring him it was "only fruit juice." He gulped it down and asked for another, then a third glass, telling Marion, "I don't know when I've had anything as refreshing."

Lovers, Flings, or Just Friends?

- Charlie Chaplin, actor-director
- Clark Gable, actor (costar of *Polly of the Circus,* '32)
- Lawrence Gray, actor (costar in *The Florodora Girl,* '30)
- William Randolph Hearst, newspaper-chain magnate (her pet names for him included Poopsie and Droopy Drawers)
- Leslie Howard, actor (costar in *Five and Ten,* '31)
- Joseph Kennedy, businessman and father of John F. Kennedy
- Dick Powell, actor (costar in *Hearts Divided,* '36)
- Rudolph Valentino, actor

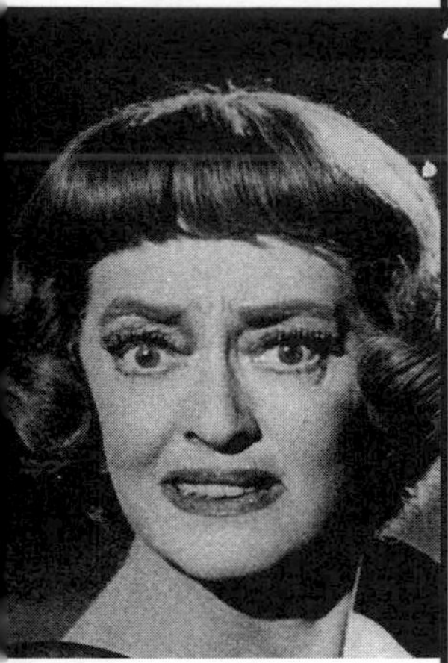

Bette Davis 1908–1989

✦ She Said

Until you're known in my profession as a monster, you're not a star.

✦ They Said

That dame is too uptight. What she needs is a good screw from a man who knows how to do it. —Humphrey Bogart, actor, seeing her on the set of her first film, *Bad Sister* ('31)

She's an egotistical little bitch. —Barbara Stanwyck, on the set of *So Big* ('32)

A no-good, sexless son of a bitch! —Michael Curtiz, director, famed for mangling his words and genders

She was like a greedy little girl at a party table who just has to sample other women's cupcakes. —Miriam Hopkins, irate about Davis's affair with Hopkins's hubby, director Anatole Litvak

I hear she screws like a mink. —Jack Carson, recounting what a Marine said when asked why all the servicemen clustered around Davis during her work at the Hollywood Canteen during World War II

✦ First Sexual Experience

Lost her virginity to her first husband, Harmon Oscar Nelson.

✦ Husbands

Harmon Oscar Nelson, professional musician (trumpet)
Arthur Farnsworth, innkeeper
William Grant Sherry, boxer-painter-physiotherapist
Gary Merrill, actor (costar in *All About Eve*, '50)

✦ Did You Know?

Davis's first husband, "Ham" Nelson, was a chronic masturbator, given to premature ejaculation, whom Bette had to "train" for several months after marriage until he could adequately satisfy her.

The origins of her famed feud with Joan Crawford seem to reside in Davis's having had an affair with Franchot Tone (who was married to Joan at the time) when they costarred together in *Dangerous* ('35).

While swearing and using filthy language, Davis would fellate Howard Hughes, who would close his eyes and pretend she was a man.

Lovers, Flings, or Just Friends?

- George Brent, actor (costar in *Housewife*, '34)
- Henry Fonda, actor (costar in *Jezebel*, '38)
- Howard Hughes, aviator–cinema mogul
- Bruce Lester, minor actor
- Anatole Litvak, director (directed her in *The Sisters*, '38)
- Johnny Mercer, songwriter
- Lewis A. Riley, U.S. Army corporal
- Vincent Sherman, director (he directed her in *Mr. Skeffington*, '44)
- Barry Sullivan, actor (costar in *Payment on Demand*, '51)
- Bob Taplinger, publicity man
- Richard Tate, actor
- Franchot Tone, actor (costar in *Dangerous*, '35)
- William Wyler, director (directed her in *Jezebel*, '38)
- Gig Young, actor (costar in *Old Acquaintance*, '43)
- *plus* an ongoing parade of younger (mostly homosexual) men when she was in her sixties, some of whom Davis would propose marriage to after three or four dates, and quite a few of the servicemen she met while working at the Hollywood Canteen during World War II

Nancy Davis (Reagan) 1921–

✦ She Said

I knew that being his wife was the role I wanted to play. —Commenting on how she decided to forsake film roles for the role as wife to an actor (with political ambitions)

✦ They Said

If I had a nickel for every Jew Nancy was under, I'd be rich. —George Cukor, director

She just wasn't star material. —Pandro Berman, producer

Nancy was one of those girls whose phone number got handed around a lot. —Anne Edwards, writer

That woman! Who on earth does she think she is? —Queen Elizabeth II's reputed comment after Nancy had broken with protocol by taking Prince Philip's arm preceding the Queen and President Reagan

✦ First Sexual Experience

Unknown.

✦ Husbands

Ronald Reagan, actor, U.S. president, and costar in *Hellcats of the Navy* ('57) (and the third Mr. Jane Wyman)

✦ Did You Know?

Peter Lawford's last wife has relayed a story in her biography of Peter that she said he told her about some automobile trips that he, actor Robert Walker, and Nancy took to visit Nancy's parents in Arizona. According to Peter's tale, Nancy kept her two escorts orally entertained on their journeys. Is there any truth to Peter's claim? Well, only Peter, Nancy, and Walker know for certain–and two of them are dead. But, Peter also told his wife that Nancy was famed in Hollywood for her skill at fellatio.

Lovers, Flings, or Just Friends?

- Max Allentuck, theatrical assistant (and later Mr. Maureen Stapleton)
- Yul Brynner, actor
- Alfred Drake, actor
- Clark Gable, actor
- Peter Lawford, actor
- Dr. Daniel Ruge, physician
- Frank Sinatra, singer-actor
- Benjamin Thau, head of MGM casting
- Spencer Tracy, actor
- Robert Walker, actor
- *and* a homosexual dancer from the Broadway production of *Lute Song*

Lovers, Flings, or Just Friends?

Jack Carson, actor (costar in *Romance on the High Seas,* '48)

Tyrone Power, actor

Ronald Reagan, actor-president (costar in *Storm Warning,* '51)

Doris Day 1924–

✦ She Said

I am really appalled by some of the public exhibitions on the screen by good actors and actresses who certainly have the talent to convey the impact of what they are doing without showing us to the last detail of pubic hair and rosy nipple how they are doing it.

When I'm in love, I want to make love with that man all the time.

Yes, sir, America's la-di-da virgin.

✦ They Said

No one realized that under those dirndls lurked one of the hottest asses in Hollywood. —Ross Hunter, producer

She is the last one to know when a man is interested in her. Sad to say, I don't think my mother has had much of a sex life. —Terry Melcher, son

I knew her before she was a virgin. —Oscar Levant, Hollywood wit, mocking Day's image as a virgin in her 1960s films

✦ First Sexual Experience

Probably lost her virginity to her first husband, Al Jorden, whom she married at age seventeen.

✦ Husbands

Al Jorden, musician
George Weidler, musician
Martin "Marty" Melcher, producer-manager (who was previously Mr. Patty Andrews, of the Andrews Sisters)
Barry Comden, restaurateur

✦ Did You Know?

When Melcher, her third husband and manager, died, Day discovered that all of the approximately $20 million she'd earned during her career was gone—and he'd left her $500,000 in debt, plus committed to begin a television series in a matter of weeks.

Romantic rumors always seemed to link Day with black men like basketball player Elgin Baylor (of the LA Lakers) and rock singer Sly (of Sly and the Family Stone). Day denied all the rumors. When quizzed on why she'd be linked with the black men, she speculated that it was probably because of her father, "a staid German bigot," who had ended up married to a black woman.

Yvonne De Carlo 1922–

✦She Said

Men, no matter what their promises, rarely leave their spouses—the louses.

✦They Said

Yvonne, you can look the best of any girl I've ever known . . . and the worst. —Robert Stack

I want to place you on a pedestal where I can worship you hour after hour, and *With your goddesslike figure you should* never *wear clothes.* —Anthony Quinn, spouting seduction drivel, which De Carlo didn't fall for

✦First Sexual Experience

She would have let actor Sterling Hayden take her virginity, but he didn't make a bold enough attempt, so she let businessman Carl Anthony, whom she had met rather casually, take it.

✦Husbands

Bob Morgan, stuntman

✦Did You Know?

When De Carlo was sixteen, an elderly boarder in her grandfather's house gave her a rude start while she was sleeping. He came—totally nude—into the bedroom where she was asleep and urinated on her.

According to De Carlo, when she and Burt Lancaster had sex it was on a mink coat under an oleander bush in her backyard.

Lovers, Flings, or Just Friends?

- Carl Anthony, businessman
- Claude Boissol, French screenwriter
- Yul Brynner, actor
- Mario Cabre, Spanish bullfighter
- "Champ," Australian auto racer
- Tony Curtis, actor
- "Dinkie Die," Australian sheep rancher
- Howard Duff, actor
- Clark Gable, actor (costar in *Band of Angels,* '57)
- Van Heflin, actor
- Howard Hughes, aviation-cinema mogul
- "Jeff," NY journalist
- Prince Aly Khan, millionaire playboy and son of the Aga Khan
- Burt Lancaster, actor (costar in *Brute Force,* '47)
- Lord Lanesborough, British aristocrat
- Jocko Mahoney, actor (who later ended up as Tarzan and Sally Field's stepfather)
- Prince Abdorezza Pahlavi of Iran, half brother of the Shah of Iran
- Robert Stack, actor
- Milburn Stone, actor and later "Doc" in TV's *Gunsmoke* series
- Robert Taylor, actor
- Carlos Thompson, Argentinean actor (costar in *Fort Algiers,* '53)
- Robert Urquhart, British actor (costar in *Tonight's the Night,* '54)
- Rudy Vallee, singer-actor
- Baron Julian von Thund, German businessman
- Billy Wilder, director

Lovers, Flings, or Just Friends?

- George Brent, actor
- Luther Davis, writer-producer
- Pat de Cicco, playboy (and ex–Mr. Thelma Todd and ex–Mr. Gloria Vanderbilt)
- Edward Heath, prime minister of Great Britain
- Howard Hughes, aviation-cinema mogul
- John Huston, director
- Anatole Litvak, director (and ex–Mr. Miriam Hopkins)
- Fredric March, actor
- Maj. Joseph McKeon, U.S. military
- Burgess Meredith, actor (and ex–Mr. Paulette Goddard)
- James Stewart, actor

Olivia de Havilland 1916–

✦ She Said

Can you imagine what it's like to be an elder sister and have your younger one do everything first? —Remarking on how it felt to have her younger sister, actress Joan Fontaine, lose her virginity first, sign a lucrative studio contract first, be the first to marry, the first to win an Oscar, and the first to bear a child

✦ They Said

Her face was so beautiful, all I could do was stand and stare. —Ernie Pyle, war correspondent

I don't think she has a hole between her legs. —Errol Flynn, commenting to a friend after de Havilland kept rebuffing his sexual advances

✦ First Sexual Experience

Unknown.

✦ Husbands

Marcus Goodrich, writer
Pierre Paul Galante, French editor

✦ Did You Know?

When Errol Flynn, who had the unrequited hots for her, asked Olivia, who had a crush on him, how he could get into her pants, she replied, "The same as you with yours—you know, one leg at a time."

Much has been made of the long-standing rivalry between Olivia and her sister Joan. There's the classic photo of Olivia holding her Oscar, which she won for *To Each His Own* ('46), walking past Joan and ignoring her outstretched hand of congratulations. Sometimes their rivalry reached absurd proportions. On location in Spain, Olivia refused to occupy the most lavish suite, which had been reserved for her, in a hotel merely because sister Joan had stayed in it when she was there earlier on location.

Dolores Del Rio 1905–1983

✦ She Said

As long as a woman has twinkles in her eyes, no man notices whether she has wrinkles under them.

Take care of your inner beauty, your spiritual beauty, and that will reflect in your face.

✦ They Said

I thought she was the most beautiful woman I had ever seen. —Orson Welles, director-actor

As a beauty, Dolores Del Rio is in a class with Garbo. Then she opens her mouth and becomes Minnie Mouse. —John Ford, director

"Every part of her was beautiful—even her toes."—Erich Marie Remarque, novelist

✦ First Sexual Experience

Probably lost her virginity to first husband Jaime Del Rio, whom she married when she was only sixteen.

✦ Husbands

Jaime Del Rio, writer and son of a wealthy Mexican family
Cedric Gibbons, MGM art director
Lewis Riley, businessman

✦ Did You Know?

Real name: Lolita Dolores Martinez Asunsolo Lopez Negrette

Del Rio introduced the two-piece bathing suit for women when she first wore one on-screen in *Flying Down to Rio* ('33).

The superelegant Del Rio became irked at Fred Othman, a Hollywood columnist, who wrote items in his columns claiming that she ate orchid omelettes and used butterfly wings as a back scratcher, so she invited him to interview her during lunch at her home. When the meal was served, it appeared on a silver platter and consisted of a mound of perfect gardenias. She ate them and so did Othman. Nothing else was served, but the butler did pass the platter again in case Othman desired another helping.

Lovers, Flings, or Just Friends?

- Bruce Cabot, actor
- Edwin Carewe, director
- Walt Disney, studio head
- Joel McCrea, actor (costar in *Bird of Paradise,* '32)
- Greta Garbo, actress
- Erich Marie Remarque, novelist
- Porfirio Rubirosa, Dominican diplomat and playboy
- George Sanders, actor (costar in *Lancer Spy,* '37)
- Orson Welles, director-actor

Lovers, Flings, or Just Friends?

Michael des Barres, actor

Johnny Halliday, the French Elvis Presley

Dean Martin, singer-actor

Marcello Mastroianni, actor (costar in *It Only Happens to Others,* '72)

Roman Polanski, director (directed her in *Repulsion,* '65)

Burt Reynolds, actor (costar in *Hustle,* '75)

Omar Sharif, actor (costar in *Mayerling,* '68)

Roger Vadim, French director (he directed her in *Vice and Virtue,* '62)

Catherine Deneuve 1943–

✦ She Said

Life is a jungle. You eat or you get eaten. Passion is the only way out.

All men are Arabs.

I want to please. I desperately *want to please, but if I gave everything to a film or to a person, I would retain nothing for myself—the mystery of who I am and what I want would be lost and something would have flown out of me.*

One is old the moment she is no longer desirable.

✦ They Said

She looks like a professional virgin, but sexy. —Roman Polanski, director

I remember thinking, I'd never seen such beautiful breasts. —Roger Vadim, on making love with her for the first time

Catherine Deneuve is an iceberg. Gorgeous, but an iceberg. —Steve McQueen, actor

✦ First Sexual Experience

Possibly lost her virginity to Roger Vadim, since they began going together when she was only seventeen.

✦ Husbands

David Bailey, British fashion photographer (she wore black for the wedding, and Mick Jagger was the best man)

✦ Did You Know?

Deneuve is mother to an illegitimate child fathered by actor Marcello Mastroianni, which caused another one of his flings, actress Faye Dunaway, to pout, "I wanted a child by him. He gave one to Deneuve instead."

Angie Dickinson 1931–

✦ She Said

I dress for women, and undress for men.

I've never knowingly dated a Republican.

✦ They Said

She has more sex appeal than anyone I've ever directed. —Roger Vadim, who directed her in *Pretty Maids All in a Row* ('71)

She has a lusty sense of humor. —Earl Holliman, actor and costar of her television series *Police Woman*

✦ First Sexual Experience

Unknown.

✦ Husbands

Gene Dickinson, college football star
Burt Bacharach, composer-singer-performer

✦ Did You Know?

Rumor says Dickinson keeps an autographed photo of the late John F. Kennedy inscribed "Angie: To the only woman I've ever loved."

Lovers, Flings, or Just Friends?

Johnny Carson, entertainer–television personality

David Janssen, actor

John F. Kennedy, U.S. president

Frank Sinatra, singer-actor

Lovers, Flings, or Just Friends?

Cecil Beaton, photographer-designer
Yul Brynner, actor
Jo Castairs, female racing driver
Maurice Chevalier, French entertainer (who was impotent)
Colette, French author
Ronald Colman, actor (costar in *Kismet,* '44)
Gary Cooper, actor
Mercedes D'Acosta, author
Lily Damita, actress
Joe DiMaggio, baseball player
Kirk Douglas, actor
Douglas Fairbanks Jr., actor
Eddie Fisher, singer
Gen. James Gavin, U.S. military
John Gilbert, actor
Howard Hughes, aviation-cinema mogul
John F. Kennedy, U.S. president
Joseph P. Kennedy, financial finagler–ambassador
Burt Lancaster, actor
Fritz Lang, director
Burgess Meredith, actor
Edward R. Murrow, newsman
Gen. George Patton Jr., U.S. military
Edith Piaf, French chanteuse
Otto Preminger, director
George Raft, actor (costar in *Manpower,* '41)
Erich Maria Remarque, writer
Edward G. Robinson, actor
William Saroyan, author
George Bernard Shaw, author
Frank Sinatra, singer-actor
Barbara Stanwyck, actress
Adlai Stevenson, politician
James Stewart, actor
Mike Todd, showman-producer
Josef von Sternberg, director
John Wayne, actor
Orson Welles, director-actor
Michael Wilding, actor

Marlene Dietrich 1901–1992

✦ She Said

No man falls in love with me that I don't want to have fall in love with me.

They [men] *always want to put their things in. That's all they want.*

In Europe it doesn't matter if you're a man or a woman. We make love with anyone we find attractive.

It's a mistake to try to please everyone. Besides being impossible, there's more of a mystique attached to someone who's got a bit of temperament in her personality. People admire the nonconformist.

✦ They Said

She has sex without gender. —Kenneth Tynan, who should know since she gave it to him

I always did want to get into Marlene's pants. —Tallulah Bankhead's teasing—but pointedly lesbian—remark on replacing Dietrich in *A Very Different Woman* ('31)

I wish I had slept with [Marlene Dietrich]. *She had a very masculine thing about her, but she maintained a sexual allure.* —Madonna

✦ First Sexual Experience

Lost her virginity at age fifteen to Prof. Robert Reitz, a violinist and music teacher in Weimar, Germany.

✦ Husbands

Rudolf (Rudy) Sieber, chicken farmer

✦ Did You Know?

Her method for avoiding pregnancies, considering all the lovers she had? Dietrich was obsessed with ice water and vinegar douches, purchasing Heinz vinegar by the case. Yul Brynner was the exception to her douches; even in her fifties, she dreamed of (and tried to) get pregnant by him.

Dietrich preferred fellatio, as she felt it allowed her to control the sexual situation. According to her husband, she only met George Bernard Shaw once. As was her custom on meeting and talking with someone with whom she was impressed, Dietrich knelt at his feet. When she met George Bernard Shaw, she knelt, unbuttoned his fly, and removed his penis. "Of course I had to do it before we could talk," she said.

Doris Duke 1912–1993

✦ She Said

American men have no talent for being married to a rich woman.

It appalls me to be so spoken of. It is terrifying. —How she felt about being called "the richest girl in the world"

I am not a recluse. I'm a loose wreck.

✦ They Said

She was frigid. —Jimmy Cromwell, her first husband

Doris had the most beautiful legs in the world. —Brian Aherne, actor, who had them wrapped around his neck on occasion

✦ First Sexual Experience

Probably lost her virginity to Elmer F. Quinn, a New York politician with whom she was involved.

✦ Husbands

James H. R. (Jimmy) Cromwell, socialite
Porfirio Rubirosa, Dominican playboy-diplomat

✦ Did You Know?

Duke liked to have her toes tongued and sucked furiously.

Duke, who once had a screen test at MGM, had a lifelong fascination with artistic performing and always tried to "improve" the scarcity of talent she possessed. To further that dubious talent she took dancing lessons from Bill (Bojangles) Robinson and singing lessons from Aretha Franklin's father.

Duke, among all her other possessions, always kept at least four tons (eight thousand pounds) of pure gold bars stored in a Swiss bank.

When she died, Duke was living in her Hollywood home, Falcon's Lair, the former home of Rudolph Valentino.

It didn't always pay to stand too close to Duke. One of her servants and rumored lover was run over and killed by an automobile she was driving, while he was opening the gate to one of her estates. Of course, it was all ruled an accidental death.

Lovers, Flings, or Just Friends?

- Brian Aherne, actor
- Leon Amar, decorator
- Louis Bromfield, novelist
- Peter Byrne, wildlife conservationist
- Joey Castro, jazz pianist
- Alec Cunningham-Reid, British member of Parliament
- Errol Flynn, actor
- Luis Gastral, Brazilian banker
- John Gomez, companion and employee
- Cary Grant, actor
- Captain Henderson, British soldier
- Duke Kahanamoku, Hawaiian Olympic medalist in swimming
- Charles MacArthur, writer and husband of actress Helen Hayes
- Tex McCrary, radio performer
- David Niven, actor
- Aristotle Onassis, Greek shipping tycoon
- Gen. George C. Patton, U.S. military
- Elvis Presley, singer-actor
- Taylor A. (Tap) Pryor, socialite
- Gilbert Roland, actor
- Franco Rossellini, who was part owner of the notorious film *Caligula* ('80)
- George Sanders, actor
- Jay Sims, newsreel commentator
- Eduardo Tirella, set designer
- *and* lots of Hawaiian beach-boy types because Duke highly favored "dark meat"

Lovers, Flings, or Just Friends?

Desi Arnaz Jr., actor and son of Lucille Ball and Desi Arnaz

Gene Kirkwood, producer

Frank Sinatra, singer-actor

Patty Duke 1946–

✦ She Said

I was very poor when I was little, and if I hadn't become a child star, I don't know what I would have been. I might have turned into a prostitute or something.

I had days when I did nothing but cry for nine hours straight.

✦ They Said

I thought she was a "Method actress." Afterwards somebody informed me she was merely a manic-depressive. —Elsa Lanchester, actress

✦ First Sexual Experience

Lost her virginity to Harry Falk, a television director, whom she later married.

✦ Husbands

Harry Falk, television director

Michael Tell, rock promoter (but since she hardly knew him, it only lasted fifteen days)

John Astin, actor

Michael Pearce, U.S. military

✦ Did You Know?

It's hard to think of "little" Patty as the older, femme fatale—but she was once upon a time. During her affair with Desi Arnaz Jr., Duke was twenty-three—and the older woman—to young Desi's seventeen. And how did comedienne Lucille Ball react when she discovered her son was conducting an affair with an older woman? To put it mildly, she was less than thrilled.

Faye Dunaway 1941–

✦ She Said

Sex isn't everything. Love isn't everything. Nothing can be everything.

I want no fences around me, unless I erect them myself.

When I was young, I rebelled a lot. I purposely tried to do the opposite of what my mother had done, just to be different, to maybe find myself.

I have had work, possessions, love, sex, and men. I worked during the day and I had a man to share my bed at night because I need love and sex—but never one without the other.

✦ They Said

I have loved many women, but Faye was the one I loved the most. —Marcello Mastroianni

Next to her, the rest of us are mere fawn-yearlings. —Candice Bergen

Faye Dunaway is the most unprofessional actress I ever worked with, and that includes Miriam Hopkins, even! —Bette Davis

✦ First Sexual Experience

Unknown.

✦ Husbands

Peter Wolf, rock musician (of the J. Geils Band)
Terry O'Neill, photographer

✦ Did You Know?

Faye got into a tiff at a celebrity fashion show with Raquel Welch, when they began arguing over which of them would end up wearing a specific outfit they both liked. Faye proclaimed that she should wear it, because she "knew how to sell" it. Raquel got the last word, because she enquired about "with what body" was Faye going to wear the dress.

Lovers, Flings, or Just Friends?

- Marlon Brando, actor
- Andrew Braunsberg, producer
- Lenny Bruce, comedian
- Michael Caine, actor (costar in *Hurry Sundown,* '67)
- Marcello Mastroianni, actor (costar in *A Place for Lovers,* '69)
- Steve McQueen, actor (costar in *The Thomas Crown Affair,* '68)
- Jack Nicholson, actor (costar in *Chinatown,* '74)
- Miguel (Mike) O'Brian, actor-waiter
- Jerry Schatzberg, fashion photographer
- Renzo Soria, Italian architect
- Harris Yulin, actor (costar in *Doc,* '71)

Britt Ekland 1942–

✦ She Said

Sex is a man's supreme game.

I said I don't sleep with married men, but what I meant was I don't sleep with happily married men.

✦ They Said

She's a professional girlfriend and an amateur actress. —Peter Sellers, actor and husband

Mum goes for boy lovers. —Victoria Sellers, daughter, on her mom's "affairs"

As an actress you symbolize all that we are looking for in Europe. You are not only beautiful, but your name means a great deal at the box office. —Count Ascanio Cicogna, Italian producer, spouting the typical flattery to which actresses are subjected

✦ First Sexual Experience

Lost her virginity to a crew-cut boy in Stockholm, Sweden, who played drums in a jazz club at night and sold cars during the day. She said, "The first time with any man is always a disappointment."

✦ Husbands

Peter Sellers, actor (costar in *The Bobo,* '67)

Jim McDonnell (Slim Jim Phantom), rock musician with the Stray Cats

✦ Did You Know?

Ekland appears to have been pursued ardently by Sellers because a clairvoyant had told him that he would soon marry a woman with the initials BE.

Victoria Sellers, Britt's daughter by actor Peter Sellers, is a good friend and sometimes roommate of Heidi Fleiss, the latest in a long line of infamous Hollywood madams.

Lovers, Flings, or Just Friends?

- Lou Adler, record producer
- Warren Beatty, actor
- Boris, her ballet tutor in Sweden
- Count Ascanio "Bino" Cicogna, Italian producer
- Dick Ebersol, television producer
- Ron Ely, actor
- Gio, an Italian gigolo
- George Hamilton, actor
- Lord Patrick Lichfield, cousin of Queen Elizabeth II
- Lee Majors, actor
- Ryan O'Neal, actor
- Jaime Ostros, son of a Spanish bullfighter
- Igi Polidori, Italian director
- Robert Rupley IV, millionaire
- Rod Stewart, rock singer (she said he regarded "every orgasm as his testimony of love for me")
- *plus* assorted actors, students, and other men

Frances Farmer 1913–1970

✦ She Said

It's a little sad to think that people are so lonely that they'll sit down and write to people they've never met. —Remarking on how she viewed fan mail

✦ They Said

Whatever it is that makes a star, she had it, and you knew it the minute she looked at you. —Glenn Hughes, head of the drama department at the University of Washington and one of Farmer's first drama instructors

The nicest thing I can say about Frances Farmer is that she is unbearable. —William Wyler, director, who assumed the helm of *Come and Get It* ('36) after Howard Hawks left the film

✦ First Sexual Experience

Unknown for certain, but possibly lost her virginity while a student at the University of Washington to a member of the radical, "artistic" crowd, a star of campus plays named Chet Huntley, who later achieved fame as a television newscaster.

✦ Husbands

Leif Erickson, actor
Alfred Lobley, Seattle city engineer
Lee Mikesell, show-business promoter

✦ Did You Know?

Farmer's bizarre mother, Lillian, who was responsible for her many incarcerations, was quite a character. Once she interbred three strains of chicken (a Rhode Island Red, a White Leghorn, and an Andalusian Blue) and created a red, white, and blue chicken. She called it the Bird Americana and lobbied to have it replace the eagle as the U.S. national emblem.

While she was incarcerated by her mother, supposedly for her "mental illness," Farmer was sexually assaulted by hundreds of orderlies, friends of orderlies, and patients (both male and female) at the Western Washington State Hospital at Steilacoom. The orderlies also sold her sexual favors to many, many drunken soldiers from nearby Fort Lewis Army Base, who were allowed to gang-rape her.

Lovers, Flings, or Just Friends?

Howard Clurman, producer

Bing Crosby, actor (costar in *Rhythm on the Range,* '36)

John Garfield, actor (costar in *Flowing Gold,* '40)

Howard Hawks, director (who began directing her in *Come and Get It,* '36, before being removed)

Clifford Odets, playwright

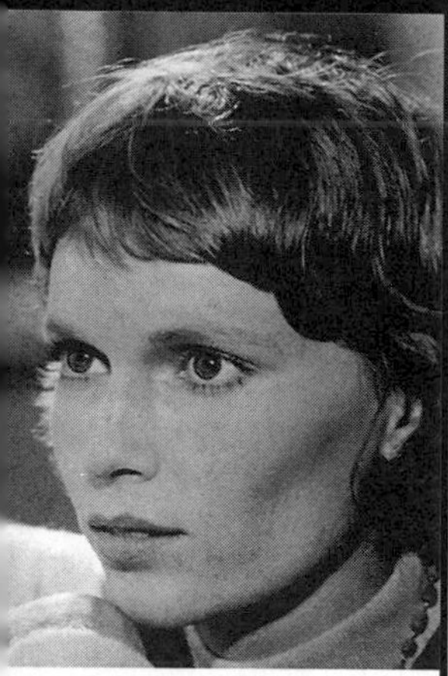

Mia Farrow 1945–

✦ She Said

I can match bottoms with anyone in Hollywood. —Evidently assessing one of her physical attributes against those found on other actresses

Now I know why I was born. —Her only remark at the party where she and Sinatra "officially" announced their engagement

✦ They Said

There are 127 varieties of nuts; she's 116 of them. —Roman Polanski, expressing (surprisingly) his high opinion of her

I always knew Frank [Sinatra] *would end up in bed with a little boy.* —Ava Gardner, commenting on her ex-husband Frank Sinatra, who married Mia

I've got Scotch older than she is. —Dean Martin's telegram to Sinatra, teasing about the age discrepancy between the bride and groom

I'll get you down from that drug if I have to pull you down by your pubic hairs. —Peter Sellers, discovering that Mia had done mescaline with John Phillips (of the Mamas and the Papas)

✦ First Sexual Experience

Unknown.

✦ Husbands

Frank Sinatra, singer-actor (who was also the third Mr. Ava Gardner)

Andre Previn, conductor-composer

✦ Did You Know?

Mia's godmother was Hollywood gossip columnist Louella Parsons, and her godfather was homosexual director George Cukor. Her father, director John Farrow—who had a reputation as a womanizer—was made a papal prince by the Vatican in reward for a book he wrote on Catholicism.

Mia, wearing a long, white dress, and accompanied by Salvador Dali, once watched a Greenwich Village orgy.

After having her husband, Andre, stolen by Mia, Dory Previn wrote a song called "Beware of Young Girls." Given what later happened to Mia's relationship with Woody Allen, Dory's song is quite ironic.

Lovers, Flings, or Just Friends?

- Woody Allen, director-actor (costar in *Broadway Danny Rose,* '84)
- Eddie Fisher, singer
- Sven Nykist, Swedish cinematographer
- John Phillips, singer (of the Mamas and the Papas)
- Roman Polanski, director (directed her in *Rosemary's Baby,* '68)
- Peter Sellers, actor

Sally Field 1946–

✦ She Said

"I look like the people you might have grown up with."

This country has a very adolescent attitude toward sexuality. [American men] *are like fifteen-year-old boys with a hard-on twenty-four hours a day.*

I was young and not wise, and the people around me wanted me to stay the darling, little adorable person forever.

✦ They Said

I don't entirely agree with a friend of mine who says that Miss Field is simply a Mary Tyler Moore someone has stepped on. —Vincent Canby, critic

I'm not going to get into a pissing contest with Sally, because I'd lose. —Burt Reynolds, commenting on the breakup of their relationship

✦ First Sexual Experience

Probably lost her virginity to her high school sweetheart, Steve, since he was also her first husband. She has said, "I must have lost my virginity around fifteen. It was terrible, terrible."

✦ Husbands

Steve Craig, high school sweetheart
Alan Griesman, producer

✦ Did You Know?

Sally has said that she was truly scared when she won her first Oscar for *Norma Rae* ('79). "All I could think of was, 'Don't fall down,' because I didn't have any underwear on."

Lovers, Flings, or Just Friends?

Johnny Carson, entertainer–television personality

Kevin Kline, actor

Burt Reynolds, actor (costar of *Smokey and the Bandit*, '77)

Jane Fonda 1937–

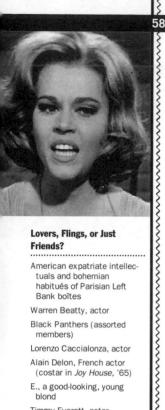

✦ She Said

I can only play love scenes well when I am in love with my partner.

Working in Hollywood does give one a certain expertise in the field of prostitution.

I went wild. —Describing her reaction to discovering that she was attractive to males

✦ They Said

Jane had a reputation for being easy. —Brooke Hayward, on Jane's years as a student at Vassar

It's not easy being married to Joan of Arc. —Roger Vadim, on the experience of being married to Fonda during her antiwar-activist period

Daughter? I don't have a daughter. —Henry Fonda, answering a reporter's query on how he felt about her activities

✦ First Sexual Experience

Lost her virginity to a much older, divorced man, a European (possibly an Italian), probably in the fall of 1955, when she was a student at Vassar.

✦ Husbands

Roger Vadim, French director (directed her in *Barbarella,* '68)
Tom Hayden, antiwar activist–politician
Ted Turner, television mogul

✦ Did You Know?

The first time they went to bed, Vadim couldn't perform. His impotence—caused, he claimed later, by Jane's sexually aggressive behavior—lasted for three frustrating weeks.

Did Jane engage in lesbian activities when Vadim began bringing other women home to bed while married to Fonda? After all, he said, "She seemed to understand and, as always, went all out—*all the way.*" Actress Jennifer Lee (and later wife of Richard Pryor) claims in her book that she successfully evaded being lured into sexual fun and games with the Vadims, but goes on to speculate whether or not such people as Eric Emerson, a Warhol groupie, and actress Patti D'Arbanville were as lucky as she.

Lovers, Flings, or Just Friends?

- American expatriate intellectuals and bohemian habitués of Parisian Left Bank boîtes
- Warren Beatty, actor
- Black Panthers (assorted members)
- Lorenzo Caccialonza, actor
- Alain Delon, French actor (costar in *Joy House,* '65)
- E., a good-looking, young blond
- Timmy Everett, actor
- James Franciscus, actor
- Fred Gardner, part-time screenwriter–Marxist activist
- Christian Marquand, French actor
- Baron Matalon, hairdresser
- Huey Newton, criminal–Black Panther activist
- Bob Scheer, magazine editor
- Jay Sebring, hairstylist
- Donald Sutherland, actor (costar in *Klute,* '71)
- U.S. servicemen she met while performing with the F.T.A. troupe
- Andreas Voutsinas, acting teacher
- Sandy Whitelaw, socialite

Joan Fontaine 1917–

✦ She Said

I married first, won the Oscar before Olivia did, and if I die first, she'll undoubtedly be livid because I beat her to it!

Obviously a wife has to do a lot of pretending to be successful; to make a difficult, selfish husband of hers feel that he is the greatest man alive even when she knows damned well that he isn't.

Marriage, as an institution, is as dead as the dodo bird.

✦ They Said

She's the kind of woman who, inevitably, winds up alone. —William Dozier, her second husband

She pranced in one day when we were shooting and said she was sorry for being late, but after all, the whole picture rested on her shoulders and it was a heavy responsibility. —Mitch Leisen, recalling an incident while he was directing her in *Frenchman's Creek* ('44)

✦ First Sexual Experience

Lost her virginity to much older actor Conrad Nagel.

✦ Husbands

Brian Aherne, actor

William Dozier, director (who later became the second Mr. Ann Rutherford)

Collier Young, writer-producer (she's called him her "favorite husband") (who was also the second Mr. Ida Lupino)

Alfred Wright, writer

✦ Did You Know?

The day before their wedding, Brian Aherne tried to back out. Then, on their wedding night, he lay in bed with Joan and discussed the torrid affair he'd been having with Marlene Dietrich. Next, he bounced out of bed and demonstrated ballet steps he'd taught Dietrich's daughter, Maria. Joan has written, "I grew increasingly numb." She had to wait several more nights before the marriage was finally consummated.

Lovers, Flings, or Just Friends?

- George "Slim" Aarons, photojournalist
- Charles Addams, cartoonist
- Gustavo Berckemeyer, Peruvian importer
- Harry Crocker, writer
- John Houseman, actor-producer
- Ben Kean, physician
- Prince Aly Khan, playboy-socialite
- Jose Maria Martarell, Spanish bullfighter
- Conrad Nagel, actor
- David O. Selznick, producer
- George Stevens, director
- Adlai Stevenson, politician
- Peter Viertal, writer (who later became the second Mr. Deborah Kerr)
- Tom Wanamaker, department-store heir

Lovers, Flings, or Just Friends?

Dennis Allen, actor

Joel Ashley, actor

Baron Raven Erik Angus Barnekow, German aircraft manufacturer (whom she met at one of the Countess di Frasso's parties)

Charles Baskerville, writer-illustrator

George Brent, actor (costar in *Living on Velvet,* '35)

Maurice Chevalier, singer-actor

Eddie Chodorov, screenwriter

Delmer Daves, writer-producer-director

Howard "Hap" Graham, stage manager

Leslie Howard, actor (costar in *British Agent,* '34)

Herbert Marshall, actor

"Prince" Alexis (Alec) Mdivani, Georgian pseudoroyalty and fortune hunter

McKay Morris, actor

William Powell, actor

Allan A. Ryan Jr., businessman

Edgar Selwyn, theatrical producer

Perc Westmore, makeup specialist of the Westmores of Hollywood family

Kay Francis 1899–1968

✦ She Said

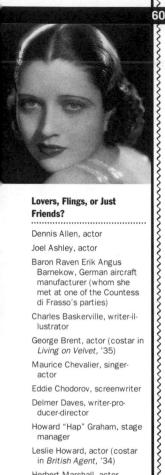

I'm not a star. I'm a woman. *And I want to get fucked!* —Screaming in a rage in her London hotel room during a publicity tour

I didn't give a shit. I wanted the money. —Responding to a comment from Bette Davis, who'd said that she "cared" personally for the career, not the money it made

The one thing I have is that I will never have to worry about money as long as I live. —And she didn't; her will left a bequest of a million dollars to train Seeing Eye dogs

I can't wait to be forgotten. —Adding to her reputation as being almost as "reclusive" as Garbo about personal publicity

✦ They Said

In many ways she was a lonely lady. People were afraid to approach her. —Ouida Rathbone, Hollywood hostess and wife of actor Basil

Despite her lisp, despite her background as a model, despite her inexperience in the theater, she had that indefinable presence that somehow enabled her to be convincing as well as beautiful. —Edward G. Robinson, actor and costar in *I Loved a Woman* ('33)

✦ First Sexual Experience

Unknown.

✦ Husbands

James Dwight Francis, playboy (who later married the daughter of poet Robert Frost)

William Gaston, socialite

John Meehan, playwright-actor

Kenneth MacKenna, producer-actor (costar in *Virtuous Sin,* '30)

plus, at one time or another, Francis was rumored to have been secretly married to anywhere from one to three other men

✦ Did You Know?

During a magazine interview, Francis advised women not to throw away their old ermine coats. If they were cut up, she said, they'd make divine bath mats.

Eva Gabor 1922(?)–1995

✦ She Said

Marriage is too interesting an experiment to be tried once or twice.

All any girl needs at any time in history is simple velvet and basic diamonds.

We Gabors are supposed to do nothing but take bubble baths and drip with jewels, but I've worked like a demon. I didn't have time to sit in the bubbles.

I know scandal makes you famous, but it wasn't for me. I must sound terribly square, but I'm not.

✦ They Said

The Gabor sisters are highly competitive. There is, I would say, a strong sibling rivalry. —Richard Brown, ex-spouse

Marriage is for bores—I mean Gabors. —Oscar Levant, wit

Their husbands and their dalliances have made a loose-leaf address book a necessity. —Fred De Cordova, producer-director, on the demands of being friends with the Gabor sisters

✦ First Sexual Experience

Unknown.

✦ Husbands

Dr. Eric Drimmer, psychologist (who was also the in-house shrink at MGM Studios at one time)
Charles Isaac, Realtor
Dr. John E. Williams, surgeon
Richard Brown, stockbroker
Frank Jamieson, vice president, North American Rockwell

✦ Did You Know?

Eva once got caught swimming in the nude by two gentlemen. When they saw her, they said, "Hi, Eva," to which she replied devilishly, "No, dahling . . . it's Zsa Zsa."

Lovers, Flings, or Just Friends?

Stuart Barthelmess, son of silent-screen star Richard Barthelmess
Glenn Ford, actor
Merv Griffin, entertainer
John Hodiak, actor
Tyrone Power, actor
Frank Sinatra, singer-actor

Lovers, Flings, or Just Friends?

- Mustafa Kemal Atatürk, dictator of Turkey
- Greg Bautzer, Hollywood attorney–escort of beautiful women
- Richard Burton, actor
- Sean Connery, actor
- Hal Hayes, construction millionaire
- Nicky Hilton, hotel-chain heir and stepson (son of the second Mr. Zsa Zsa Gabor)
- John F. Kennedy, president
- Prince Aly Khan, millionaire playboy
- Mario Lanza, actor-singer (costar in *For the First Time*, '59)
- William S. Paley, head of CBS
- Porfirio Rubirosa, Dominican diplomat-playboy
- Willi Schmidt-Kentner, German composer
- Frank Sinatra, singer-actor
- Robert Stralie, businessman
- Franchot Tone, actor
- Rafael Trujillo Jr., son of the dictator of the Dominican Republic

Zsa Zsa Gabor 1917 (?)–

✦She Said

I believe in large families; every woman should have at least three husbands.

I don't mind sleeping with him, dollink, but he vants to be seen *with me! Imagine, a headvaiter!*

✦They Said

She's unbelievable—you can't believe a damn thing she says. —Earl Wilson, columnist

Zsa Zsa knew more days on which gifts can be given than appear on any holiday calendar. —Conrad Hilton, wealthy hotelman and second gift-giving husband

Zsa Zsa Gabor has discovered the secret of perpetual middle age. —Oscar Levant, actor-musician-wit

"I don't know how she does it, but she can make more fuss about nothing than anyone in Hollywood—and, believe me, I've known them all." —Louella Parsons, gossip columnist

✦First Sexual Experience

Has claimed, at various times, that she lost her virginity to several different men. One time it was first husband Burhan Belge, a Turkish diplomat; another time it was Turkish dictator Kemal Atatürk.

✦Husbands

Burhan Belge, Turkish diplomat
Conrad Hilton, hotel-chain magnate
George Sanders, actor (who was also later married—briefly—to her older sister, Magda)
Herbert Hutner, businessman
Joshua Cosden Jr., Texas businessman
Jack Ryan, inventor of the Barbie doll and Chatty Cathy
Michael O'Hara, attorney
Frederick von Anhalt, German nobleman

✦Did You Know?

One of Zsa Zsa's greatest performances came at a Las Vegas press conference, where she displayed—or rather hid under an eyepatch—the black eye that lover Rubirosa gave her. Their argument came about over Rubi's impending marriage to heiress Barbara Hutton.

Greta Garbo 1905–1990

✦ She Said

I give them everything I've got on the screen, why do they try to usurp my privacy?

I have tried everything at various times of my life, but my body and my thoughts were never satisfied.

I do not want to be a silly temptress. I cannot see any sense in getting dressed up and doing nothing but tempting men in pictures.

✦ They Said

She had extraordinary intuitions, especially in the realm of erotic expression. —Melvyn Douglas, costar in *Ninotchka* ('39)

I thought that in most of her films she looked a little like Snow White's stepmother. —Marcello Mastroianni, actor

The most inhibited person I have ever worked with. —Ernst Lubitsch, director

She was lousy in bed. —Erich Marie Remarque, author

✦ First Sexual Experience

Lost her virginity one summer in her early teens, when she and her sister Alva had sex outdoors in a tent. Garbo also used to masturbate frequently—in her early teens—while looking at photos of her favorite film actors.

✦ Husbands

Garbo never married, but she did leave John Gilbert standing at the altar on their scheduled wedding day.

✦ Did You Know?

Garbo, while in her teens, discovered she had a most unusual menstrual cycle; it came almost once a week. She consulted gynecologists, who informed her that while this affliction was rare, it did occur in some women and was virtually untreatable. She then developed a regimen to treat herself; she walked a lot, spent lots of time alone, and developed a fondness for "natural" foods. Since she was plagued throughout her life with this unnatural cycle, she never married, feeling that she wouldn't make either a proper wife or mother. Her decision, due to her shyness, not to reveal her condition—and the methods she developed to cope with it—all added up to giving her the mystique of being an aloof almost-recluse.

Lovers, Flings, or Just Friends?

- Max Baer, boxer-actor
- Cecil Beaton, British photographer
- George Brent, actor (costar in *The Painted Veil,* '34)
- Louise Brooks, actress
- Fifi D'Orsay, actress
- Mercedes de Acosta, lesbian writer
- Dolores Del Rio, actress
- Marie Dressler, actress
- Paulette Duval, actress
- John Gilbert, actor (costar in *Flesh and the Devil,* '27)
- Lilyan Fashman, actress
- Einar Hanson, Swedish actor
- Gayelord Hauser, health guru
- Leland Hayward, agent-producer
- Maria Huxley, wife of author Aldous Huxley
- Joseph P. Kennedy, financier and father of president
- Beatrice Lillie, actress
- Rouben Mamoulian, director
- Carson McCullers, author
- Ramon Novarro, actor (costar in *Mata Hari,* '31)
- William S. Paley, businessman and later head of CBS
- Erich Marie Remarque, author
- George Schlee, husband of couturier Valentina
- Dorothy Sebastian, actress (costar in *A Woman of Affairs,* '29)
- Prince Sigurd, Duke of Upland, Swedish royalty
- Mauritz Stiller, director
- Leopold Stokowski, conductor
- Robert Taylor, actor (costar in *Camille,* '36)
- Salka Viertel, lesbian actress-writer

Lovers, Flings, or Just Friends?

Greg Bautzer, attorney–Hollywood escort

Turhan Bey, Turkish actor

Richard Burton, actor (costar in *Night of the Iguana,* '64)

Mario Cabre, Spanish bullfighter

Walter Chiari, Italian actor

Luis Miguel Dominguin, Spanish bullfighter

Howard Duff, actor (later became third Mr. Ida Lupino)

Robert Evans, producer

Anthony Franciosa, actor (costar of *The Naked Maja,* '59)

Clark Gable (costar in *The Hucksters,* '47)

Farley Granger, actor

Howard Hughes, aviation-cinema mogul

John Huston, director (directed her in *The Bible,* '66)

Fernando Lamas, actor

Peter Lawford, actor

Robert Mitchum, actor (costar in *My Forbidden Past,* '51)

David Niven, actor

Porfirio Rubirosa, diplomat

George C. Scott, actor (costar in *The Bible,* '66)

Omar Sharif, actor (costar in *Mayerling,* '68)

Johnny Stompanato, minor gangster

Robert Taylor, actor (costar in *The Bribe,* '49)

Mel Torme, singer

Peter Viertel, screenwriter (who later became the second Mr. Deborah Kerr)

Robert Walker, actor (costar in *One Touch of Venus,* '48)

plus many, many other actors, bullfighters, and assorted men *including* a Mexican beach boy during the filming of *Night of the Iguana* ('64) who beat up her in public

Ava Gardner 1922–1990

✦ She Said

Some people say Liz and I are whores, but we are saints. We do not hide our loves hypocritically, and when love we are loyal and faithful to our men.

I'm one Hollywood star who hasn't tried to slash her wrists or take sleeping pills.

That's what attracts 'em, honey chile. —Replying to a taunt from Humphrey Bogart that she was just a "li'l hillbilly girl"

✦ They Said

She can't act, she can't talk. She's terrific. —Louis B. Mayer, on seeing her first screen test

She also had big brown nipples, which, when aroused, stood out like some double-long, golden California raisins. —Mickey Rooney

Ava has been completely victimized by the kind of life she has led and, as a result, has become the kind of person she is today. —Artie Shaw, her second husband, who was no paragon of virtue and clean living himself

✦ First Sexual Experience

Lost her virginity at age nineteen to first husband Mickey Rooney, on January 10, 1942, their wedding day.

✦ Husbands

Mickey Rooney, actor

Artie Shaw, musician (who was also the first Mr. Lana Turner and the fourth Mr. Evelyn Keyes)

Frank Sinatra, singer-actor (who was also the first Mr. Mia Farrow)

✦ Did You Know?

When she lived in Madrid, Ava's downstairs neighbor was exiled Argentinean dictator Juan Perón (and widower of Eva "Evita" Perón, ex–film actress). Although he was ensconced with some unsavory doings of his own—he kept both his mistress, Isabel, and the body of Evita in a crystal coffin in his apartment—Perón still complained about all the noise and shenanigans erupting constantly from Ava's place upstairs.

Howard Hughes once slapped Ava so hard that he dislocated her jaw; Ava grabbed a vase and shattered it over his head.

Judy Garland 1922–1969

✦ She Said

I have to take them, but I hate them. I hate the wake-up pills the worst, because they make me hop around like a Mexican jumping bean.

If I get fat, I couldn't work. So, I mustn't get fat.

All my life I've done everything to excess.

✦ They Said

For God's sake, darling, watch Judy, because if she goes into the bathroom, she'll eat up every single pill I have in there. —Lauren Bacall to Zsa Zsa Gabor at a party in Bacall's home

Judy, you keep this up and you're going to hurt yourself. —A physician chiding her after one of her "suicide" attempts

Judy got around. She tried to make people fall in love with her, and she was quite successful at it. —Chuck Walters, a friend and professional colleague

There's wasn't a thing that gal couldn't do—except look after herself. —Bing Crosby

✦ First Sexual Experience

Possibly lost her virginity to ten-years-older musician Artie Shaw, who was her first serious love and a notorious womanizer.

✦ Husbands

David Rose, musician (who was also the second Mr. Martha Raye)
Vincente Minnelli, director (directed her in *The Pirate,* '48)
Sid Luft, producer (who had previously been married to actress Lynn Bari)
Mark Herron, actor
Mickey Deans, nightclub manager

✦ Did You Know?

Judy's father, Frank Gumm, was a homosexual, as was her second husband, Vincente Minnelli, as was her first son-in-law.

Garland claimed her first marriage to David Rose failed because he was repulsed when she asked him to perform cunnilingus on her.

Garland aborted pregnancies by David Rose, Tyrone Power, and Sid Luft.

Lovers, Flings, or Just Friends?

Carleton Alsop, producer
Betty Asher, personal publicist
Greg Bautzer, attorney–Hollywood escort
David Begelman, agent
Dirk Bogarde, actor (costar on *I Could Go on Singing,* '63)
Yul Brynner, actor
Jackie Cooper, actor
Fred Finkelhoffe, playwright-screenwriter
Eddie Fisher, singer
Glenn Ford, actor
Tom Green, personal manager
Aly Khan, socialite-playboy
Mario Lanza, singer-actor
Peter Lawford, actor
Oscar Levant, pianist-composer
Joseph Mankiewicz, writer-director
James Mason, actor (costar in *A Star Is Born,* '54)
Ethel Merman, singer-actress
Johnny Meyer, musician
André Phillipe, cabaret singer
Tyrone Power, actor
Harry Rubin, electrician–general factotum
Artie Shaw, musician
Frank Sinatra, actor-singer
Robert Stack, actor
Kay Thompson, writer–cabaret star
Robert Walker, actor (costar *The Clock,* '45)
Orson Welles, director-actor
plus lots of other men and women in all sorts of professions

Lovers, Flings, or Just Friends?

Louis B. Mayer, head of MGM
Laurence Olivier, actor
Benny Thau, MGM executive

Greer Garson 1908–

✦ She Said

I thought of Hollywood as Babylon-on-the-Pacific.

On the whole I do not enjoy actors who seek to commune with their armpits, so to speak. —Expressing her contempt for Method actors

✦ They Said

One of the most richly syllabled queenly horrors of Hollywood. —Pauline Kael, film critic

You don't get any cussing from her. I've worked with some of the biggest dames in the business, and you'd be surprised what they say when they're hot under the collar. Not her. —An electrician in the crew of one of her films

I must say she is a clever, witty, erudite lady, and I like that in people. —Maureen O'Sullivan, actress and mother of Mia Farrow

There are actors who work in movies. And there are movie stars. She was a movie star. —Teresa Wright, who costared with her in *Mrs. Miniver* ('42)

✦ First Sexual Experience

Unknown.

✦ Husbands

Edwin Alec Snelson, British civil servant on leave from India (it lasted less than thirty days)
Richard Nye, actor (costar in *Mrs. Miniver,* '42)
Elijah E. "Buddy" Fogelson, Texas businessman

✦ Did You Know?

When Greer Garson arrived at MGM, someone in the publicity department thought it would be good to have her photographed with John Garfield, who was well-known for his amorous adventures in studio dressing rooms. Garson, being British, promptly sent Garfield a note requesting he join her for tea in her dressing room. He misunderstood the note, assuming he was being invited for something more, and arrived at the specified time. When Garson turned her back to make the tea, Garfield grabbed her saying, "Let's not fool around, Greer. I want to fuck you right now!" Garson broke free, and her commands of "Get out! Get out!" issued louder and louder, until Garfield stumbled from her dressing room thoroughly chagrined.

Paulette Goddard 1905–1990

✦ She Said

Never, ever sleep with a man until he gives you a pure white stone [diamond] *of at least ten carats.* —Advice given to Marlene Dietrich

Every woman needs jewels. They're small, easy to carry—easy to hide, in case the woman has a falling out with the man whom she regards as a keystone in her life.

I never discuss my private life. I feel that my life is one thing and my career another. —Snapping at the press when asked questions about her marriage to Charlie Chaplin

✦ They Said

When Paulette hit Hollywood, all the other starlets lost their novelty. —Anita Loos, playwright-screenwriter

Mmmm. She's nice. Me likee. —George Gershwin's description of his first meeting with Paulette in a note to a friend

Now she's rich as Croesus and can rot in her luxury. —Marlene Dietrich, on hearing of the death of Goddard's husband, author Erich Maria Remarque, who had once had a torrid affair with Dietrich

✦ First Sexual Experience

Unknown for certain. Probably lost her virginity to her first husband, one E. James, occupation uncertain, as she married him when she was in her late teens.

✦ Husbands

E. James, occupation uncertain, but rumored to have been a gambler who used Goddard as his shill

Charlie Chaplin, actor (costar in *Modern Times,* '36)

Burgess Meredith, actor

Erich Maria Remarque, author

✦ Did You Know?

The under-the-table fellatio scene in *Shampoo* ('75) was supposedly inspired by an incident that occurred when Goddard was dating director Anatole Litvak. Rumors abound over what happened, but one thing's for certain: Goddard did disappear under the table at Ciro's nightclub and something did go on down under, but nobody's been able to determine exactly what.

Lovers, Flings, or Just Friends?

- Greg Bautzer, attorney–Hollywood escort
- Bruce Cabot, actor
- Constance Collier, actress–acting coach
- Gary Cooper, actor (costar in *Northwest Mounted Police,* '40)
- Clark Gable, actor
- George Gershwin, composer
- John Hertz Jr., Yellow Cab and rental-car heir
- Cy Howard, screenwriter-producer
- John Huston, director
- Aldous Huxley, author
- Frida Kahlo, artist
- Sir Alexander Korda, producer
- Anderson Lawler, wealthy homosexual tobacco heir and one of Gary Cooper's old flames
- Charles Lederer, screenwriter (and nephew of actress Marion Davies)
- Mervyn LeRoy, director
- Anatole Litvak, director
- John McClain, newspaperman
- David Niven, actor
- Aristotle Onassis, shipping magnate
- Ramón Ortega, Mexican bullfighter
- Diego Rivera, Mexican painter
- Joseph Schenck, studio executive
- Artie Shaw, musician
- Spencer Tracy, actor
- John Wayne, actor (costar in *Reap the Wild Wind,* '42)
- H. G. Wells, author
- John Hay (Jock) Whitney, socialite-businessman

Lovers, Flings, or Just Friends?

- Desi Arnaz, singer-actor
- Rory Calhoun, actor
- Oleg Cassini, fashion designer
- Dan Dailey, actor (costar in *Mother Wore Tights,* '47)
- Dick Haymes, singer-actor (costar in *The Shocking Miss Pilgrim,* '47)
- Charlie Mace, musician
- Victor Mature, actor (costar in *Wabash Avenue,* '50)
- Jeff Parker, dancer
- Tyrone Power, actor (costar in *A Yank in the RAF,* '41)
- Charles Price, musician
- George Raft, actor (costar in *Palmy Days,* '31)
- Bob Remick, Las Vegas dancer
- Mickey Rooney, actor
- Artie Shaw, musician
- Robert Stack, actor
- Lee Thompson, millionaire playboy
- *plus* lots of dancers, actors, chorus boys and rough men she met in bars

Betty Grable 1916–1973

✦ She Said

Honey, Coogan taught me more tricks than a whore learns in a whorehouse.

I'm a truck driver's delight.

It wasn't that Mother pushed me, I was just raised to obey, no matter what it was.

✦ They Said

It was impossible to sit next to her and not want to get to know her better. —Desi Arnaz

The worst actress to give the most consistently bad performances. —*The Harvard Lampoon*

✦ First Sexual Experience

Probably lost her virginity to older actor George Raft, whom she started dating when she was fifteen.

✦ Husbands

Jackie Coogan, child actor (costar in *Million Dollar Legs,* '39)
Harry James, bandleader-trumpeter

✦ Did You Know?

Unknown to her until found by a physician, Grable once had a condom stuck inside her. Over a period of several months it created such a bad vaginal odor that Tyrone Power finally ceased his affair with her.

She aborted a baby fathered by Artie Shaw when he dropped her (amid their affair) to elope with Lana Turner. Shaw was also conducting an affair with Judy Garland at the same time.

Grable had a lifelong affection for chorus boys and dancers, many of whom were homosexual. When she couldn't find other sex partners, she'd press her demands on them to service her. But she really preferred rough men of the truck-driver and bartender type and especially liked to fellate them.

During a meeting in his office, Darryl Zanuck pulled out his large endowment, asking Grable if she thought it was "beautiful." She agreed it was, then said, "You can put it away now."

Sheilah Graham 1908–1988

✦ She Said

Personally, given the choice between a donkey and a chipmunk, I might choose the chipmunk. —Referring, obliquely, to her preference in the size of men's penises

When you are a columnist, especially a gossip columnist, you are never quite relaxed, even when you are supposed to be enjoying yourself.

✦ They Said

It's hard to believe that a girl as pretty as you is the biggest bitch in Hollywood. —Constance Bennett, who objected to some items about her in Graham's column, on first being introduced to the columnist. Graham quickly replied, "Not the biggest bitch, Connie, the *second*-biggest bitch!"

A chorus girl who missed the bus. —Joseph L. Mankiewicz, director-screenwriter

✦ First Sexual Experience

Unknown.

✦ Husbands

Maj. John Graham Gillam, businessman
Trevor Cresswell Lawrence Westbrook, British bureaucrat
Wojciechowicz Stanislaus (Stanley) Wojtkiewicz, football coach

✦ Did You Know?

The rumor bounced around Hollywood for years that Graham's lover F. Scott Fitzgerald suffered his fatal heart attack while they were in bed having sex. She said it was not so. According to her, Fitzgerald's attack came while he was sitting in a chair reading the *Princeton Alumni Weekly* magazine. Wherever he died, Fitzgerald did so without having ever seen Graham completely nude—she always kept her bra on during sex with him.

Lovers, Flings, or Just Friends?

- A. J. Ayer, British empiricist philosopher
- Savington Crampton
- Marquess of Donegall, British nobleman
- F. Scott Fitzgerald, author
- John Garfield, actor
- Eddie Mayer, screenwriter
- John O'Hara, author
- King Vidor, director
- John Hay "Jock" Whitney, millionaire socialite

Lovers, Flings, or Just Friends?

- George Englund, producer
- Frank Lovejoy, actor (costar in *In a Lonely Place,* '50)
- Jim McKenzie, producer
- Robert Mitchum, actor (costar in *Crossfire,* '47) (her sister was married to his brother)
- Jack Palance, actor
- Stanley Rubin, writer
- Peter Turner, British actor

Gloria Grahame 1925–1981

✦ She Said

It wasn't the way I looked at a man, it was the thought behind it.

To look sexy you've got to be thinking sexy while you're playing the scene.

✦ They Said

She has the manners of a schoolgirl and the eyes of a sorceress. —Cecil B. DeMille, who directed her in *The Greatest Show on Earth* ('53)

She's sexy in a strange way. Like a woman who's begging you to wallop her in the mouth 'cause she'd just love it. —Kris Kristofferson

She just seemed to prefer to be around men. —Shirley Jones, remarking on how Gloria didn't make friends with women

✦ First Sexual Experience

Unknown.

✦ Husbands

Stanley Clemets, actor
Nicholas Ray, director
Cy Howard, TV sitcom creator
Tony Ray, son of second husband Nicholas Ray

✦ Did You Know?

When she was twenty-eight and married to Nicholas Ray, her stepson Tony—aged thirteen—came to visit. Tony and Gloria promptly ended up in bed, until husband Nicholas came home and caught them. He threw Tony out of the house, and his marriage with Gloria soon collapsed. Several years later, Gloria and Tony married, and she bore him two sons. Thus, Tony became stepfather to his own stepbrother, who was only about ten years younger than Tony.

Melanie Griffith 1957–

✦ She Said

Sure I used to do drugs. I used to drink. I was wild. I could do anything I wanted and did.

Young girls in Hollywood can be very deceiving. You look like a woman, but you're still a child inside.

It's amazing the people who crawl out of the woodwork once there's a nude scene. —Remarking on how film crews grow in size while filming certain scenes

✦ They Said

Being a dumb blonde must run in that family. —Derek Jarman, director, sneering about Griffith and her mother, actress Tippi Hedren

✦ First Sexual Experience

Lost her virginity to actor (and future husband) Don Johnson when she was about fifteen.

✦ Husbands

Don Johnson, actor
Steven Bauer, actor
Don Johnson, actor

✦ Did You Know?

How did Melanie have the divorce papers served on hubby Don Johnson during their latest breakup? One tabloid claimed that she used a stunning—and blond—private detective, who presented them to Johnson while he was at a Planet Hollywood party in Washington, D.C.

Lovers, Flings, or Just Friends?

Antonio Banderas, actor
Warren Beatty, actor
Ryan O'Neal, actor

Jean Harlow 1911–1937

✦ She Said

All they are after is getting their hands underneath my dress.

My God, must I always wear a low-cut dress to be important?

✦ They Said

I'd have liked to have gone to bed with Jean Harlow. She was a beautiful blonde. The fellow who married her was impotent and he killed himself. I would have done the same. —Groucho Marx

Jean liked sex as much as the next person, but she wasn't the kind of girl to go around unzipping men's flies. —Kay Mulvey, MGM publicist

When it came to kissing—Harlow was the best. —Jimmy Stewart, actor

She didn't have enough ego to survive, and so the movies' greatest femme fatale simply died of sex starvation. —Anita Loos, screenwriter and author

✦ First Sexual Experience

Lost her virginity at age sixteen to Charles McGrew, a young man she married. She didn't enjoy her first sexual experience, saying, "I thought it was awful messy. A nothing."

✦ Husbands

Charles McGrew, playboy-socialite

Paul Bern, studio executive (she said she liked him because "he doesn't talk fuck, fuck, fuck all the time")

Harold Rosson, cinematographer (who was called Long Dong by some friends who'd seen him nude)

✦ Did You Know?

Harlow never wore a brassiere and always rubbed her nipples with ice cubes—to make them erect—before filming a scene. Many people who saw them commented that they were "remarkable."

Harlow died of uremic poisoning because her mother, a Christian Scientist, delayed medical treatment for her. Some say her illness was a result of a botched abortion, with fiancé William Powell the father of the unborn child.

Lovers, Flings, or Just Friends?

- Lew Ayres, actor
- Max Baer, boxer-actor
- William Bakewell, actor
- Marino Bello, stepfather-manager
- Roy Fox, bandleader
- Donald Friede, publisher
- Clark Gable, actor (costar in *Red Dust,* '32)
- James Hall, actor
- Howard Hawks, director
- Howard Hughes, aviation-cinema mogul
- Jesse Lasky Jr., son of film pioneer Jesse Lasky Sr.
- Chester Morris, actor (costar in *Red-Headed Woman,* '32)
- William Powell, actor (costar in *Reckless,* '35)
- Harry Richman, singer-actor
- Benjamin "Bugsy" Siegel, mobster
- Jimmy Stewart, actor (costar in *Wife vs. Secretary,* '35)
- Ernest Torgler, stockbroker
- Thomas Wolfe, author
- Abe "Longy" Zwillman, racketeer
- *plus* lots of salesmen, taxi drivers, and other assorted men she picked up at random

Pamela Digby Churchill Hayward Harriman 1920–

✦ She Said

Everybody talks about the rich men I have slept with, no one ever talks about the poor men I have slept with.

I've had quite a lot of what might be called global experience.

✦ They Said

Pamela's a geisha girl who made her man happy. They just didn't want to marry her. —Truman Capote, author–social gadfly

She's the ultimate gold digger. —Kenneth Wagg, husband of actress Margaret Sullavan

When Pamela met a man she adored, she just unconsciously assumed his identity, as if she were putting on a glove. —Leonora Hornblow, friend

✦ First Sexual Experience

Unknown.

✦ Husbands

Randolph Churchill, son of Sir Winston

Leland Hayward, agent-producer (and the third Mr. Margaret Sullavan)

W. Averell Harriman, businessman-politician

✦ Did You Know?

Pamela's open involvements with a number of well-known and powerful men raised some eyebrows, particularly when President Clinton appointed her U.S. Ambassador to France. While many who had known her in Britain during her marriage to Winston Churchill's son considered her a "tart," it was assumed that the French would be more understanding of her past sex life.

Lovers, Flings, or Just Friends?

- Gianni Agnelli, head of FIAT
- Frederick L. Anderson, U.S. Army general
- J. Carter Brown, director of the National Gallery of Art
- William Cahan, surgeon (who was once Gertrude Lawrence's son-in-law)
- Robert Capa, photographer
- Count Rudolfo Crespi, Italian socialite
- Carlos de Beistegui, socialite
- Elie de Rothschild, French banker
- Maurice Druon, French author
- Prince Aly Khan, socialite
- Joseph Kennedy, businessman (and father of President John F. Kennedy)
- Henry Luce, founder of *Time* and *Life*
- George McCullagh, newspaper owner
- Edward R. Murrow, journalist
- Stavros Niarchos, Greek shipping tycoon (and brother-in-law to Aristotle Onassis)
- Aristotle Onassis, Greek shipping tycoon
- William Paley, head of CBS
- Sir Charles Portal, British chief of air staff
- Frank Sinatra, singer-actor
- John Hay "Jock" Whitney, socialite-businessman

Lovers, Flings, or Just Friends?

Warren Beatty, actor (costar in *Shampoo,* '75)

Kurt Russell, actor (costar in *Overboard,* '87)

Goldie Hawn 1945–

✦ She Said

I used to dance in sequin pasties on tabletops with guys exposing themselves. —Reflecting on her days as a go-go dancer earning $25 a night in a New Jersey sleaze joint

Just because a man has something that sticks out doesn't mean he's got to put it anywhere and everywhere.

✦ They Said

Goldie Hawn is as bright as a dim lightbulb. —Totie Fields, comedienne

Ditsy, my eye, she's the brightest dumb blonde since Queen Boadicea sliced Roman kneecaps. —Victor Davis, British journalist

✦ First Sexual Experience

Unknown.

✦ Husbands

Gus Trikonis, director
Bill Hudson, comedian

✦ Did You Know?

When Hawn interviewed with Al Capp, who originated the comic strip, for a spot in the Broadway show based on his creation *Li'l Abner,* the one-legged cartoonist exposed his penis to her. Years later, after Capp was convicted of indecent exposure in another case, many other women came forward with similar tales of having suffered the same indignity from Capp.

While viewed primarily as a comedic actress, Hawn has a rather extensive—and varied—background in dance; she's run a dancing school, cancanned at a world's fair, go-goed in a cage, and chorined it in Las Vegas.

Susan Hayward 1918–1975

✦ She Said

Men! I'd like to fry 'em all in deep fat.

Oh, I know I've got big boobs, and I'm glad.

When you're dead, you're dead. Nobody is going to remember me when I'm dead.

✦ They Said

Anything I have to say about Susan Hayward you couldn't print. —Robert Preston, costar in *Tulsa* ('49)

She was distant, nontalkative, no sense of humor. —Robert Cummings, costar in *The Lost Moment* ('47)

✦ First Sexual Experience

Lost her virginity to a young man she almost eloped with in 1936, at age eighteen.

✦ Husbands

Jess Barker, actor
Eaton Floyd Chalkley Jr., businessman-lawyer

✦ Did You Know?

When Hayward was on her deathbed, dying from brain tumors and not permitted any nonfamily visitors, except Katharine Hepburn, a mysterious woman dressed in black arrived one day to see her. It was Greta Garbo, who was quickly admitted into the house. Since she and Hayward had never been friends, and most probably hadn't even met, it was a most unusual gesture on Garbo's part.

Lovers, Flings, or Just Friends?

- Donald "Red" Barry, actor
- John Beck, producer
- John Carroll, actor (costar of *Change of Heart,* '43)
- Oleg Cassini, fashion designer
- Jeff Chandler, actor (costar of *Thunder in the Sun,* '59)
- Richard Egan, actor
- Larry Ellis, actor
- Jorge Guinale, Brazilian millionaire
- Hal Hayes, businessman
- William Holden, actor (costar in *Young and Willing,* '43)
- Howard Hughes, aviation-cinema mogul
- John F. Kennedy, U.S. president
- Edward Lahey, politician
- Benny Meford, agent
- Dr. Frederick Meyer, academician
- Bob Neal, millionaire
- Ron Nelson, charity executive
- Ronald Reagan, actor
- Porfirio Rubirosa, Dominican diplomat-playboy
- Walter Wanger, producer
- Gordon White, publisher

Lovers, Flings, or Just Friends?

- Caryl Chessman, California's "Red Light" bandit, executed in the 1950s
- Luis Dominguin, Spanish bullfighter
- Kirk Douglas, actor
- Charles Feldman, agent
- Glenn Ford, actor (costar in *The Loves of Carmen,* '48)
- Bill Gilpin, artist
- Raymond Hakim, producer
- Hal Hayes, architect
- Howard Hughes, aviation-cinema mogul
- Mac Krim, businessman
- Peter Lawford, actor
- Tony Martin, singer (costar in *Music in My Heart,* '40)
- Victor Mature, actor (costar in *My Gal Sal,* '42)
- Gary Merrill, actor and the fourth Mr. Bette Davis
- Robert Mitchum, actor (costar in *Fire Down Below,* '57)
- David Niven, actor
- Mahmud Pahlevi, brother of the Shah of Iran
- Tyrone Power, actor (costar in *Blood and Sand,* '41)
- Manuel Rojas, Chilean polo player
- Gilbert Roland, actor
- Bob Scheffer, makeup man
- Wilfred Sheehan, vice president of production at 20th Century–Fox
- Teddy Stauffer, bandleader
- Jimmy Stewart, actor
- Count José-Maria Villapadierna, Spanish nobleman

Rita Hayworth 1918–1987

✦ She Said

All I ever wanted to be was myself.

Basically, I am a good, gentle person, but I am attracted to mean personalities.

Every man I've known has fallen in love with Gilda and wakened up with me.

✦ They Said

All her life was pain. —Orson Welles, who regretted the pain he himself had caused Rita during their marriage

The worst lay in the world. She was always drunk and she never stopped eating. —Peter Lawford

Her only security was knowing someone would want to be with her. That's the only thing that meant anything to her. —Shifra Haran, Orson Welles's secretary and close observer of Orson and Rita's marriage

✦ First Sexual Experience

Lost her virginity to her father, Eduardo Cansino.

✦ Husbands

Edward Judson, salesman–con man

Orson Welles, actor-director (directed her in *The Lady From Shanghai,* '48)

Prince Aly Khan, wealthy playboy and son of the Aga Khan

Dick Haymes, singer (who had previously been Mr. Joanne Dru)

James Hill, producer

✦ Did You Know?

Harry P. Cohn, head of Columbia Pictures, was obsessed with possessing Rita. Her first husband, who made Rita sleep with lots of men to further her career, ordered her into Cohn's bed, but she refused. From then on, Cohn chased her and used every chance possible to degrade and humiliate her, even putting secret microphones into her dressing room. Despite all his tries, Cohn was never able to bed Hayworth.

Hayworth's likeness was stamped on the first bomb dropped on Hiroshima, Japan.

Lillian Hellman 1905–1984

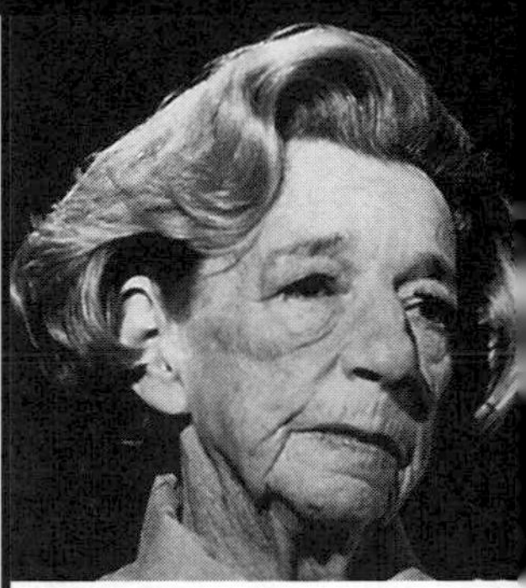

✦ She Said

You know, in the nineteenth century, no proper hostess, no proper woman, would let an actor into her sitting room.

I was always jealous of great beauties.

The forms of fucking do not need my endorsement. —Answering a query as to why she had never "endorsed" the gay rights movement. She also once threatened to expose a theater columnist's homosexuality if he did not retract a story he'd written that had annoyed her.

✦ They Said

If you want to know what the secret of Lillian's power over people was, it was an extraordinary gift for intimacy—even when you didn't have it, she made it. —Diana Trilling, social and literary critic

All I wanted was a docile woman, and look what I got. —Dashiell Hammett, author and longtime lover

If I spent the rest of my life in a room with this writer, she'd never bore me. She's the toughest, softest person I ever met. She transcends sex. —Dustin Hoffman, actor

✦ First Sexual Experience

Lost her virginity when she was nineteen to a "tall man of twenty-three," out of college, and on his way to earning a Ph.D.

✦ Husbands

Arthur Kober, magazine editor

✦ Did You Know?

Hellman claimed that because she was not invited to a party on Frank Sinatra's yacht one summer when it was docked near her home on Martha's Vineyard, she phoned in an anonymous threat that a bomb had been planted on the boat to spoil the actor's party.

Hellman claimed to Diana Trilling that author Norman Mailer had once tried to rape her.

Lovers, Flings, or Just Friends?

- George Backer, financier
- David Cort, writer-editor
- Arthur Cowan, businessman
- Peter Feibleman, novelist
- Stephen Greene, painter
- Dashiell Hammett, author
- Jed Harris, theatrical director
- Ernest Hemingway, author
- Harry Hopkins, wartime adviser to Franklin D. Roosevelt
- Ralph Ingersoll, journalist
- Louis Kronenberger, author
- John Melby, U.S. government Foreign Service officer
- Howard Meyer, architectural student
- Philip Rahv, political activist
- Herman Shumlin, theatrical producer
- Randall "Pete" Smith, political activist and union official
- Gerald Sykes, roommate of Louis Kronenberger
- Nathanael West, novelist (who wrote *Day of the Locust* about Hollywood)
- Richard Wilbur, poet

Lovers, Flings, or Just Friends?

Desi Arnaz, actor-singer
Stuart Barthelmess, son of silent-screen star Richard Barthelmess
Greg Bautzer, attorney–escort of beautiful women
Marshall Beard, ice-skater
Lee Bowman, actor
Fred De Cordova, producer
Richard Greene, actor (costar in *My Lucky Star,* '38)
Dick Haymes, singer-actor
Van Johnson, actor
John F. Kennedy, U.S. president
Michael Kirby, ice-skater
Liberace, overly showy pianist
Vic Orsatti, agent
Tyrone Power, actor (costar in *Thin Ice,* '37)
Stewart Reburn, Canadian ice-skater
Claude Terrail, French restaurateur
plus many, many other ice-skaters, ski instructors, and studio employees

Sonja Henie 1912–1969

✦She Said

They're all jealous because I didn't spend years in those dreary actors' study groups to become a star. —Stating why she believed Hollywood didn't appreciate her acting talents

It is the irresistible lure of making love to a star that has him under my spell. —Snapping at Darryl F. Zanuck, who had chastised her for conducting an affair with a film crew member

Jewelry takes people's minds off your wrinkles.

✦They Said

Among other things, this guileless, simple girl was one of the most voracious sexy broads in town. She really loved to fuck. —Milton Sperling, screenwriter of her film *Thin Ice* ('37)

A Degas ballerina on ice skates. —B. R. Crisler, in a profile in the *New York Times*

Slap some keys on her and we'll have a grand piano. —Darryl F. Zanuck, making fun of Henie's bulging leg muscles

✦First Sexual Experience

Lost her virginity to Jackie Dunn, a young British skater whom she considered marrying.

✦Husbands

Dan Topping, sportsman-socialite
Winthrop Gardiner Jr., socialite
Niels Onstad, Norwegian businessman

✦Did You Know?

During her affair with Tyrone Power, the couple had quaint nicknames for each other's sexual parts: hers was "Betsy" and his was "Jimmy."

While touring with her ice show, Henie was notorious for stripping her hotel suites when she left. She took silverware, bed linens, towels, bath mats, thermos bottles, and even toilet paper. When she was in Cuba, she pulled her "collecting" stunt, but the government of Batista—also known for its looting—demanded that she return everything before she would be allowed to leave the country.

Sonja once announced to the press that she and Liberace had fallen in love and were to be married.

Audrey Hepburn 1929–1993

✦ She Said

I probably hold the distinction of being one movie star who, by all laws of logic, should never have made it. At each stage of my career, I lacked the experience.

I've never thought of myself as glamorous or anything. I think Ava Gardner and Elizabeth Taylor are glamorous, but I don't fit into that category at all, not at all.

I never wanted to be divorced. To this day, I hate the word; I cringe when it's applied to me.

✦ They Said

Titism has taken over the country. But Audrey Hepburn single-handed may make bozooms a thing of the past. —Billy Wilder, who directed her in *Love in the Afternoon* ('57)

She is every man's dream of the nymph he once planned to meet. —Walter Kerr, theater critic

Audrey Hepburn is the patron saint of the anorexics. —Orson Welles

✦ First Sexual Experience

Unknown for certain. Possibly lost her virginity to Marcell Le Bon, a French singer.

✦ Husbands

Mel Ferrer, actor (costar in *War and Peace,* '56)
Dr. Andrea Mario Dotti, Italian psychiatrist

✦ Did You Know?

Audrey had a particularly trying and personally taxing habit: she always liked to be surrounded by her possessions. Whenever she traveled, she was accompanied by in excess of twenty large trunks and crates. On arrival in a hotel suite, or on location, she would carefully unpack them, then arrange the contents (pictures, vases, etc.) to make her accommodations more like home. Before leaving, everything would be repacked (by her) and sent on to her next place of call, to be unpacked and repacked again.

Lovers, Flings, or Just Friends?

- Prince Alfonso de Bourbon-Dampierre, Spanish nobleman
- Albert Finney, actor (costar in *Two for the Road,* '66)
- Ben Gazzara, actor (costar in *Bloodline,* '79)
- James Hanson, British heir to a truck-building fortune
- William Holden, actor (costar in *Sabrina,* '54)
- Antonio Ordonez, Spanish bullfighter
- Peter O'Toole, actor (costar in *How to Steal a Million,* '66)
- Robert Wolders, Dutch actor and last husband of Merle Oberon

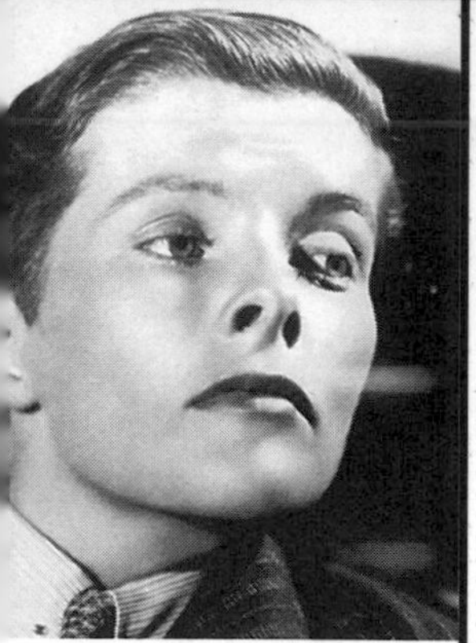

Lovers, Flings, or Just Friends?

- Charles Boyer, actor (costar in *Break of Hearts,* '35)
- John Ford, director (directed her in *Mary of Scotland,* '36)
- Laura Harding, American Express heiress
- Jed Harris, producer
- Leland Hayward, agent
- Van Heflin, actor
- Howard Hughes, aviation-cinema mogul
- Jane Loring, film editor
- Robert McKnight, sculptor
- George Stevens, director
- Jimmy Stewart, actor
- Spencer Tracy, actor (costar in *Guess Who's Coming to Dinner,* '67)

Katharine Hepburn 1907–

✦She Said

My father doesn't want me to make babies. —Turning aside an attempted seduction by John Barrymore

My privacy is my own and I am the one to decide when it shall be violated.

As for me, prizes mean nothing. My prize is my work. —Commenting on why she doesn't attend the awards ceremonies

If you survive, you become a legend. I'm a legend because I've survived over a long period of time.

✦They Said

Goddamnit, Kate, why do you always talk like you have a feather up your ass? —Spencer Tracy, tweaking his longtime lover

I didn't like the "glamour" side of Kate. I loved the fresh, natural Kate when she forgot to be a movie queen. —George Cukor

I just adore her, even when she does hit me. —Peter O'Toole, who starred with her in *The Lion in Winter* ('68). During shooting he nicknamed her Old Nag, while she called him Pig.

✦First Sexual Experience

Lost her virginity to her husband, Ludlow Ogden Smith.

✦Husbands

Ludlow Ogden Smith, businessman

✦Did You Know?

Hepburn was the first person to sing the word *shit* on a Broadway stage. She did it during a song in her musical *Coco.* The lyric was originally written in French, but she changed it to English.

Many people have wondered about Hepburn's sexuality, speculating on whether she was ever involved with other women, but no one has ever uncovered any definite proof of such. Actress Margaret Sullavan, who ended up marrying agent Leland Hayward, to whom Hepburn was "close," once referred to Kate as "that dikey bitch."

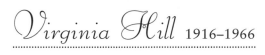

Virginia Hill 1916–1966

✦ She Said

I'm the best damn cocksucker in Chicago and I've got the diamonds to prove it.

✦ They Said

What I remember about this girl is that she had the swingingest parties in town and had a purse so full of new hundred-dollar bills that at least one Wilshire Boulevard store thought they were counterfeit. —Hedda Hopper, gossip columnist

A sexy-looking blonde in mink and diamonds who was always the life of the party and carried a roll of bills that would choke a horse. —Robert Stack, actor

She was the only woman who could be trusted to keep her mouth shut. —Jack Dragna, mobster, on why Virginia was so popular, aside from her sexual skills, with mobsters

✦ First Sexual Experience

Unknown for certain, but probably lost her virginity around age thirteen to a local boy in Marietta, Georgia.

✦ Husbands

Osgood Griffin, football player at the University of Alabama
Miguelito Carlos Gonzales Valdez, Mexican dancer
Benjamin "Bugsy" Siegel, mobster
Hans Hauser, Austrian ski instructor

✦ Did You Know?

During her tenure as Bugsy's girlfriend, Hill was "stashed" at Harry Cohn's Columbia Studio, ostensibly as a starlet under contract. Want to see the "real" Virginia Hill in person? Catch *Ball of Fire* ('41) with Barbara Stanwyck and Gary Cooper, because she has a small role in it.

One of Virginia's favorite put-downs to the men who pursued her: she would flush the expensive gifts of jewelry, and even money, that they had given to her down the toilet—usually in front of them.

To prove that she was just "one of the guys" to her Chicago mobster friends, Virginia fellated Charlie Frischetti, one of the biggest Chicago gangster bosses, at a Christmas party in front of a roomful of people attending the bash. Most of the other women and mobster wives in attendance fled the room in disgust.

Lovers, Flings, or Just Friends?

- Joseph "Joey" Adonis, New York City mobster
- Major Luis Amezcuna, Mexican politician
- Bruce Cabot, actor
- John Carroll, actor
- Joe Epstein, Chicago mobster
- Errol Flynn, actor
- Nicholas Fouillette, French heir to a wealthy family
- Charlie Frischetti, Chicago mobster
- Chato Juarez, Mexican playboy
- Gene Krupa, drummer
- Carl Laemmle Jr., millionaire and son of Universal Studios founder Carl Sr.
- Victor Mature, actor
- Anthony Quinn, actor
- George Raft, actor
- Maj. Arterburn Riddle, trucking-company tycoon
- George Rogers (Randall), Georgia boyfriend
- Johnny Rosetti, Los Angeles mobster
- *plus* lots of young men in Marietta, Georgia, *and* multitudes of mobsters in several American cities, *along with* many, many other men in various places like Mexico, Europe, Miami, Sun Valley, and Las Vegas

Judy Holliday 1922–1965

✦ She Said

Well, I guess these belong to you, too! —Removing her falsies and throwing them into Darryl F. Zanuck's face before fleeing his office. The studio mogul had cornered Holliday, informing her that all the women at the studio "belonged" to him.

I like writers. I don't like actors. They're impossible. They're vain exhibitionists, and they all live in a big vacuum. You need them onstage, but do you have to have them in your life?

✦ They Said

Well, I guess I worked with fat asses before! —Harry P. Cohn, who always nagged and threatened Holliday about her weight problem

✦ First Sexual Experience

Lost her virginity to Yetta Cohn, an employee of the New York Police Department, when she was twenty. A year or so later she had her first sexual experience with a man when actor John Buckmaster raped her—or so she claimed.

✦ Husbands

David Oppenheim, musician

✦ Did You Know?

In March 1952, when Holliday was called to testify before the House Un-American Activities Committee, she performed her greatest acting stunt. She played almost a parody of Billie Dawn, her Oscar-winning role. Her attorney had convinced her to sublimate her near-genius IQ and give the committee just what he felt they expected: a dumb blonde. She succeeded magnificently, and within a short time her involvement with the Red-hunting committee was over.

Lovers, Flings, or Just Friends?

- Heywood Hale Broun, journalist
- John Buckmaster, actor
- Sydney Chaplin, actor and son of Charlie
- Yetta Cohn, policewoman
- Arnold Krakower, attorney
- Peter Lawford, actor (costar in *It Should Happen to You,* '53)
- Gerry Mulligan, jazz musician–composer
- Freddie Wakeman, novelist (who dedicated his novel *The Hucksters* to her)

Libby Holman 1904–1971

✦ She Said

Singers don't have romances. They inspire them.

I'm a lady, and whether I'm drunk in public or swear in church, I expect to be treated like one.

✦ They Said

Loving Libby is like loving chocolate mousse. Soft to the touch and sweet to the eye, but the pleasure is fleeting. —Eugenia Bankhead, Tullalah's sister

She was selfish and a menace to men and women alike, whenever she thought it to her advantage to exert her sensuous allure. —Anonymous female college mate

No one in the theater was more discussable than Libby Holman, who came from Cincinnati and was game for anything. —Howard Dietz, lyricist

✦ First Sexual Experience

Holman remained a virgin until she was twenty-two, then she planned a seduction in order to lose her virginity. She chose Robert Brandeis, an actor, to perform the deed, then never let him touch her again after the one night.

✦ Husbands

Zachary Smith Reynolds, aviator and RJ Reynolds tobacco heir
Ralph Holmes, pilot and brother of her lover Phillips Holmes
Louis Schanker, artist

✦ Did You Know?

Holman once told friends that she believed that the penis and vagina should have been located in the neck. That way, when friends hugged, they could copulate at the same time.

Temperamental Lupe Velez, who hated Holman with a passion, starred with her in the Broadway production of *You Never Know.* Velez knew Holman was near-sighted and refused to wear glasses, so she urinated in the hallway outside Holman's dressing room each night in hopes that the singer would slip and injure herself. Much to the Mexican Spitfire's annoyance, Holman never slipped on Velez's piddle.

Lovers, Flings, or Just Friends?

- Josephine Baker, singer
- Tallulah Bankhead, actress
- Ted Bendict, dance instructor
- Marcus Blechman, photographer
- Jane Bowles, writer and wife of avant-garde author Paul Bowles
- Robert Brandeis, actor
- Montgomery Clift, actor
- Gary Cooper, actor
- Jeanne Eagles, singer-actress
- Ross Evans, writer
- Lisabeth White Guthrie, her secretary
- Phillips Holmes, actor-producer
- Alan Jackson, magazine writer
- Louisa Carpenter du Pont Jenney, heiress (who also had an affair with Tallulah Bankhead's sister, Eugenia)
- Beatrice "Bea" Lillie, actress-comedienne
- Johnny Martin, magazine editor
- John McClain, reporter
- Nicholas Ray, director
- Clifton Webb, homosexual dancer-actor
- Ahmed Yacoubi, Moroccan painter
- *and* lots of men she picked up for quickies and one-night stands whose names and faces she immediately forgot

Miriam Hopkins 1902–1972

✦ She Said

When I can't sleep, I don't count sheep, I count lovers. And by the time I reach thirty-eight or thirty-nine, I'm asleep.

How can a motion picture reflect real life when it is made by people who are leading artificial lives?

If I had to do it all over again, I'd do everything different.

✦ They Said

She was beautiful. All men were in love with her. —Jean Negulesco, director

I think she exhausted husbands. I don't mean sexually, it was just too much vitality to live with. —Hank Potter, stage manager

Miriam is a perfectly charming woman socially. Working with her is another story. —Bette Davis, actress

The least desirable companion on a desert island. —Awarded by the 1940 *Harvard Lampoon*

✦ First Sexual Experience

Unknown.

✦ Husbands

Brandon Peters, actor
Austin Parker, playwright-screenwriter
Anatole Litvak, director (directed her in *The Woman I Love,* '37)
Raymond B. Brock, reporter

✦ Did You Know?

Part of the ongoing feud between Hopkins and fellow actress Bette Davis, which carried on into several of their films together, stemmed from an incident early in Davis's career. She was an ingenue appearing in a stock company, of which Hopkins was the star, that presented stage presentations in upper New York. Hopkins was sexually attracted to Davis, who rejected the advances and was ultimately fired because, as one actor put it, "she didn't put out."

Hopkins was a most unusual shopper: when she decided to adopt a child, she sent a close friend to Chicago to pick one out for her.

Lovers, Flings, or Just Friends?

- Bennett Cerf, publisher and longtime panelist on *What's My Line*
- Maurice Chevalier, singer-actor
- Bing Crosby, singer-actor (costar in *She Loves Me Not,* '34)
- John Gilbert, actor
- John Gunther, author of the *Inside* books
- Leland Hayward, agent-producer
- William Randolph Hearst, publishing magnate
- Patrick Kearney, dramatist
- Ernst Lubitsch, director (directed her in *Design for Living,* '33)
- Fredric March, actor (costar of *Dr. Jekyll and Mr. Hyde,* '32)
- Herbert Marshall, actor
- Edwin J. Mayer, playwright
- Robert Montgomery, actor
- Henry C. "Hank" Potter, stage manager
- B. P. Schulberg, production head at Paramount
- Franchot Tone, actor (costar in *The Stranger's Return,* '33)
- King Vidor, director (directed her in *The Stranger's Return,* '33)

Hedda Hopper 1885–1966

✦ She Said

Louella Parsons is a reporter trying to be a ham. Hedda Hopper is a ham trying to be a reporter.

I shall not set myself up as a judge or critic, but I'd like you to know the people of Hollywood as I do. —From the blurb announcing the beginning of her column

Nobody is interested in sweetness and light.

✦ They Said

Take one black widow spider, cross it with a scorpion; wean their poisonous offspring on a mixture of prussic acid and treacle, and you'll get the honeyed sting of Hedda Hopper. —Donald Zec, British author

Hedda was imperious. She was a dynamic, aggressive, humorless, essential bitch, with a knife in both hands. She was truly an impossible woman. —Henry Rogers, press agent

When we cursed them [Hedda and Louella Parsons] *collectively, we referred to them as Lulu Poppers.* —Lili Palmer, actress

✦ First Sexual Experience

Probably lost her virginity to her husband, since she told her son at his wedding, "For God's sakes, don't take your wife by force like your father did."

✦ Husbands

DeWolf Hopper, stage actor

✦ Did You Know?

Hopper insinuated in her book that actor Michael Wilding was homosexual, and that she had warned Elizabeth Taylor of that fact before she married him. When Stewart Granger, a close friend of Wilding's, heard of the assertion, he immediately phoned Hopper and said, "I just called to say that I think you're a monumental bitch. How bloody dare you call a friend of mine a queer, you rattled, dried-up, frustrated old cunt." Wilding—who wasn't gay—sued Hopper and won his case.

Hopper, so the story goes, was told by a doctor that if she had sex with a young man, she'd stay young forever. From then on, her escorts to film premieres, parties, and such were always much, much younger men—with whom she was usually involved.

Lovers, Flings, or Just Friends?

Harold Grieve, decorator

Robert Q. Lewis, comedian

and a bevy of much younger men, mostly homosexual, who enjoyed escorting Hedda and trying on her many, many hats

Lena Horne 1917–

✦She Said

I looked exactly like everybody else in Hollywood, except I was bronze.

I was a sepia Hedy Lamarr.

I'd like to do a good serious role in a mixed-cast movie instead of being confined to cafe-singer parts.

✦They Said

She is a honeypot for the bees. —Elsa Maxwell, society gadabout and columnist

✦First Sexual Experience

Probably lost her virginity to her first husband, Louis Jones, since she married him very young and her mother always accompanied her on her singing jobs to ensure nobody "tampered" with her darling.

✦Husbands

Louis (Lewis) Jones, friend of her father's
Leonard George (Lennie) Hayton, MGM musical arranger

✦Did You Know?

When Horne first signed with MGM in 1942, she was the first black woman to obtain a term contract with a major studio. Only one other black woman, Madame Sul-Te-Wan, had ever signed a term contract and that was a personal one with D. W. Griffith in 1915.

Lovers, Flings, or Just Friends?

- Harry Belafonte, singer
- Duke Ellington, composer-musician
- David Janssen, actor
- Quincy Jones, musician–record producer
- Joe Louis, boxer
- Paul Robeson, singer-actor
- Orson Welles, director-actor

Barbara Hutton 1912–1979

✦She Said

I only had to look once at a decent, attractive man and he would run as fast as he could in the opposite direction.

I won't say my husbands thought only of my money, but it had a certain fascination for them.

American men don't understand me. European men are more sophisticated, more aware.

Money can't buy you happiness.

✦They Said

Barbara Hutton lived a fairy-tale existence, a second-rate fairy tale at that. —Douglas Fairbanks Jr., actor

Men were the chief stimulus in Barbara's life. She bought and sold them, bartered them, or replaced them in much the same way a stockbroker operates on the Exchange. —Oleg Cassini, designer

✦First Sexual Experience

Lost her virginity to Peter Storey, an English socialite–tennis instructor, when she was sixteen, on August 2, 1929.

✦Husbands

"Prince" Alexis (Alec) Mdivani, Russo-Georgian pseudoroyalty and one of the "marrying Mdivani" brothers

Count Kurt Haugwitz-Reventlow, Danish nobleman

Cary Grant, actor

Prince Igor Troubetzkoy, Lithuanian nobleman

Profirio Rubirosa, Dominican playboy-diplomat

Baron Gottfried von Cramm, German nobleman

"Prince" Raymond Doan, Laotian chemist-painter

✦Did You Know?

While she was married to Haugwitz-Reventlow, he forced her into the bathroom after one of their arguments, then made her sit nude on his lap while he had a bowel movement.

Hutton said that on one of the evenings she and actor Michael Rennie spent together, he emerged from another room "wearing a rubber diving suit, with a bullwhip in one hand and a jar of Vaseline in the other." She didn't specify what exact "games" the couple indulged in after that.

Lovers, Flings, or Just Friends?

Count Manolo Borromeo-d'Atta, Italian nobility

James Dean, actor

Prince Henri de la Tour d'Auvergre, French aristocrat

Count Alain d'Eudenville, French aristocrat from the Moët et Chandon champagne family

James H. Douglas III, son of the secretary of the air force

Errol Flynn, actor

Raymond Guest, socialite

Hal B. Hayes, architect

Prince Frederick Hohenzollern of Prussia, German royalty

Howard Hughes, aviation-cinema mogul

Prince Muassam Jah, Indian nobleman and grandson of the Nizam of Hyderabad

Fred McEvoy, playboy (who during one marriage kept the body of his dead baby on display in a Mexico City house)

David Niven, actor (who said she had the smallest feet he'd ever seen)

Stanley Page, stockbroker

Phil Morgan Plant, playboy

David Pleydell-Bouverie, British architect

Phillip Reed, actor

Michael Rennie, actor

Gilbert Roland, actor

Prince Girolami Rospigliosi, Italian nobleman

Robert Sweeney, amateur golf champion

Michael Wilding, actor

and a security guard she seduced who left her, as she put it, "black and blue and torn and tattered and covered with stickiness"

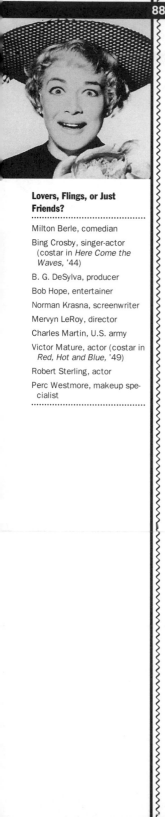

Lovers, Flings, or Just Friends?

Milton Berle, comedian

Bing Crosby, singer-actor (costar in *Here Come the Waves,* '44)

B. G. DeSylva, producer

Bob Hope, entertainer

Norman Krasna, screenwriter

Mervyn LeRoy, director

Charles Martin, U.S. army

Victor Mature, actor (costar in *Red, Hot and Blue,* '49)

Robert Sterling, actor

Perc Westmore, makeup specialist

Betty Hutton 1921–

✦ She Said

If you could treat men you want like you treat men you don't want, you could have any guy in the world.

I shoved and clawed my way up.

Nobody loved me unless I bought them, so I bought everybody.

Talent is my social security. When I run out of talent, I'll be dead.

✦ They Said

Betty Hutton was the most self-destructive star of them all. —Billy De Wolfe, comedian

If they put a propeller on Hutton and send her over Germany, the war would be over by Christmas. —Bob Hope, during World War II, joking about Hutton's "frenetic" singing-dancing style

Working with Betty Hutton keeps anybody moving. —Fred Astaire

✦ First Sexual Experience

Unknown, but possibly lost her virginity while she was touring with the Vincent Lopez band, since she started with them when she was about sixteen years old.

✦ Husbands

Ted Briskin, camera manufacturer

Charles O'Curran, choreographer (who later married singer Patti Page)

Alan W. Livingston, record company executive

Peter Candoli, trumpeter (who later married entertainer Edie Adams)

✦ Did You Know?

Hutton proved that success can be fleeting. While in her heyday in Hollywood, and after starring in two of the biggest films of the early fifties (*Annie Get Your Gun,* '50, and *The Greatest Show on Earth,* '52), she stomped off the Paramount lot and broke her contract with them because they wouldn't let her husband, a choreographer, direct her films. She wound up broke and destitute, working as a cook/housekeeper in a Rhode Island Catholic rectory.

Bianca (Blanca) Pérez Morena de Macias Jagger 1944–

✦ She Said

I was brought up in a terrible way: brainwashed by sexual repression. I was taught that virginity was the biggest asset in life and I believed it.

It's hard being beautiful.

I don't want to be a rock-'n-roll wife.

✦ They Said

I married her because I looked like her. —Mick Jagger, her rocking spouse

I think she had a bigger negative influence on Mick than anyone would have thought possible. —Keith Richards, musician

✦ First Sexual Experience

Unknown.

✦ Husbands

Mick Jagger, singer-actor

✦ Did You Know?

October 12, 1977: according to a court document, the last time Bianca and Mick had sexual relations.

Lovers, Flings, or Just Friends?

- Eddie Barclay, record executive
- Warren Beatty, actor
- Bjorn Borg, tennis player
- Michael Caine, actor
- Donald Cammell, painter
- Jack Ford, son of President Gerald Ford
- Ryan O'Neal, actor
- Tony Portago, socialite
- Mark Shand, brother of Camilla Parker-Bowles, the Prince of Wales's intimately "close" friend
- Robert Torricelli, U.S. congressman

Lovers, Flings, or Just Friends?

Montgomery Clift, actor (costar of *Indiscretion of an American Wife,* '54)

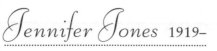

Jennifer Jones 1919–

✦ She Said

When they make actors or actresses, they should give them that other ingredient—the one that enables them to cope with publicity. They left that out of me.

Nobody likes me! —Crying after receiving bad press, and catty remarks, about having left husband Robert Walker for lover David O. Selznick

✦ They Said

Jennifer Jones was the Meryl Streep of her day. —Laurence Olivier

I personally felt that, as they say, "it takes two to tango." And in my opinion, Jennifer was a greedy, self-centered bitch. —Jim Henaghan, Hollywood columnist and close friend of Robert Walker's

✦ First Sexual Experience

Probably lost her virginity to Robert Walker, her first real romantic involvement.

✦ Husbands

Robert Walker, actor (costar of *Since You Went Away,* '44)
David O. Selznick, producer
Norton Simon, millionaire businessman

✦ Did You Know?

Truman Capote claimed that while filming *Indiscretion of an American Wife* ('54) Jones "got some kind of crush on Monty [Montgomery Clift]," her costar. She didn't realize he preferred guys. But, when she did find out, Capote related, she went into her "portable dressing room and stuffed a mink jacket down the portable toilet."

Selznick, in the midst of his affair with Jones, used to take a perverse delight in coming to the sets of *Since You Went Away* ('44) and *Duel in the Sun* ('46) to watch her love scenes with other men. King Vidor, director of *Sun,* said that he could hear Selznick panting during the steamy love scenes between Jones and costar Gregory Peck.

Janis Joplin 1943–1970

✦She Said

I didn't have any tits at fourteen.

✦They Said

When she picked up someone, it was a punk, an alcoholic-looking guy or a speed freak. —Unnamed close friend

That girl has problems. . . . Bein' heard ain't one of 'em. Like me, she gives an audience their money's worth. —Ethel Merman, singer-actress

✦First Sexual Experience

Probably lost her virginity around age fourteen to a Port Arthur, Texas, schoolmate, probably a fellow student at Thomas Jefferson High.

✦Husbands

Joplin was never married, but was engaged to Seth Morgan at the time of her death.

✦Did You Know?

Janis was scheduled to appear on the cover of the *Newsweek* dated April 7, 1969, then ex-president Dwight Eisenhower died. The magazine pulled her cover, substituting one on Ike instead. Her reaction: "Motherfuck! Fourteen heart attacks and the son of a bitch has to croak in my week. In *my* week!"

Lovers, Flings, or Just Friends?

- Frank Andrews, high school friend
- Tom Baker, actor
- Mark Braunstein, college student
- Peggy Caserta, storeowner
- Patrick Cassidy, beatnik
- Dick Cavett, television personality
- Kim Chappell, ex-lover of Joan Baez
- Eric Clapton, musician-singer
- Nick Gravenites, songwriter
- Albert Grossman, personal manager
- James Gurley, rock musician, Big Brother and the Holding Company
- Chet Helms, beatnik poet
- Jimi Hendrix, rock musician
- Howard Hesseman, actor
- George Hunter, founder of the Charlatans band
- Richard Kermonde, keyboardist, Kozmic Blues Band
- Kris Kristofferson, singer-actor
- Joe McDonald, musician, Country Joe McDonald and the Fish
- Seth Morgan, author-convict
- Jim Morrison, singer, The Doors (who preferred anal sex with women, but once fellated Jimi Hendrix onstage)
- Joe Namath, athlete-actor
- Michael J. Pollard, actor
- Bob Siedemann, photographer
- Powell St. John, college friend
- Paul Whaley, drummer, Blue Cheer

Lovers, Flings, or Just Friends?

Woody Allen, director-actor (costar in *Annie Hall,* '77)

Warren Beatty, actor-director (costar in *Reds,* '81)

Albert Finney, actor (costar in *Shoot the Moon,* '82)

Al Pacino, actor (costar in *The Godfather,* '72)

Diane Keaton 1946–

✦ She Said

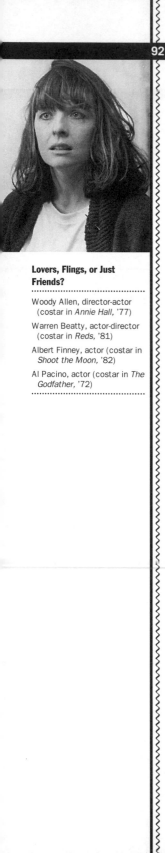

There are some nice things about being a woman with a man that are not about being fair or equal. They're about tricks and seduction and fun and some playing out of fantasies and, you know, like dreams.

In my past I've done an awful lot of apologizing. I have always liked to say "I'm sorry" before anything happened, but I don't do that as much anymore.

✦ They Said

A homely girl who in normal times would never get the boy. —Taki, society writer

She has an uncanny understanding of people—when they are vulnerable, when they are covering up, when they are hostile. —Woody Allen, actor-director, who directed and costarred with her in *Manhattan Murder Mystery* ('93)

✦ First Sexual Experience

Unknown.

✦ Husbands

Keaton has remained single thus far.

✦ Did You Know?

Keaton appeared on Broadway in *Hair,* but she refused to join in the cast's striptease at the end of each performance.

Grace Kelly 1928–1982

✦She Said

As an unmarried woman, I was thought to be a danger. Other women looked on me as a rival. And it pained me a great deal.

I felt like a streetwalker. —Describing how she felt when many people in Hollywood had an adverse reaction to her affair with Ray Milland, since he and his popular wife were regarded as one of the town's happiest married couples

Hollywood amuses me. Holier-than-thou for the public and unholier-than-the-devil in reality.

✦They Said

She screwed everybody she came into contact with who was able to do anything good for her. . . . She screwed agents, producers, directors. And there was really no need for it. She was already on her way. —Don Richardson, describing his disenchantment with his ex-lover

Looked like she was a cold dish with a man until you got her pants down, then she'd explode. —Gary Cooper

Grace almost always laid the leading man. She was notorious for that in this town. —Gore Vidal, author

✦First Sexual Experience

She lost her virginity to an older, married man, the husband of a close girlfriend, one afternoon at his house when his wife was away.

✦Husbands

His Most Serene Highness Rainier I (Rainier Louis Henri Maxence Bertrand Grimaldi), Prince of Monaco

✦Did You Know?

Although she maintained a prissy, prim white-gloves-wearing image to the public, Grace was widely known as an "easy lay," especially for her male co-stars. Not everyone looked kindly on the two faces of Grace. For example, Clara Bow, who knew something about torrid affairs herself, said, "It's been 20 years since the trial that broke my heart. If it happened today, I'd still be a whore. Grace Kelly, however, will get away with having many lovers. Know why? The damn public will never believe it." Director Henry Hathaway's wife said, "She wore those white gloves, but she was no saint."

Lovers, Flings, or Just Friends?

- Jean-Pierre Aumont, French actor
- Oleg Cassini, fashion designer
- Gary Cooper, actor (costar in *High Noon,* '52)
- Bing Crosby, actor (costar in *The Country Girl,* '54)
- Alexander D'Arcy, actor
- Robert Dornhelm, director
- Robert Evans, producer
- Jeffory Martin FitzGerald, business executive
- Clark Gable, actor (costar in *Mogambo,* '53)
- Cary Grant, actor (costar in *To Catch a Thief,* '55)
- William Holden, actor (costar in *The Bridges at Toko-Ri,* '54)
- Prince Aly Khan, playboy
- Frederick Knott, playwright
- Gene Lyons, actor
- Per Mattsson, Swedish actor
- Jim McMullen, restaurateur
- Ray Milland, actor (costar in *Dial M for Murder,* '54)
- Mark Miller, actor (who later fathered actress Penelope Ann Miller)
- David Niven, actor
- Mohammed Reza Pahlavi, the Shah of Iran
- Bud Palmer
- Claudius Charles (Claude) Phillipe, banquet manager, Waldorf-Astoria Hotel
- Don Richardson, drama instructor
- Frank Sinatra, actor-singer (costar in *High Society,* '56)
- Jimmy Stewart, actor (costar in *Rear Window,* '54)
- Spencer Tracy, actor

Deborah Kerr 1921–

Lovers, Flings, or Just Friends?

Stewart Granger, actor (costar in *King Solomon's Mines,* '50)

David Niven, actor (costar in *Bonjour Tristesse,* '58)

✦ She Said

I didn't fight Hollywood because I soon realized that if I did, I would wear myself out and maybe destroy myself.

If you're paid an enormous sum of money every week under a seven-year contract, you do as you're told—that's the way I was brought up.

All the most successful people seem to be neurotic these days. Perhaps we should stop being sorry for them and start being sorry for me—for being so confounded normal.

The camera always seemed to find an innate gentility in me.

✦ They Said

Her name will rhyme with star *and not with* cur. —Louis B. Mayer, on bringing her to Hollywood from England

Miss Kerr is a good actress. She is also unreasonably chaste. —Laurence Olivier, describing her to her fiancé

✦ First Sexual Experience

Unknown.

✦ Husbands

Anthony Bartley, RAF squadron leader
Peter Viertel, novelist-screenwriter

✦ Did You Know?

Take a close look at the gold gown Kerr wears as Lygia, the Christian slave-girl in *Quo Vadis* ('51). It was made from a fabric which had been soaked in 14-karat gold to achieve a "special effect."

Evelyn Keyes 1919–

✦ She Said

I always took up with the man of the moment—and there were many such moments.

I have often wondered what would have happened to me if I had needed a size-38 bra instead of a modest 34.

✦ They Said

You're a Hollywood product, don't you know that? —Artie Shaw, snapping at her during their marriage

✦ First Sexual Experience

Lost her virginity to a boy she met at a dance in Atlanta, when they were in their teens. The couple adjourned to a motel to complete their passion.

✦ Husbands

Barton Bainbridge, businessman
Charles Vidor, director
John Huston, director
Artie Shaw, musician (who was also the first Mr. Lana Turner and the second Mr. Ava Gardner)

✦ Did You Know?

Harry Cohn, head of Columbia, once shoved his hand between Keyes's legs and rubbed her vagina saying, "Save some of that for me 'cause I'm gonna marry you." She was repulsed by his action and was determined that he'd never sleep with her, much less marry her. Soon, Cohn's lust turned to anger, and he was calling her names every time her name was linked with another man's.

While married to Huston, Keyes once caught him in a restaurant with a blonde perched on his lap. Annoyed at the antics of her husband—who already had an eighteen-year-old mistress on the side—Keyes went storming over and pulled the blond tootsie off Huston, saying, "Listen, you, I'm his wife, and that's his mistress over there, and you are one too many!"

Lovers, Flings, or Just Friends?

- Kirk Douglas, actor
- Carlos Guinle, Brazilian millionaire
- Bob Neal, businessman
- David Niven, actor
- Dick Powell, actor
- Anthony Quinn, actor
- Mike Todd, producer

Nastassja Kinski 1959–

✦ She Said

I am a very independent girl. No one ever tells me what to do. No one forces me to do anything.

I was brought up to believe that there is nothing shameful about the naked human body.

✦ They Said

Her mother is a poet, her father is possessed. —Armand Assante, actor

She blackens my name in the press and makes me think abortion is a good idea. —Klaus Kinski, father

You have to assume the star is intensely fuckable. —Paul Schrader, who directed her in *The Cat People* ('82)

She excites me more than any other person in the movies today. —Gene Siskel, film critic

✦ First Sexual Experience

Unknown for certain; possibly lost her virginity to Roman Polanski, who directed her in *Tess* ('79).

✦ Husbands

Ibrahim Moussa, Egyptian talent agent–producer

✦ Did You Know?

Nastassja's father, actor Klaus Kinski, named her for Nastassja, the young woman who burns with passion in *The Idiot* by Dostoeyevsky.

Lovers, Flings, or Just Friends?

- Jean Jacques Beineix, French director
- Gerard Depardieu, French actor
- Milos Forman, Czech director
- Quincy Jones, musician–record producer
- Andrei Konchalovsky, Russian director
- Rob Lowe, actor (costar of *Hotel New Hampshire,* '84)
- Marcello Mastroianni, Italian actor (costar of *Stay As You Are,* '79)
- Ian McShane, British actor
- Dudley Moore, actor
- Roman Polanski, director (directed her in *Tess,* '79)
- Paul Schrader, director (directed her in *The Cat People,* '82)
- Wim Wenders, German director (directed her in *Paris, Texas,* '84)

Eartha Kitt 1928–

✦ She Said

The most exciting men in my life have been the men who have never taken me to bed.

You don't have to hit anybody on the head with four-letter words to be sexy.

✦ They Said

You represent all women of all ages. You have no place in time. — Orson Welles

✦ First Sexual Experience

Unknown.

✦ Husbands

William McDonald, real estate mogul

✦ Did You Know?

After she harangued Lady Bird Johnson at a White House luncheon about poverty and American involvement in Vietnam, Kitt was characterized in a CIA dossier on her as "a sadistic, sex nymphomaniac" and "rude, crude, shrewd, difficult."

Kitt is known for her wicked tongue, which she wields whenever she thinks she's been slighted. After being turned down for a hotel room in England, which she assumed was because she was a black woman, she informed the clerk, "By the way, I'm not black, I'm Spanish." When he challenged her to say something in Spanish, she did: "Adios, motherfucker."

Lovers, Flings, or Just Friends?

- Bayeux Baker, student
- Sammy Davis Jr., singer-actor
- James Dean, actor
- Tommy Gomez, dancer
- Arthur Loew Jr., cinema-chain heir
- Chris O'Donnell, British socialite
- Charles Revson, cosmetics magnate
- Porfirio Rubirosa, diplomat-playboy
- John Barry Ryan, socialite
- Orson Welles, actor-director

Lovers, Flings, or Just Friends?

- Rita Beery, lesbian ex-wife of Wallace Beery
- Milton Berle, comedian-actor
- William Dozier, producer
- Andy Elickson, merchant seaman
- Raymond Hakim, producer
- Robert Hakim, producer
- Victor Mature, actor
- Dr. McGee, physician
- Jean Negulesco, director
- Aristotle Onassis, millionaire shipowner
- Nat Perlow, magazine editor–writer
- Porfirio Rubirosa, Dominican diplomat-playboy
- *plus* lots of studio technicians who attended the booze and sex orgies at her home

Veronica Lake 1919–1973

✦ She Said

Hollywood gives a young girl the aura of one giant, self-contained orgy farm, its inhabitants dedicated to crawling into every pair of pants they can find.

I wasn't a sex symbol. I was a sex zombie.

If I had written everything I know about this town, there'd be a rash of divorces and at least a hundred people would die of apoplexy. —Stating that she certainly didn't tell all she knew in her autobiography

✦ They Said

She and her hair have destroyed this scene. They go or I go. —Eddie Cantor, who got disgusted when Lake's hair kept falling in her face while she was a chorus girl in one of his pictures

She's nothing much in real life—a quiet, rather timid little thing. But the screen transforms her, electrifies her, and brings her to life. —Preston Sturges, director

She was known as "the bitch" and deserved the title. —Eddie Bracken, actor

Veronica was a nice enough lady burdened with more bosoms than brains. —John Engstead, studio art supervisor

✦ First Sexual Experience

Probably lost her virginity to first husband John Detlie.

✦ Husbands

John Detlie, studio art director
André DeToth, director (directed her in *Ramrod*, '47)
Joe McCarthy, music publisher
Robert Carlton-Monroe, British sea captain

✦ Did You Know?

Lake was diagnosed as a "classic" schizophrenic while still a teenager, but her mother chose not to have her committed or held for treatment. As she grew older, Lake began to exhibit the signs of her illness quite frequently—drinking heavily, abusing her first child, and picking up men randomly.

Hedy Lamarr 1913–

✦ She Said

The men in my life have ranged from a classic case history of impotence, to a whip-wielding sadist who enjoyed sex only after he tied my arms behind me with the sash of his robe.

If you use your imagination, you can look at any actress and see her nude. I hope to make you use your imagination.

American men, as a group, seem to be interested in only two things, money and breasts.

✦ They Said

People like Hedy Lamarr do our industry a great disservice by publicizing their sexual conquests. Sure, a lot of stars have made it that way, but not all. —Ann Miller, dancer-actress

When she spoke, one did not listen, one just watched her mouth moving and marveled at the exquisite shapes made by her lips. —George Sanders, who starred with her in *Samson and Delilah* ('49)

✦ First Sexual Experience

Lost her virginity at age fourteen in her family's house, when she was raped by a laundryman. He had already tried once to attack Lamarr, but she fought him off; he succeeded on the second attempt.

✦ Husbands

Fritz Mandl, Austrian munitions magnate (who said, "A lady is a woman who knows what jewels go with the right clothes.")

Gene Markey, screenwriter (who was also the second Mr. Joan Bennett and the third Mr. Myrna Loy)

Sir John Loder, British actor (costar in *Dishonored Lady,* '47)

Ted Stauffer, orchestra leader–restaurateur

W. Howard Lee, oil businessman (who was also the second Mr. Gene Tierney)

Lewis J. Boles, attorney

✦ Did You Know?

While married to Fritz Mandl, Lamarr—due to her husband's business interests—socialized with both Hitler and Mussolini. She called Hitler "posturing" and Mussolini "pompous."

Lovers, Flings, or Just Friends?

Jean-Pierre Aumont, French actor

Charles Boyer, actor (costar of *Algiers,* '38)

Charlie Chaplin, actor

Errol Flynn, actor

Clark Gable, actor (costar in *Boom Town,* '40)

Reginald Gardiner, British actor

John Garfield, actor (costar in *Tortilla Flat,* '42)

Grisha Goluboff, female friend

Howard Hughes, cinema-aviation mogul

John F. Kennedy, later U.S. president

Burgess Meredith, actor

George Montgomery, actor (who later became Mr. Dinah Shore)

David Niven, actor

Otto Preminger, director

George Sanders, actor (costar in *The Strange Woman,* '46)

Sam Spiegel, producer

Mark Stevens, actor

Rudy Vallee, singer-actor

Walter Wanger, producer

John Hay "Jock" Whitney, socialite-businessman

plus the father of her best childhood friend, a female roommate at a Swiss boarding school, several studio wardrobe women, several starlets at MGM, an impotent Texan, and various and sundry other men and women

Lovers, Flings, or Just Friends?

Greg Bautzer, attorney–Hollywood escort

Bing Crosby, singer-actor (costar in *The Road to Zanzibar*, '41)

William Holden, actor (costar in *The Fleet's In*, '42)

Bob Hope, comedian-actor (costar in *Caught in the Draft*, '41)

Robert Preston, actor (costar in *Typhoon*, '40)

Randolph Scott, actor

Rudy Vallee, singer-actor

Dorothy Lamour 1914–

✦ She Said

Glamour is just sex that got civilized.

My hips are too big, my feet aren't very pretty, and my shoulder blades stick out.

Someday I hope the critics will say of me not only that I wear a sarong becomingly, but also that I give a good performance.

✦ They Said

I saw her films over and over, wrote to her once a month, and drooled over the signed photos she sent me. —Ken Russell, director, on his youthful "love" for her

I knew the jungle was full of rare flowers, but what kind of bush did she grow on? —Bitchy line delivered about Dorothy's character in *Moon Over Burma* ('40) by a female antagonist

✦ First Sexual Experience

Unknown.

✦ Husbands

Herbie Kaye, orchestra leader
William Ross Howard III, U.S. Army captain

✦ Did You Know?

One of Lamour's sarongs sold at a charity auction in the early 1970s for $50,000, while another one resides in the Smithsonian Institution.

Carole Landis 1919–1948

✦ She Said

I want a fair chance to prove myself as an actress rather than as a "curvaceous cutie."

Dearest Mommie: I'm sorry, really sorry to put you through this. But there is no way to avoid it. I love you darling. You have been the most wonderful Mom ever. Everything goes to you. Look in the files, and there is a will which declares everything. Goodbye, my angel. Pray for me. Your Baby —Her suicide note, found after she killed herself over her affair with actor Rex Harrison

✦ They Said

I don't say she was a talented actress, but she was a beautiful girl, and full of life. —Rex Harrison, over whom Landis ended her life

She seemed very happy-go-lucky all the time. —Fannie Mae Bolden, Landis's personal maid

✦ First Sexual Experience

Unknown.

✦ Husbands

Irving Wheeler, student (whom she married at age fifteen; it lasted only twenty-five days)

Willie Hunts Jr., yacht broker (whom she divorced after five months)

Thomas Wallace, U.S. Air Force captain

W. Horace Schmidlapp, businessman

✦ Did You Know?

Landis once worked as a call girl in San Francisco for a short spell. Rumors about her past kept dogging her in Hollywood and even led Busby Berkeley's mother to stop the proposed marriage between her son and Landis. She kept prostituting herself in Hollywood—frequently making her sexual favors available to high studio execs at both Warner Bros. and 20th Century–Fox, in hopes of obtaining larger and better roles.

Lovers, Flings, or Just Friends?

- Busby Berkeley, choreographer
- Charlie Chaplin, actor
- Errol Flynn, actor (costar in *Four's a Crowd*, '38)
- Rex Harrison, actor
- Huntington Hartford, grocery chain heir
- Dick Haymes, singer-actor
- Victor Mature, actor (costar in *One Million B.C.*, '40)
- Louis Schurr, agent
- Jacquelin Susann, author
- Franchot Tone, actor (who was also the third Mr. Joan Crawford)
- Darryl F. Zanuck, studio head

Lovers, Flings, or Just Friends?

- Mikhail Baryshnikov, Russian ballet dancer
- Bob Fosse, choreographer-director (directed her in *All That Jazz*, '79)
- Antonio Lopez, fashion illustrator
- Jack Nicholson, actor (costar in *The Postman Always Rings Twice*, '81)
- Sam Shepard, playwright-actor

Jessica Lange 1949–

✦ She Said

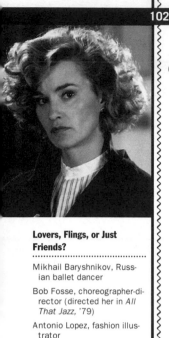

It angers me when I run into women who are totally submissive, completely dependent. What angers me more are men who like that kind of woman.

Romance was a trap for me. As long as it was passionate. Either positive or negative. Then I knew it was love. It had to be extreme. That was its validity.

It's hard to feel too terrible with one of these around. —Referring to her baby and remarking on the thrill of being a mother

✦ They Said

Beautiful face, no brains, big bosoms. —Dino De Laurentiis, who was responsible for *King Kong* ('76), which almost scuttled Lange's career at its inception

Jessica is one of the few actresses I've ever met who is completely unself-conscious about her sexuality. —Bob Rafelson, who directed her in *The Postman Always Rings Twice* ('81)

Few are the men who don't want to fall at her feet. —Jack Nicholson, who played her murderous lover in *The Postman Always Rings Twice* ('81)

✦ First Sexual Experience

Unknown for certain; possibly lost her virginity to Paco Grande, whom she met while a student in college.

✦ Husbands

Paco Grande, Spanish filmmaker

✦ Did You Know?

Lange trained as a mime for two years in Paris with Etienne Decroux, considered one of the inventors of the performing art and a trainer of Marcel Marceau.

Gertrude Lawrence 1898–1952

✦ She Said

There may be glamour and romance about certain phases of it, but let nobody imagine that it isn't mostly hard and tireless work. —Remarking on being a "star"

✦ They Said

She spent money like an entire fleet of drunken sailors. —Fanny Holtzmann, noted show-business attorney

She was a darling, but she sometimes behaved like the empress of China. —Bea Lillie, performer and close friend

She gave me an orange and told me a few mildly dirty stories, and I loved her from then onwards. —Noel Coward, on their first meeting (and she also seduced him)

✦ First Sexual Experience

Unknown.

✦ Husbands

Francis Gordon-Hawley, dance director
Richard Aldrich, theatrical director

✦ Did You Know?

Lawrence, though not a racist, once appeared in a London revue dressed in a Ku Klux Klan costume and singing a hymn to lynching.

When Lawrence appeared on Broadway starring in *Lady in the Dark,* her chum Noel Coward sent her a telegram that said, "Hope you get a warm hand on your opening."

Lovers, Flings, or Just Friends?

- Capt. Philip Astley, British military man
- Noel Coward, actor-playwright
- Prince George, Duke of Kent, British nobleman
- Prince Edward, Duke of Windsor, British nobleman
- Sir Gerald du Maurier, actor
- Earl of Dudley and Marquis de Casa Maury, British nobleman
- Douglas Fairbanks Jr., actor (costar in *Mimi,* '35)
- Vinton Freedley, theatrical producer
- George Gershwin, composer
- Benn Levy, director
- William Powell, actor
- Bert Taylor, banker (and brother of Dorothy, Countess diFrasso, who "tossed" her own charms around Hollywood)
- Viscount Wimbourne, British nobleman

Lovers, Flings, or Just Friends?

Lex Barker, actor
Peter Lawford, actor
Arthur Loew Jr., cinema-chain heir
Barry Nelson, actor
Bob Quarry, actor
Robert Scheerer, dancer

Janet Leigh 1927–

✦ She Said

The size of the part had no bearing. Alfred Hitchcock was enough incentive for me. —Describing what lured her into *Psycho* ('60), and a part where the star is killed off unexpectedly in the first half of the film

✦ They Said

They were fearfully ambitious kids, so determined to make it, they were tiresome. —Unnamed Hollywood columnist remarking on Leigh and husband Tony Curtis

I am going to Hollywood and marry Janet Leigh. —Alex Illes, member of the 1960 Hungarian Olympic soccer team being interviewed on Hungarian radio

✦ First Sexual Experience

Lost her virginity to Kenneth Carlyle, a young student she married at age fourteen.

✦ Husbands

Kenneth Carlyle, student
Stanley Reames, U.S. Navy
Tony Curtis, actor (costar in *Houdini,* '53)
Robert Brandt, stockbroker

✦ Did You Know?

Johnny Stompanato, the minor hood fatally stabbed by Lana Turner's daughter, once made a big play for Leigh's affections, asking her to be his "girl." After one date, during which she discovered he was involved in underworld activities, Leigh declined to have anything else to do with Stompanato. Another male who pursued her, almost to the point of harassment, was the reclusive Howard Hughes.

Vivien Leigh 1913–1967

✦ She Said

Her Ladyship is fucking bored with such formality and prefers to be known as Vivien Leigh. —Commenting at a press conference before *A Streetcar Named Desire* ('51) in answer to a question about being called Lady Olivier

I was barely out of my teens when Larry started fucking me. —Snapping at a friend who had debunked her suspicion that Olivier was having an affair with a teenage costar

✦ They Said

If ever there was a flawed masterpiece, it was Vivien. —Peter Finch, who began costarring with Leigh in *Elephant Walk* ('54) before she had her nervous breakdown and was forced to withdraw from the film

I'll never forget that first look. —David O. Selznick, on the night he first laid eyes on Vivien Leigh, who was introduced with, "David, here's your Scarlett O'Hara."

✦ First Sexual Experience

Lost her virginity to her first husband on her wedding night, December 20, 1932. She was eighteen.

✦ Husbands

Herbert Leigh Holman, British businessman
Sir Laurence Olivier, actor (costar in *That Hamilton Woman,* '41)

✦ Did You Know?

During her stay in Los Angeles while filming *Gone With the Wind* ('39), Leigh invented a bizarre parlor game she liked to play with her friends: Ways to Kill a Baby. The players had to concoct unusual and inventive methods of slaughtering infants.

In December 1993 the Oscar she won for Best Actress as Scarlett O'Hara in *Gone With the Wind* ('39) was auctioned off at Sotheby's in New York; it brought $560,000 from an unnamed bidder.

Toward the end of her life, when Leigh was suffering from bouts of depression, she became notorious for picking up men she met casually in the street for sex, much to the consternation of her friends, who feared for her safety.

Lovers, Flings, or Just Friends?

- Jean-Pierre Aumont, actor
- Warren Beatty, actor (costar in *The Roman Spring of Mrs. Stone,* '61)
- John Buckmaster, British actor
- Don Cunningham, actor
- Peter Finch, actor
- Rex Harrison, actor
- Sir Alexander Korda, British producer
- Jack Merivale, actor
- Edmund Purdom, actor
- Peter Wyngarde, actor

Lovers, Flings, or Just Friends?

- Judith Anderson, actress
- Tallulah Bankhead, actress
- Larry Ceballos, dance director
- Katharine Cornell, actress
- Eddie Duryea Dowling, stage director–personal manager
- Greta Garbo, actress
- James Gardiner, socialite producer
- Reginald Gardiner, actor
- Rolf Gérard, stage designer
- John Gilbert, actor
- Bob Goldstein, 20th Century–Fox executive
- Libby Holman, singer
- John Philip Huck, actor-singer
- Buster Keaton, silent-film comedian
- Gertrude Lawrence, actress
- Eva Le Gallienne, actress
- Charles MacArthur, playwright (and later Mr. Helen Hayes)
- Rupert Bloomfield McGunigle, advertising theatrical writer
- Clifford Odets, playwright
- Rudolph Valentino, actor
- Tim Whalen, writer

Beatrice (Bea) Lillie 1894–1989

✦ She Said

What time does this place get to New York? —An example of Lillie's humor; she was traveling on the *Queen Mary* ocean liner when she made the quip

Darling, if I should die before Gertrude Lawrence, I want you to be very sure in my obituary that they put my correct age, that I am four years younger than Gertrude. Gertrude will lie about it and say that I am four years older just because she was once was my understudy. —Instructing a close friend to make certain that her "good" friend Gertrude Lawrence didn't attempt to upstage Lillie on her death

✦ They Said

She's seventy-five and completely mad. —Noel Coward, annoyed at being asked how "old" Lillie was during a student symposium at Harvard

✦ First Sexual Experience

Unknown.

✦ Husbands

Sir Robert Peel, British baron

✦ Did You Know?

After her operation for hemorrhoids Lillie encountered her doctor at a party. When he seemingly didn't recognize her, she gently reminded him of their "acquaintance" only a few weeks before. He calmly replied, "I never remember faces." Lillie thought the incident vastly amusing, repeating the story for years afterward.

Gina Lollobrigida 1927–

Lovers, Flings, or Just Friends?

Dr. Christian Barnard, South African surgeon (who pioneered heart transplants)

Yul Brynner, actor (costar in *Solomon and Sheba,* '59)

Fidel Castro, dictator of Cuba

Richard Johnson, actor

Jean Sorel, actor (costar in *Le Bambole,* '65)

✦She Said

My whole life is big, long battle to tell men I don't wish to take off the clothes. . . . I cannot help the way I look.

Sex appeal I do not do on purpose. I do it sincerely. I am always dressed in my pictures.

I get very irritated when people think I must be the same women I portray on the screen.

✦They Said

She's like a modern apartment building with outside balconies. —John Huston, director

She looks good in anything. —King Vidor, director

Gina's personality is limited. She is good playing a peasant, but is incapable of playing a lady. —Sophia Loren, doing a little Italian sniping

✦First Sexual Experience

Unknown.

✦Husbands

Dr. Milko Skofic, Yugoslavian physician
George S. Kaufman, real-estate executive

✦Did You Know?

In tribute to her "assets," the French coined the term *lollobrigidienne,* meaning "curvaceous."

Gina was the third-place winner in the 1947 Miss Italy contest.

Carole Lombard 1908–1942

✦ She Said

Okay, bring me my breasts. —Yelling at the wardrobe crew on her films. Lombard was relatively flat-chested and had to be equipped with falsies in some films

I think that e *made the whole fucking difference.* —Telling how her name helped

I don't know why everybody thinks this is so great. It's like a dry fuck. —Describing how she felt about her first bareback horse ride

✦ They Said

She had one of the sexiest, most sensational figures I've ever seen in my life. —George Raft, actor

She photographed like a virginal princess, but she lived like a tiger and fluttered like a colorful butterfly. —William "Billy" Haines, Hollywood interior decorator and close friend

✦ First Sexual Experience

Probably lost her virginity to Howard Hughes, when she was about twenty or twenty-one.

✦ Husbands

William Powell, actor (costar in *Man of the World,* '31)
Clark Gable, actor (costar of *No Man of Her Own,* '32)

✦ Did You Know?

George Raft has said he was astounded the day he found out Lombard wasn't a natural blonde. She undressed in front of him, then made up a peroxide mixture, which she began to apply with a cotton dab to her pubic hair. Seeing his surprise, Lombard said, "Relax, Georgie, I'm just making my collar and cuffs match."

Lombard's fabled "blue" tongue was a deliberate calculation on her part. Annoyed by men making sexual advances to her, she enlisted the aid of her two brothers to teach her all the vulgar and obscene terms they knew. Her ploy served her well. For example, when Harry Cohn of Columbia made a move on Lombard, she said she was going to be in his "shitty little picture, but fucking you isn't part of the deal." Cohn liked her spunk, and they went on to become friends.

Lovers, Flings, or Just Friends?

- John Barrymore, actor (costar in *Twentieth Century,* '34)
- Russ Columbo, singer-actor
- Gary Cooper, actor
- Henry D'Arrast, director
- John Gilbert, actor
- Howard Hughes, aviation-cinema mogul
- Horace Liveright, publisher–story researcher
- Ernst Lubitsch, director (directed her in *To Be or Not to Be,* '42)
- David Niven, actor
- George Raft, actor (costar in *Bolero,* '34)
- Robert Riskin, screenwriter (and the second Mr. Fay Wray)
- Charles "Buddy" Rogers, actor
- Cesar Romero, actor
- David O. Selznick, producer
- Preston Sturges, director

Sophia Loren 1934–

✦ She Said

I am not just another cheesecake pot.

Sex appeal is fifty percent what you've got and fifty percent what people think you've got.

Everything you see, I owe to spaghetti.

I will never announce my plans in public, like some other people. If I decide to quit, I will just tiptoe out quietly the way I came in.

✦ They Said

It's like being bombed by watermelons. —Alan Ladd, costar in *Boy on a Dolphin* ('57), about acting with Sophia's breasts

Women don't like her. She makes them nervous. She's too sexy. —Lou Schreiber, studio executive

She should have been sculpted in chocolate truffles, so that the world could devour her. —Noel Coward

✦ First Sexual Experience

Unknown for certain, but probably lost her virginity to Carlo Ponti, since she met him when she was fifteen or sixteen years old.

✦ Husbands

Carlo Ponti, producer

✦ Did You Know?

For her fortieth birthday, hubby Carlo Ponti gave Sophia a unique present—a custom-fitted, 14K-gold toilet seat.

Lovers, Flings, or Just Friends?

Emile Bouryour, French physician

Rosanno Brazzi, (costar in *Legend of the Lost*, '58)

Cary Grant, actor (costar in *The Pride and the Passion*, '57)

Peter Sellers, actor (costar in *The Millionairess*, '61)

Omar Sharif, actor (costar in *More Than a Miracle*, '69)

Gig Young, actor (costar in *Five Miles to Midnight*, '62)

Lovers, Flings, or Just Friends?

Gerard Damiano, film producer–director

Sammy Davis Jr., singer-actor

Al Goldstein, *Screw* publisher

Hugh Hefner, *Playboy* publisher

Harry Reems, porno actor

and many, many others, both male porno stars and "customers" she was forced to service

Linda Lovelace 1952–

✦ She Said

Living in Hollywood you begin to forget that outside there is still a normal world with normal people. California is the land of the superfreak, and they all seem to come to Hollywood sooner or later.

Today I still can't go to a supermarket or a bus station or a high school basketball game without the risk—the whispers, the pointed fingers, the stampede.

Each time someone sees that movie, they're watching me being raped. —Referring to her appearance in the porn film *Deep Throat*

✦ They Said

A woman is supposed to do everything for her husband. —Chuck Traynor, her spouse

✦ First Sexual Experience

Unknown.

✦ Husbands

Charles "Chuck" Traynor, photographer–personal manager
Larry Marchiano, blue-collar worker

✦ Did You Know?

Lovelace was once forced to have sex with a dog for a porno movie; her husband tried to restage the event live for Hugh Hefner's entertainment, but the dog that time wasn't as cooperative.

Myrna Loy 1905–1993

✦ She Said

This myth about Hollywood people being so bacchanalian is ridiculous. We worked hard.

I became known as an American girl gone native in an Easterly direction. —Remarking on her early roles playing Asian and other exotic characters

I've never quite gotten over it, freckled face, slanted eyes, and red hair—being redheaded isolates you.

I think that carrying on a life that is meant to be private in public is a breach of taste, common sense, and mental hygiene.

✦ They Said

She's not a movie queen, you know. She's not that. She's a real *person.* —George Cukor, director

✦ First Sexual Experience

Unknown.

✦ Husbands

Arthur Hornblow, producer
John Hertz Jr., rental-car heir
Gene Markey, screenwriter (who was also the second Mr. Joan Bennett and the second Mr. Hedy Lamarr)
Howland Sargeant, U.S. State Department official

✦ Did You Know?

The scientists working on the Manhattan Project, which developed the atomic bomb during World War II, gave all the radioactive elements they worked with code names; they called thorium "Myrnaloy."

Lovers, Flings, or Just Friends?

- Montgomery Clift, actor (costar in *Lonelyhearts,* '58)
- Helmut Dantine, actor
- Leslie Howard, actor (costar in *The Animal Kingdom,* '32)
- George Kogel, scion of a construction fortune
- Louis B. Mayer, studio head
- Ramon Novarro, actor
- William Powell, actor (costar in *The Thin Man,* '34)
- Tyrone Power, actor (costar in *The Rains Came,* '39)
- Adlai Stevenson, politician–presidential candidate
- Dwight Taylor, screenwriter

Lovers, Flings, or Just Friends?

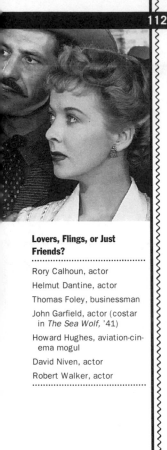

- Rory Calhoun, actor
- Helmut Dantine, actor
- Thomas Foley, businessman
- John Garfield, actor (costar in *The Sea Wolf,* '41)
- Howard Hughes, aviation-cinema mogul
- David Niven, actor
- Robert Walker, actor

Ida Lupino 1914–1995

✦ She Said

It was frightening going to a place with the terrifying name of Hollywood.

I don't care a fig about looking pretty on the screen.

You could pack the bags under my eyes and go off to Las Vegas on holiday.

✦ They Said

She's a pro's pro and can be as bossy as any man when she needs to be. —Rosalind Russell

✦ First Sexual Experience

Unknown.

✦ Husbands

Louis Hayward, actor

Collier Young, writer-producer (who was also the third Mr. Joan Fontaine)

Howard Duff, actor

✦ Did You Know?

Lupino's father Stanley, also an actor, hosted the party that actress Thelma Todd attended shortly before she was mysteriously murdered.

In moments of annoyance over her career, Lupino often referred to herself as a "poor man's Bette Davis."

Jeanette MacDonald 1903–1965

✦ She Said

All my other costars are either old enough to be my father or queer. —Commenting on frequent costar—and lover—Nelson Eddy

Woman, like man, can only be free when she follows her finest and strongest instincts. To have these smothered because of the faddish frenzy of the moment is ludicrous.

I did not have a particularly hard time achieving anything in my career.

✦ They Said

Jeanette was the easiest lay in Hollywood. —Rouben Mamoulian, director

That silly horse Jeanette MacDonald, yakking away at wooden-peg Eddy, with all that glycerine running down her Max Factor makeup. —Judy Garland, making fun of her singing rival at MGM

I never thought she had much of a sense of humor. —Maurice Chevalier, who was her first cinema singing partner in several films. She called him "the fastest derriere pincher in Hollywood"

✦ First Sexual Experience

Possibly lost her virginity to Thorn, an architectural student at NYU to whom she was semi-engaged for a couple of years in her early twenties.

✦ Husbands

Gene Raymond, actor (costar in *Smilin' Through,* '41)

✦ Did You Know?

In the middle 1920s, the virginal appearing MacDonald worked as an "escort" in New York City.

Raymond's mother didn't attend MacDonald's marriage to her twenty-nine-year-old son because she thought the thirty-four-year-old actress was a "cradle snatcher."

Raymond spent his honeymoon with MacDonald, who was crying and pining over true love Nelson Eddy, having sex with Buddy Rogers, Mary Pickford's new husband, while the two couples were on a joint honeymoon cruise to Hawaii.

Lovers, Flings, or Just Friends?

- Maurice Chevalier, singer-actor (costar in *The Love Parade,* '29)
- Nelson Eddy, singer-actor (costar of *Naughty Marietta,* '35)
- Duke Ellington, composer-musician
- Henry Fonda, actor
- Allan Jones, singer-actor (and father of singer Jack Jones) (costar of *The Firefly,* '37)
- Ernst Lubitsch, director (directed her in *The Love Parade,* '29)
- Louis B. Mayer, head of MGM
- Robert "Bob" Ritchie, booking agent (they first had sex on April 7, 1928—he kept a record of all the women he slept with)
- Jimmy Stewart, actor
- Irving Stone, wealthy heir

Lovers, Flings, or Just Friends?

- Robin Clark, actor
- "Jamie," professor-poet
- Jordan Kalfus, photographer's assistant
- Ryan O'Neal, actor (costar in *Love Story,* '71)
- Mickey Raphael, musician
- Larry Spangler, producer
- Peter Weller, actor (costar in *Just Tell Me What You Want,* '80)
- *and* a "world-class" quarterback

Ali MacGraw 1938–

✦ She Said

Romance, for me, was usually just heat.

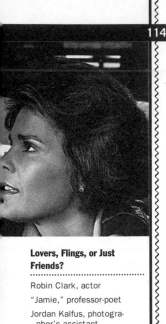

The sex buzzing around Hollywood doesn't interest me at all.

With me and Steve, confrontation was the norm.

✦ They Said

Ali MacGraw is proof that a great model is not necessarily a great, or even an average, actress. —Peter Sellers

You have a great ass, but you better start working out now, because I don't want to wake up one day with a woman who's got an ass like a seventy-year-old Japanese soldier. —Steve McQueen, passing along physical fitness advice to MacGraw

✦ First Sexual Experience

Probably lost her virginity to her first husband, a banker, whom she dubs with the pseudonym of Alex in her autobiography.

✦ Husbands

Alex, a pseudonym for her first husband, a banker
Robert (Bob) Evans, producer
Steve McQueen, actor (costar in *The Getaway,* '72)

✦ Did You Know?

MacGraw had her toes sucked by surrealist artist Salvador Dalí in a room at New York's St. Regis Hotel. After the encounter, he sent her a fully grown, live iguana, its tail covered with imitation pearls, in a flower box.

Shirley MacLaine 1934–

✦ She Said

I have only one vice: fucking.

I don't have to worry about my husband growing tired of me because I never see him. —Telling why her nearly thirty-year marriage to Steve Parker has been successful, because he's lived in Japan almost the whole time

I have mostly used relationships to learn, and when that process is over, so is the relationship.

✦ They Said

Shirley—I love her, but her oars aren't touching the water these days. —Dean Martin, actor-singer

The most difficult and unpleasant star I have ever worked with . . . she hasn't a grain of gratitude in her. —Hal Wallis, producer

Shirley MacLaine is a disaster, a fucking ovary with a propeller who leaves a trail of blood wherever she goes. A half-assed chorus girl, a pseudo-intellectual who thinks she knows politics, thinks she knows everything, wears clothes from the ladies of the Good Christ Church Bazaar. —Martin Rackin, producer

✦ First Sexual Experience

Unknown.

✦ Husbands

Steve Parker, film producer (in Japan)

✦ Did You Know?

MacLaine is the classic case of the "understudy who became a star." She was actress-dancer Carol Haney's understudy for the Broadway show *The Pajama Game.* Three days after it opened, Haney sprained her ankle and MacLaine went on for her that night. Producer Hal Wallis happened to be in the audience, saw MacLaine, and liked what he saw. MacLaine's now been a star for more than thirty years, but who remembers Haney?

MacLaine, in one of her books, claims that producer Hal Wallis, to whom she was under contract at the time, once chased her around his desk. Wallis retorted, in his autobiography, that he was younger then and could have certainly caught her if the incident had ever occurred.

Lovers, Flings, or Just Friends?

- Alain Delon, actor (costar in *The Yellow Rolls-Royce,* '65)
- Pete Hamill, columnist-author
- Elton John, singer-actor
- Danny Kaye, actor
- Andrei Konchalovsky, director
- Robert Mitchum, actor (costar in *Two for the Seesaw,* '63)
- Andrew Peacock, Australian prime minister
- Frank Sinatra, actor (costar in *Some Came Running,* '58)
- Kenneth Tynan, British critic and essayist
- Sander Vanocur, telejournalist

Lovers, Flings, or Just Friends?

Jean-Michel Basquiat, artist
Warren Beatty, actor-director (costar in *Dick Tracy,* '90)
Eric Bell, friend
John "Jellybean" Benitez, musician
Sandra Bernhard, comedienne
Steve Bray, waiter
Norris Burroughs, graffiti artist
Jose Canseco, baseball player
Ingrid Casaros, makeup artist
Ken Compton, artist-musician
Oliver Crumes, dancer
Dan Gilroy, musician
Mick Jagger, singer-actor
Nick Kamen, model-singer
Mark Kamins, disc jockey–music producer
John F. Kennedy Jr., son of President John F. Kennedy
Bobby Martinez, graffiti artist
Lenny McGurr, graffiti artist
Moira McPharlin, childhood friend
Esai Morales, actor
Steve Newman, journalist
Jack Nicholson, actor
Prince, singer-composer (she referred to him as "the midget")
Bob Riley, drummer
Martin Schreiber, photographer
Tony Ward, model (appeared on the cover and inside the gay magazine *In Touch* in 1985)
Dr. Tim Willocks, psychiatrist-author
David Wolinski, songwriter
and lots and lots of Hispanics and light-skinned black males

Madonna 1958–

✦ She Said

I don't like *blow jobs, but I do like* getting *head—for a day and a half.*

Guys get to do everything. They get to be altar boys. They get to stay out late. Take their shirts off in summer. They get to pee standing up. They get to fuck a lot of girls and not worry about getting pregnant.

All those men I stepped on to get to the top—every one of them would take me back because they still love me and I still love them.

Feel comfortable with yourself . . . whether it's with another man . . . another woman . . . with three people.

✦ They Said

She could afford to be a little more magnanimous and a little less of a cunt. —Cher

Madonna loves beautiful women, and she is into anyone sexually, male or female, who is beautiful. —Camille Barbone, music producer

It's no joke, size counts to her. She's not interested in somebody who's not above average. —A former friend

✦ First Sexual Experience

Lost her virginity, first, to a female friend, Moira McPharlin, who, as Madonna put it, "finger-fucked" her. Her first male was seventeen-year-old Russell Long, a high school boyfriend in 1973, when she was fifteen. She's said, "I saw losing my virginity as a career move."

✦ Husbands

Sean Penn, actor (costar in *Shanghai Surprise,* '86)

✦ Did You Know?

What led to the split between Sean Penn and Madonna? Among other incidents, there were claims that Penn tied the Material Girl up to a chair and "abused" her for several hours.

Anna Magnani 1908–1973

✦ She Said

I have so much boiling inside, if I hadn't chosen acting, I think I would have been a great criminal.

I was a whore before you were born! —Yelling at a beautiful younger woman, who had been ogling Magnani's lover Roberto Rossellini

I am not an animal, so why should I wear a cage. —Answering why she refused to wear a brassiere

✦ They Said

A human Vesuvius. —Edith Head, costume designer

Anna had a difficult personality, she was more pagan than Christian, she was vigorous and primitive and noisy. —Luchino Visconti, director

Magnani is the last of the shameless emotionalists. You have to go back to silent movies for that kind of acting. —William Dierterle, director

✦ First Sexual Experience

Unknown.

✦ Husbands

Goffredo Alessandrini, director (directed her in *Cavalleria,* '36)

✦ Did You Know?

When she was signed to make *The Fugitive Kind* ('59), Magnani, who was having an affair with Anthony Franciosa, dropped him abruptly. She arrived on the set all prepared for an affair with costar Marlon Brando, who wasn't interested—which really got her temper up. She had the same problem on *The Rose Tattoo* ('55); she fancied costar Burt Lancaster, but he wasn't interested.

Magnani was never reticent about venting her anger. When she was rudely pushed aside by fans and photographers at a reception where Marilyn Monroe was being presented a film award, Magnani directed her ire at Monroe screaming, "*Puta! Puta!* (Whore! Whore!)" in the sex siren's face.

And how did Magnani often express her fabled temper? During the filming of *Wild Is the Wind* ('57), she would throw plates of pasta against the walls of her motel room. By the end of the shoot, the walls were streaked with spaghetti sauce.

Lovers, Flings, or Just Friends?

Anthony Franciosa, actor (costar in *Wild Is the Wind,* '57)

Robert Rossellini, Italian director

Massimo Serato, Italian actor

Luchino Visconti, director (directed her in *Bellissima,* '51)

Lovers, Flings, or Just Friends?

Greg Bautzer, Hollywood attorney-escort

Enrico Bomba, Italian producer

Samuel Brody, attorney (who was driving the car the night she was killed)

Jim Byron, press agent

Oleg Cassini, fashion designer

Steve Cochran, actor

Richard Egan, actor

John F. Kennedy, president

Anton LaVey, noted satanist

Tommy Noonan, comedian-actor-director (costar in *Promises! Promises!* '63)

Douglas Olivares, Venezuelan student

Nicholas Ray, director

Robby Robertson, airline pilot (who later became the third Mr. Linda Darnell)

Profirio Rubirosa, Dominican playboy

Nelson Sardelli, Brazilian or Italian singer

Raymond Straight (aka Rusty Ray), press agent–author

Stephen Vlabovith (aka Count Stephano V. Tirone), church sexton

Jayne Mansfield 1932–1967

✦ She Said

Men want women pink, helpless, and to do a lot of deep breathing.

Men are those creatures with two legs and eight hands.

I'm a big girl and I have to have a big guy.

When I was told about sex, first I laughed and then I cried. I couldn't see the point. Fortunately, I changed.

✦ They Said

There was something overblown about her figure, something not sexy, but pathetic. I would have rather gone to bed with Agnes Moorehead. —Greg Bautzer, Hollywood attorney, who always had a beautiful star or starlet on his arm

This country knows more about Jayne's statistics than about the Second Commandment. —The Reverend Billy Graham, evangelist

She's just for truck drivers to drool over. She's too cheap looking. —Paul Wendkos, director, rejecting Mansfield for a part

Miss United Dairies, herself. —David Niven, referring to Mansfield's two biggest claims to fame

✦ First Sexual Experience

Lost her virginity at age sixteen to a twenty-four-year-old man she called Inky—because of his black hair—whom she met at a party. Within a few days she was also probably having sex with future first husband Paul Mansfield, whom she married a short time thereafter.

✦ Husbands

Paul Mansfield, high school student
Mickey Hargitay, Hungarian bodybuilder
Matt Cimber, director–personal manager

✦ Did You Know?

Jayne called her vagina Suzi.

Want to see Jayne's two biggest treasures in their prime? Then find a copy of the February 1955 *Playboy*—she's the centerfold.

Mary Martin 1913–1990

✦ She Said

I think every baby girl is born knowing how to flirt . . . first with her father, then with every other male in sight.

I tried so hard in Hollywood that they called me Audition Mary.

It was all so boring, so wasteful, so enervating. —On the "tedium" of making movies

✦ They Said

She got to live every dyke and fairy's dream combined. I mean all that running around onstage dressed as a man and getting to fly, too, Dahling. —Tallulah Bankhead, actress

✦ First Sexual Experience

Lost her virginity at age sixteen to her first husband, Ben Hagman.

✦ Husbands

Benjamin Jackson Hagman, student, later attorney
Richard Halliday, story editor–personal manager

✦ Did You Know?

When Martin married her second husband, she was surprised when she saw how he spelled his name—Halliday—at the marriage license bureau; she'd always thought it was Holiday.

The long-time love of Martin's life appears to have been actress Janet Gaynor, winner of the first Oscar for Best Actress. Even though Gaynor was married to famed costume designer Adrian, and Martin to Halliday, the two ladies maintained a "close" relationship until Gaynor's death.

Lovers, Flings, or Just Friends?

Bing Crosby, actor (costar in *Rhythm on the River*, '40)

Frederick Drake, publisher *Harper's Bazaar*

Janet Gaynor, actress

Richard Kollman, actor (who later married columnist Dorothy Kilgallen)

Winthrop Rockefeller, millionaire

Laurence Schwab, producer

Lovers, Flings, or Just Friends?

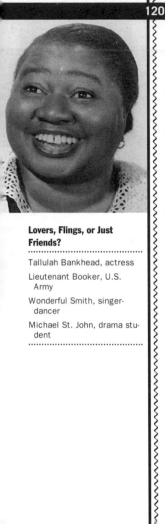

- Tallulah Bankhead, actress
- Lieutenant Booker, U.S. Army
- Wonderful Smith, singer-dancer
- Michael St. John, drama student

Hattie McDaniel 1895–1952

✦ She Said

Always remember this: There are only eighteen inches between a pat on the back and a kick in the rump. —Her oft-stated motto

Hell, I'd rather play a maid than be one! —Snarling at fellow blacks who criticized her for the roles she played

I have never gotten over my crush on Hollywood. I suppose I am still just a tourist from Milwaukee.

✦ They Said

She lacks dignity, age, nobility . . . and she hasn't the right face for it. —Susan Myrick, dialect expert for *Gone With the Wind* ('39), describing McDaniel's unsuitability for her role as Mammy

✦ First Sexual Experience

Unknown.

✦ Husbands

George Langford, scion of a wealthy black Denver family
Howard Hickman, occupation unknown
James Lloyd Crawford, real estate broker
Larry Williams, interior decorator

✦ Did You Know?

Hattie had at least one white lover who has remained unnamed thus far. She returned home one evening and caught him in bed at her house with another woman. After throwing the couple out, she tried to burn the house down.

Ethel Merman 1908–1984

✦She Said

If they could do what I do, they'd be up here. —Frequent boast about her audiences

Men, you can have them!

The audience expects Ethel Merman every night. Sometimes there's not enough left to share with a husband.

✦They Said

Never, but never, go see a singing teacher. —George Gershwin, after hearing her sing "I Got Rhythm" for the first time

Merman was something that was so special in a real sort of way—like Mount Rushmore. —Farley Granger, actor

✦First Sexual Experience

Unknown.

✦Husbands

William (Bill) Jacob Smith, talent agent
Robert Levitt, newspaper circulation manager
Robert Six, Continental Airlines president
Ernest Borgnine, actor

✦Did You Know?

Merman was an avid gum chewer (Wrigley's Spearmint) and voracious eater of peanut brittle. She could perform any of her songs with a mouthful of either treat. Once on Johnny Carson's TONIGHT show, she crammed her mouth full of peanut brittle, then proceeded to sing "I Got Rhythm", holding the high-C note for the full 16 bars.

Devoted to her family, Merman performed a strange ritual after their deaths. When her mother and daughter died, she had them cremated and their ashes placed in a vault in Colorado. At her father's death she had him cremated, too, then retrieved the other two urns and placed all three of them in a closet in her apartment. Much to the consternation of close friends, Merman said she liked being able to open the closet door and see those she loved the most.

Lovers, Flings, or Just Friends?

- Walter Annenberg, newspaper magnate
- Sherman Billingsley, owner of NY's Stork Club
- Charles Cushing, investment banker
- Ernest Gann, author
- Judy Garland, actress
- Alter Goetz, Wall Street broker
- Winthrop Rockefeller, millionaire
- Cesar Romero, actor
- Jacqueline Susann, author
- Billy Sussman, wholesale furniture broker

Lovers, Flings, or Just Friends?

- Greg Bautzer, attorney
- Alfred Bloomingdale, mercantile mogul
- Ernie Byfield Jr., screenwriter
- Mario Cabre, Spanish bullfighter
- Randolph Churchill, son of British prime minister Winston
- André Dubonnet, aperitif king
- Hal Hayes, architect
- Conrad Hilton, hotelier (and ex–Mr. Zsa Zsa Gabor, plus being Liz Taylor's ex-daddy-in-law)
- Charles Isaac, ex-spouse of Eva Gabor
- Harry Karl, shoe magnate
- James Kimberley, Kleenex heir
- Maharaja of Cooch Behar, Indian nobleman
- Tony Martin, singer-actor
- Louis B. Mayer, MGM studio head
- William J. O'Connor, attorney
- Frank Ryan, financier
- Jack Seabrook, frozen-food business
- Gilbert Swanson, frozen-food business
- Claude Terrail, French restaurant owner
- Antonio Vega, Brazilian millionaire

Ann Miller 1919–

✦ She Said

I used to fall in love with the best-looking man at a party, and sometimes I wound up marrying him.

I never played politics, I was never a party girl, and I never slept with any of the producers. —Commenting on why she believed she never became a larger star

I believe in being nice to your ex-husbands. If they're nice enough to marry you, why not stay on friendly terms with them?

I've danced with my toenails broken and bleeding, with swollen feet, with blood clots in my leg. Not all at the same time, of course. But I always managed to screw my earrings on tight.

✦ They Said

No one knows what will pop of her mouth, she least of all. —Janet Leigh, on Miller's extreme—and often amusing—tendency to ramble on about the most unusual subjects

✦ First Sexual Experience

Unknown, but she did get her a kiss in 1937 from Kenny Baker in the film *Radio City Revels,* and she's stated it was her *first* kiss.

✦ Husbands

Reese Milner, elevator millionaire and heir to an ironworks fortune
William Moss, oil millionaire (and ex–Mr. Jane Withers)
Arthur Cameron, millionaire

✦ Did You Know?

Jane Powell said that on her passport, under the line marked *Profession,* Miller wrote the word *star.*

Cowboy star Gene Autry told Miller that she was the first girl he ever kissed on the screen.

Miller believes in reincarnation, and that she's had an earlier Egyptian life.

Liza Minnelli 1946–

✦ She Said

My ugliness overwhelms me. I'm really weird looking. Take your average standards of beauty and that ain't it.

I prefer to be Liza Minnelli onstage and offstage. I'm not just Judy Garland's daughter, I'm me. I've made it on my own.

I never get mad. I'll chew Valium rather than throw a scene.

✦ They Said

Dear silly Liza. One week she holds a press conference to announce she is in love and the next complains that the press have broken up her romance. —Peter Allen, on her propensity to fall in love rather publicly

I can't understand how we can both be in love one day and out of love the next. —Desi Arnaz Jr., puzzled about being dumped abruptly in favor of Peter Sellers

She's a good anchor, a steady ship. She's had to be, considering plenty of people have tried to sink her. —Joel Grey, her costar in *Cabaret* ('72)

✦ First Sexual Experience

Unknown for certain.

✦ Husbands

Peter Allen, entertainer
Jack Haley Jr., producer
Mark Gero, stage manager–sculptor

✦ Did You Know?

Liza's maternal grandfather, Frank Gumm (Judy's dad), was homosexual, as was her father, Vincente Minnelli, and so was her first husband, entertainer Peter Allen. Her marriage to Peter didn't get consummated on their wedding night because the groom was out having sex with another man.

One tale about why her relationship with Peter Sellers ended: In a moment of mistaken frivolity, Liza crept up behind him one night at dinner and snatched off his toupee. Sellers was vastly underamused.

One racy biography tattled an interesting rumor about Liza. It involved Mikhail Baryshnikov, the basement at then-trendy Studio 54 disco, fellatio, and semen on Minnelli's lips.

Lovers, Flings, or Just Friends?

- Edward Albert, actor and son of actor Eddie Albert
- Adam Ant, singer
- Pedro Aquinaga, Brazilian playboy
- Desi Arnaz Jr., actor
- Charles Aznavour, French singer
- Mikhail Baryshnikov, Russian ballet dancer
- Baron Alexis de Redé, French socialite
- Tracy Everitt, dancer
- Bob Fosse, choreographer-director (directed her in *Cabaret*, '72)
- John Gary Gorton, prime minister of Australia
- Rex Kulbeth (Kramer), musician
- Edu Lobo, Brazilian composer
- Dyson Lovell, producer-actor
- Joe Pesci, actor
- Martin Scorsese, director (directed her in *New York, New York*, '77)
- Peter Sellers, actor
- Gene Simmons, rock singer
- Billy Stritch, pianist
- Ben Vereen, actor-dancer

Lovers, Flings, or Just Friends?

- Don Ameche, actor (costar in *Down Argentine Way,* '40)
- Ary Barroso, Brazilian composer
- Mario Cunha, Brazilian rower
- Arturo de Cordova, Mexican actor
- Vinicus de Moraes, Brazilian poet-diplomat
- Carlos Alberto Rocha Farias, Brazilian industrialist
- Cesar Ladeira, Brazilian announcer
- Dr. W. L. Marxer, physician
- John Payne, actor (costar of *Weekend in Havana,* '41)
- Mário Reis, Brazilian singer
- Cesar Romero, actor (costar in *Weekend in Havana,* '41)
- Asis Valenta, Brazilian singer
- Getúlio Vargas, president of Brazil
- John Wayne, actor

Carmen Miranda 1909–1955

✦ She Said

As soon as I see Hollywood, I love it.

Dey are so tall, dey are so smart! Dey are de type for me! —Her reaction to North American men

✦ They Said

In the Hollywood sense, which substitutes the word work *for tantrums induced by a swollen head, she had none.* —Maxene Andrews, of the Andrews Sisters singing fame

✦ First Sexual Experience

Probably lost her virginity to Mario Cunha, a Brazilian rower at Flamengo, a Rio rowing club, when she was twenty or twenty-one.

✦ Husbands

David Sebastian, producer

✦ Did You Know?

Carmen's disdain for underpants frequently delighted those working with her. Her flying skirts and fast dancing steps permitted them a glimpse of the Brazilian tropics south of her equator. Thanks to a photograph published by child-star-turned-author Kenneth Anger, most of her viewing public has also gazed at Carmen's private parts.

Marilyn Monroe 1926–1962

✦ She Said

That's the last cock I'll have to suck. —Commenting on what evidently had been a large part of her previous life, after signing her first big film contract

✦ They Said

A simple, decent-hearted kid whom Hollywood brought down, legs parted. —Elia Kazan, director

Copulation was, I'm sure, Marilyn's uncomplicated way of saying "Thank you." —Nunnally Johnson, director

If her hips weren't gyrating, she was winching her shoulders or swining her puzzy pink tits or making that sucking fish-pucker mouth. Everything about her stated, "I'm yours. Take me." —Carroll Baker, actress

I'm glad she died young. She could never have stood getting a wrinkle on her face. All she had was her beauty. —Sidney Guilaroff, a studio hairdresser of Marilyn's

✦ First Sexual Experience

Lost her virginity at age fifteen, when she was attacked by an older man in one of the many foster homes in which she was placed.

✦ Husbands

James Doughtery, U.S. serviceman
Joe DiMaggio, baseball player
Arthur Miller, playwright and author

✦ Did You Know?

Marilyn, in her early days, worked as a streetwalker on the side streets off Sunset Boulevard. She claimed she never took money for her favors, that she only did it for food. Once she had "connected" with a man, she'd negotiate for breakfast, lunch, or dinner, depending on the time of day.

When her lover Johnny Hyde died, Marilyn's grief led her to perform a bizarre ritual to bid him goodbye. She slipped into his house and spent the night on top of his body in his coffin. She then slipped away the next morning before any of his family awoke.

Lovers, Flings, or Just Friends?

Milton Berle, entertainer
Marlon Brando, actor
Yul Brynner, actor
Oleg Cassini, designer
Paddy Chayefsky, writer
Harry P. Cohn, head of Columbia Pictures
Tony Curtis, actor
Sammy Davis Jr., singer-actor
Blake Edwards, director
Albert Einstein, scientist
Howard Hughes, aviator-cinema mogul
John Huston, director
George Jessel, entertainer
Elia Kazan, director
John F. Kennedy, president
Robert Kennedy, U.S. attorney general
Anton LaVey, noted satanist
Natasha Lytess, drama coach
Dean Martin, singer-actor
Robert Mitchum, actor
Yves Montand, entertainer
Clifford Odets, writer
Nicholas Ray, screenwriter and director
Mickey Rooney, actor
Porfirio Rubirosa, Dominican diplomat-playboy
Damon Runyon, writer
George Sanders, actor
"Bugsy" Siegel, mobster
Frank Sinatra, entertainer
Sam Spiegel, producer
Lili St. Cyr, stripper
Franchot Tone, actor
Mel Tormé, singer-actor
Orson Welles, director-actor
Walter Winchell, columnist
Darryl F. Zanuck, studio head

Lovers, Flings, or Just Friends?

Jon Hall, actor (costar in *Arabian Nights,* '42)

Lt. Comdr. Claude Strickland, RAF pilot

Walter Wanger, producer

Orson Welles, director-actor

Darryl F. Zanuck, studio head

Maria Montez 1917–1951

✦ She Said

When I look at myself, I am so beautiful. I scream with joy.

Now I am a star. Now I am nice. I am more ladylike—and I don't like it.

I think if somebody would open a school to teach women to love, there would be fewer divorces. I have talked to American girls about these theengs, and their ideas of lovemaking are veery strange. Like dry ice.

✦ They Said

I'm always fascinated by the Montez woman. There's never a dull moment when you talk to her. —Louella Parsons, gossip columnist

Writing about Montez is the next best thing to being allowed to jot down anything that jumps into your head. —Pete Martin, columnist

Miss Montez has been a movie actress for two years and three months, and a press agent all her life. What she advertises is Miss Montez exclusively. She knows all her good points. —Frederick C. Othman, Hollywood columnist

✦ First Sexual Experience

Unknown for certain, but probably lost her virginity to her first husband, since she was raised by a strict Catholic family and married him when she was only seventeen.

✦ Husbands

William McFeeters, British Army officer

Jean-Pierre Aumont, actor (costar in *Siren of Atlantis,* '48)

✦ Did You Know?

Montez suffered the most unusual death to strike a Hollywood beauty. Enamored of hot baths, she let the water temperature reach scalding degrees. Unfortunately she did it once too often and suffered a fatal heart attack.

Demi Moore 1962–

✦She Said

I have to admit that in every relationship I've ever been in it's been me who did the breaking up. I'm so mean.

I didn't care if I shocked people with my outwardness. I'm sure I even tried *to do it.*

✦They Said

She's like a beautiful ballerina who can kickbox and talk dirty. —Anonymous director

Right now I'm completely one hundred percent gay. [But] . . . every time I see Demi Moore walk in front of my beach house, I think, "Whoa, she's really hot!" —David Geffen, entertainment mogul

✦First Sexual Experience

Unknown.

✦Husbands

Freddie Moore, rock musician
Bruce Willis, actor

✦Did You Know?

Moore's marriage to actor Bruce Willis on a Burbank soundstage heralded back to the extravagant "golden" age of spending in the film capital: The ceremony cost a reported $875,000.

Demi's certainly not a mama's girl. She and her mother have had troubles, putting it mildly, for the last several years. Mama didn't let Demi's appearances on magazine covers in various states of undress go unnoticed. She did some of her own—more blatant—which only helped their estrangement. Like daughter, like mother . . . demimonde mama.

Lovers, Flings, or Just Friends?

Emilio Estevez, actor and son of actor Martin Sheen (costar in *Wisdom*, '87)

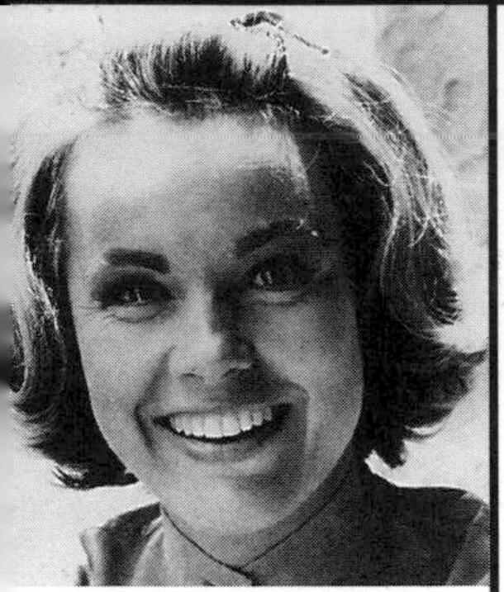

Lovers, Flings, or Just Friends?

- Greg Bautzer, attorney–Hollywood escort
- Robert Evans, producer-actor
- Nicky Hilton, playboy–hotel-chain heir and the first Mr. Liz Taylor
- David Janssen, actor
- Henry Kissinger, diplomat
- Prince Mahmud Pahlavi, brother of the Shah of Iran
- Robert Wagner, actor (costar in *Beneath the 12 Mile Reef,* '53)

Terry Moore 1929–

✦ She Said

I hate silicone, because now everyone can have what I have.

I was definitely typed as the girl next door. I was never thought to be sexy.

✦ They Said

How many times do I have to tell you all men are animals, baby? They just want to get into your pants. —Howard Hughes, who secretly married Moore, warning her about the "intentions" of other men

Stay away from that son of a bitch Hughes and you might even become a star. —Harry Cohn, head of Columbia pictures

✦ First Sexual Experience

Lost her virginity to Howard Hughes, after their secret wedding aboard his yacht.

✦ Husbands

Howard Hughes, aviation-cinema mogul

Glenn Davis, football star (who had previously been engaged to Liz Taylor)

Gene McGrath, businessman

Stuart Warren Cramer III, assistant director (who was also the first Mr. Jean Peters)

✦ Did You Know?

Hughes used to like to carefully wash, then closely examine, Moore's hands. It was apparently nothing for him to spend ten minutes on the whole procedure. He also used to quiz her thoroughly about her bowel movements. If Moore couldn't remember when she last had one, she's said it was if she had "just announced I had been bitten by a rabid dog," necessitating laxatives under Hughes's supervision.

Jeanne Moreau 1925–

✦She Said

Most people don't have the energy for sex, so they give up and go to the movies.

Age does not protect you from love. But love, to some extent, protects you from age.

It's not because you show a great orgasm in detail that you are true to facts. The mind has to be involved as well as the body. —Reflecting on her directing technique in her first film (*La Lumière,* '76)

✦They Said

Many people fall in love with her. I did. And she loves you in return. But just till the end of the film. —Marcello Mastroianni, actor

After a crying scene it is sometimes difficult for her to stop crying. —Louis Malle

✦First Sexual Experience

Unknown.

✦Husbands

Jean-Louis Richard, French actor

Theo Rubanis, actor (who was also married to Lady Sarah Churchill)

William Friedkin, director

✦Did You Know?

Given their mutual looks and sexual magnetism, Moreau and Burt Lancaster might have seemed a likely pair for an encounter during filming. It doesn't appear to have happened, given what the actress later opined. Lancaster couldn't pick up an ashtray before discussing "his motivation for an hour or so," she said. Would that be the kind of man Moreau would permit into her bedchambers?

Lovers, Flings, or Just Friends?

- Pierre Cardin, French fashion designer
- George Hamilton, actor (costar in *Viva Maria!* '65)
- Raoul Lévy, French producer
- Louis Malle, French director (directed her in *The Lovers,* '59)
- Lee Marvin, actor (costar in *Monte Walsh,* '70)
- Marcello Mastroianni, actor (costar in *La Notte,* '61)
- Tony Richardson, director (directed her in *The Sailor from Gibraltar,* '66)

Lovers, Flings, or Just Friends?

- Jack Carson, actor
- Peter Cookson, actor (who later married actress Beatrice Straight)
- Gary Cooper, actor (costar in *The Fountainhead,* '49)
- Kirk Douglas, actor
- Lewis William Douglas III, socialite-businessman
- John Gunther, author
- Bruce Hall, actor (who later married actress Kim Stanley)
- Victor Jory, actor

Patricia Neal 1926–

✦She Said

In everyone's life a lot of bad things happen. I just seemed to have had a larger dose of bad things.

Frequently my life has been likened to a Greek tragedy, and the actress in me cannot deny that comparison.

✦They Said

The power and variety of her dark brown voice, on which she plays like a master of the cello, enable her to separate the cadenza from its context and make of it a plangent cry from the depths of memory. —Kenneth Tynan, theatrical critic

✦First Sexual Experience

Lost her virginity to a young intern, who then rather unexpectedly dumped her to marry another woman.

✦Husbands

Roald Dahl, author

✦Did You Know?

One-time lover Gary Cooper—and his extra-large wonder wand, says Lupe Velez—may have been good to the last drop, but husband Roald Dahl wasn't. What happened during Neal's Maxwell House Coffee "good til the last drop" commercials shocked her better than a strong dose of caffeine. She got dropped by her husband for another woman, a member of the film crew she had befriended.

Pola Negri 1897–1987

✦ She Said

I know I am charming. I consider my work great and I am a great actress. —Replying to a woman on the street who said how "charming" she thought Negri was

Hollywood has gone from Pola to Polaroid.

I was European, and therefore, I was temperamental. —Commenting on how Hollywood "misperceived" her

The Hollywood I knew at that time was the Hollywood of dreams. It has long since vanished.

✦ They Said

A lying lesbo! A Polish publicity hound! . . . Had a mustache and couldn't act her way out of a paper bag. —Tallulah Bankhead

You're really two people. On the surface, you seem like the most worldly creature that ever lived. And what's underneath? Somebody who is more innocent girl than woman. —Charlie Chaplin

✦ First Sexual Experience

Lost her virginity to her first husband, Count Eugene Dambski, who she said used a "forcefulness that he mistook for passion."

✦ Husbands

Count Eugene Dambski, Polish nobleman

Prince Serge Mdivani, one of the Georgian "marrying Mdivani" brothers

✦ Did You Know?

Pola was the first film star to appear in public with painted toenails. When she did, one woman screamed, "Her toes are bleeding."

Pola won a libel suit against the French cinema magazine *Pour Vous,* which alleged that she had been Hitler's mistress.

Lovers, Flings, or Just Friends?

- Boris Chaliapin, Russian singer
- Charlie Chaplin, actor
- Russ Columbo, singer-actor
- Otto Froitzheim, German tennis player
- Victor Hulewicz, Polish businessman
- Glen Kidston, British millionaire aviator
- Rod La Rocque, actor (costar in *Forbidden Paradise,* '24)
- Ernst Lubitsch, director (costarred and directed her in several early German silent films)
- Harold McCormick, heir to the farm-equipment fortune
- "Prince" David Mdivani, another one of the "Marrying Mdivani" brothers
- Wolfgang George Schleber, German businessman
- Rudolph Valentino, actor
- Raoul Walsh, director
- Margaret West, Texas heiress

Lovers, Flings, or Just Friends?

Paul Bern, studio exec and later Mr. Jean Harlow

Charlie Chaplin, actor-director

Courtland Dines, socialite playboy

Sam Goldwyn, producer

Joe Kelly (Joe Greer), chauffeur–cocaine addict

Mack Sennett, director

Rollin Sturgeon, director

William Desmond Taylor, director

Mabel Normand 1894–1930

✦ She Said

Say anything you like, but don't say that I "like" to work. That sounds like Mary Pickford, that prissy bitch. Just say I like to pinch babies and twist their legs. And get drunk. —Replying about her hobbies in an interview

It was a perfectly innocent coincidence that I was the last person to see Bill Taylor alive. —Referring to the scandal, in which she was implicated and which ultimately ruined her career, over the mysterious murder of director William Desmond Taylor

✦ They Said

What a glorious, lovable, unmanageable minx! —Abraham Lehr, Sam Goldwyn's manager

When she spoke, toads came out of her mouth, but nobody minded. —Blanche Sweet, silent-film star, on Normand's racy language and love of racy jokes

That one always had the heart of a child, and like a child her heart was broken whenever anyone was unkind to her. —Marie Dressler, actress

✦ First Sexual Experience

Unknown.

✦ Husbands

Lew Cody, actor (who proposed to her drunkenly as a joke, and she accepted drunkenly as a joke)

✦ Did You Know?

After a long-running, on-off engagement with director Mack Sennett, Normand finally broke off their relationship when she caught him in bed with her best friend, actress Mae Busch. When Normand broke in on the couple, Busch picked up a vase and broke it over her friend's head, knocking her unconscious. Sennett later apologized for his craven infidelity, swearing never to do it again; she caught him in the same compromising position a few days later.

Mabel got addicted to drugs through her fondness for cocaine peanuts, a popular confection during the 1920s.

Kim Novak 1933–

✦She Said

You know why I came to Hollywood in the first place? Some guy in Chicago was bugging me to marry him, so I ran away. I was afraid of marriage.

I'd be a terribly frustrated woman today if I'd married any of the men I ever loved.

He said I was nothing but a piece of meat in a butcher shop, and that I should never forget it. I never have. —Repeating some advice Harry Cohn, her studio boss at Columbia, gave her

✦They Said

This girl has absolutely no sense of humor. She's like ice water. —William Holden, her costar in *Picnic* ('55)

She's a bitch and a spoiled brat. I will never make another picture with her. —Tyrone Power, her costar in *The Eddy Duchin Story* ('56)

That girl is the stuff of which real stars are made. —Alfred Hitchcock, her director in *Vertigo* ('58), to his wife, Alma, after entertaining Novak at dinner

✦First Sexual Experience

Unknown.

✦Husbands

Richard Johnson, British actor (costar in *The Amorous Adventures of Moll Flanders,* '65)

Dr. Robert Malloy, veterinarian

✦Did You Know?

Kim posed for some "racy" photos when she was a teenager. When they surfaced in 1954, after she had achieved stardom, Columbia supposedly paid $15,000 to suppress them.

Harry Cohn used mob influence to break up her relationship with Sammy Davis Jr. Davis was driven into the desert near Las Vegas and told, "You've only got one eye now. Wanna try for none?"

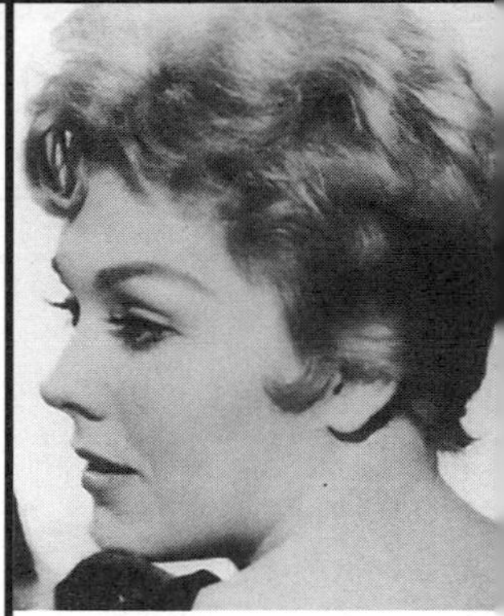

Lovers, Flings, or Just Friends?

- Mario Bandini, Italian spaghetti-sauce magnate
- Michael Brandon, actor (costar in *The Third Girl From the Left,* '73)
- Paddy Chayefsky, playwright-screenwriter
- Sammy Davis Jr., entertainer
- Cary Grant, actor
- John Ireland, actor
- Prince Aly Khan, millionaire playboy
- Mac Krim, theater magnate
- Prince Alfonso Langenberg
- Peter Lawford, actor
- Roderick Mann, British columnist
- Richard Quine, director (directed her in *Bell, Book and Candle,* '58)
- Porfirio Rubirosa, Dominican playboy
- Al Schackman, musician
- Louis Servin, fashion designer
- Frank Sinatra, singer-actor (costar in *The Man With the Golden Arm,* '55)
- Rafael "Ramfis" Trujillo, Dominican playboy
- Jack Thomas, restaurateur

Lovers, Flings, or Just Friends?

Brian Aherne, actor
Turhan Bey, Turkish actor (costar in *A Night in Paradise,* '46)
George Brent, actor (costar in *'Til We Meet Again,* '40)
Jimmy Cagney, actor
Maurice Chevalier, singer-actor
Count Giorgio Cini, Italian nobleman
Ronald Colman, actor
Gary Cooper, actor
Eddie Fisher, singer
Clark Gable, actor
George Hamilton, actor
Richard Harris, actor
Rex Harrison, actor
Richard Hillary, British RAF pilot
Leslie Howard, actor (costar in *The Scarlet Pimpernel,* '34)
Leslie A. Hutchinson, black Jamaican entertainer
Eddie Mayer, screenwriter
David Niven, actor
Prince Phillip, British consort
Dr. Rex Ross, Hollywood physician
Richard Rush, director (directed her in *Of Love and Desire,* '63)
Robert Ryan, actor (costar in *Berlin Express,* '48)
Sir Victor Sassoon, Indian mercantile prince
Joseph Schenck, producer
Charles Sweeney, golfer-tycoon
Richard Tate, actor
Rod Taylor, actor
Darryl F. Zanuck, studio head

Merle Oberon 1911–1979

✦ She Said

If you tell anyone about this, I'll tell my husband. He's more important than you and he'll ruin you. —Commend made to Eddie Mayer, a screenwriter, after they'd just finished making love

You've just made a picture with Maria Montez! If you can handle that bitch, you can handle me! —Snapping nastily at one of her directors

✦ They Said

Merle is almost a nymphomaniac. She makes love because she likes it, because of the money; she is as promiscuous as a man enjoying a quick one behind the door. —Cecil Beaton, photographer-designer

A real common piece. —Marlene Dietrich, who evidently was unimpressed by Merle's pseudoladylike affectations

She was always in awe of her fellow movie stars. When she was having an affair with Jimmy Cagney during a bond-selling tour in World War II, she interrupted their sex once by saying, "Just imagine, I'm in bed with Jimmy Cagney!" I hear it somewhat diminished his ardor. —Sheilah Graham, Hollywood columnist

✦ First Sexual Experience

Unknown.

✦ Husbands

Alexander Korda, British director-producer
Lucien Ballard, cameraman
Bruno Pagliai, Italian Mexican-based industrialist
Robert Wolders, Dutch actor

✦ Did You Know?

While making *The Lodger* ('44), Merle fancied a young carpenter who was part of the crew. She invited him home to dinner and, after feeding him, told him want she wanted. He refused, as he had just become a Christian, and left. She had him removed from the film's crew the next day.

Merle claimed that Sen. Ted Kennedy called and asked her for a date while he was still married to first wife, Joan. When she asked how he could take her out when everyone would recognize him, Teddy replied that the American people would like him whatever he did. She refused his offer and later observed that the incident occurred shortly before the senator's Chappaquiddick midnight swim.

Christina Onassis 1950–1988

✦ She Said

I've been an adult since I was nine.

If I can't be happy with all I've been given, something must be wrong with my fate—or with me.

Rich girls need it, too. —Referring to her desire for steady sex

✦ They Said

Of course, as soon as you mature, we have to get your nose fixed. —Tina Livanos Onassis, her mother

Why couldn't it have been my daughter rather than my son. —Aristotle Onassis, father, on learning his son had been killed in an airplane accident

✦ First Sexual Experience

Unknown.

✦ Husbands

Joseph Bolker, American real estate–construction company owner
Stratis Andreadis, Greek shipping heir
Sergei Kausov, Russian state maritime employee
Thierry Roussel, businessman-socialite

✦ Did You Know?

When Christina was a child, the clothes for her dolls were made by French couturier Christian Dior.

Christina was an ugly duckling compared to her mother, the beauteous Athina (Tina) Livanos. Although Tina had Christina given some cosmetic surgery, she didn't permit too much on her daughter. Otherwise her own beauty might be overshone. One item Tina never tackled was Christina's hair. Not the hair on her head, all the rest of it on her body, of which there was a lot. Many of her bed partners later derided Christina for being so monkey-like.

Lovers, Flings, or Just Friends?

- Luis Basualdo, polo player
- Warren Beatty, actor
- Jean-Paul Belmondo, actor
- Gianfranco Cicogna, playboy-socialite
- Yvon Coty, perfume heir
- David Davies, playboy
- Mick Flick, Mercedes-Benz heir
- Peter Goulandris, shipping heir
- Gunther, her helicopter pilot
- John F. Kennedy Jr., step-brother
- Danny Marentette, horse breeding agent
- Nicholas Mavroleon, shipping heir (who later married actress Barbara Carrera)
- Jack Nicholson, actor
- Jorge Tchomlekdjoglou, textile businessman
- Dovi Tubrussi, medical student

Lovers, Flings, or Just Friends?

Warren Beatty, actor

Roswell Gilpatric, businessman–government official

Pete Hamill, writer

John G. W. Husted Jr., a fiancé with whom she broke up

André Meyer, financier

David Ormsby-Gore, Lord Harlech, British diplomat

Frank Richardson, financier

Maurice Tempelsman, diamond dealer

Jacqueline Bouvier Kennedy Onassis 1930–1994

✦ She Said

My natural tendency is to be rather introverted and solitary and to brood too much.

The Kennedys are really terribly bourgeois.

I don't think there are any men who are faithful to their wives.

Anybody who is against me will look like a rat, unless I run off with Eddie Fisher.

✦ They Said

She wasn't the most glamorous nor the most beautiful woman. She had kinky hair and bad skin. —Zsa Zsa Gabor, actress, on the "young" Jackie

Everyone knew she was not cut out for dignity. You mustn't ask a woman with a touch of vulgarity to spend the rest of her life over a corpse. —Coco Chanel, couturier, on Jackie's marriage to Ari

What amazes me is that she survives while everyone around her drops. She's dangerous, she's deadly. —Christina Onassis, stepdaughter

✦ First Sexual Experience

Unknown for certain, but one published source suggests that it was author John P. Marquand Jr. who took her virginity, with Jackie saying, "Oh! Is that all there is to it?" Marquand has stated since that the published story is false.

✦ Husbands

John F. Kennedy, president of the United States
Aristotle Onassis, shipping magnate

✦ Did You Know?

The world saw Jackie's pubic hair thanks to husband Onassis. He became annoyed at what he thought where her phony protestations about being annoyed by the press. He arranged for telephoto shots to be made of her while she was nude sunbathing and then sold to tabloids. Jackie wanted to sue; he advised against it. She sued anyway and, while he paid the bills, Onassis got the final laugh: the world had seen his wife buck naked. To his Greek mind, now when Jackie berated the press, Onassis felt he would be hearing the truth from her.

Dorothy Parker 1893–1967

✦ She Said

Scratch an actor and find an actress.

Men seldom make passes at girls who wear glasses.

You can lead a whore to culture, but you can't make her think. —Retort when challenged to use the word *horticulture* in a sentence

I am cheap—you know that! —Defending her wanton ways to a friend

✦ They Said

That lady ain't a book lady, she's a bed lady, like me. —Tallulah Bankhead, actress

When Dottie fell in love, she fell in love. She didn't swim in a fishpond, you know; she went into the ocean. —Marc Connelly, writer and member of the famed Algonquin Round Table

Mark my words: Alcohol will coarsen you. —Robert Benchley, humorist and close friend, warning her about her drinking habits

✦ First Sexual Experience

Unknown.

✦ Husbands

Edwin Pond Parker II, stockbroker

Alan Campbell, actor-writer (who also had a fling with actress Estelle Winwood)

Alan Campbell, actor-writer

✦ Did You Know?

Parker, when she was drinking and under the sway of a man she desired, wasn't shy about satisfying her sexual desires. While visiting friends in their apartment one evening, she and lover Rosser Evans couldn't contain themselves. They had sex on the sofa in the same room with their friends. The hostess later remarked that Parker did have the good manners to say thanks for a nice evening before the duo departed.

Want to see Parker in a film? See *Saboteur* ('42), an Alfred Hitchcock movie. She appears with Hitchcock in his mandatory "quickie appearance scene," as a couple driving a car down a highway.

During the "Red scare" over Communism in Hollywood in the early fifties, Parker said that the only ism in Hollywood was plagiarism.

Lovers, Flings, or Just Friends?

- Heywood Broun, writer
- Joseph Bryan, writer
- Seward Collins, writer (who owned a collection of obscene English literature reputed to be the largest in the world)
- Howard Dietz, MGM publicity director
- Rosser Lynn Evans, radio announcer
- F. Scott Fitzgerald, writer
- John Wiley Garrett III, investment broker
- Gardner Jackson, left-wing journalist
- Ring Lardner, writer
- Charles MacArthur, writer (and later Mr. Helen Hayes)
- John McClain, reporter
- Elmer Rice, playwright (she dubbed him "the worst fuck I ever had")
- Thorne Smith, writer (who wrote the Topper stories)
- Deems Taylor, music critic

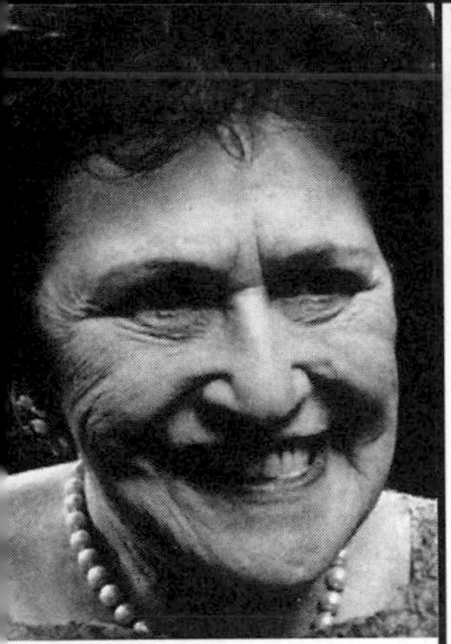

Lovers, Flings, or Just Friends?

Peter J. Brady, banker–labor leader

Clark Gable, actor

Jimmy McHugh, songwriter (who wrote "I Can't Give You Anything but Love, Baby")

Louella Parsons 1880–1972

✦ She Said

Almost everyone who has attained any kind of public stature in his or her profession can expect sometimes to see a reflection in a cracked mirror.

✦ They Said

She's a quaint old udder, isn't she? —John Barrymore Sr., unimpressed by the snoopy tattletale

Not a bad old slob. —James Mason, actor

Louella was essentially a bumbling person who had been placed in this powerful position by Mr. [William] *Hearst and was always struggling to keep this position. She could be mean and bitchy, but she was fundamentally a nice person.* —Henry Rogers, press agent

✦ First Sexual Experience

Unknown.

✦ Husbands

John Dement Parsons, real estate broker-reporter
Capt. Jack McCaffrey, steamboat captain
Dr. Harry "Docky" Martin, urologist

✦ Did You Know?

Whenever she was excited, Louella was wont to wet her panties. The older she got, the worse her problem became, until Hollywood hostesses dreaded having her visit, knowing that after she departed a large wet spot would remain to mark where she'd sat.

"Docky" Martin, Parson's third husband, was a renowned Hollywood drinker, who seemed to pass out in a drunken stupor at almost every party the couple attended. At one such affair, he was spotted on the floor with his penis exposed, prompting noted wit Wilson Mizner to point to it and quip, "There's Louella Parsons's column."

Eva "Evita" Perón 1919–1952

✦ She Said

Yes, I confess that I have one single, great ambition: I would like the name of Evita to figure somewhere in the history of my country.

Many people cannot understand the circumstances that have made my life what it is.

Before they put me to sleep—if I do not awake, "Viva Perón!" —A prime example of the typical political hyperbole she was still mouthing on her deathbed

✦ They Said

A charming horror, I thought, but I kept this opinion to myself. —Patricia Neal, actress, on meeting Perón at a South American film festival

"I think she was one of the great characters in history." —Tennessee Williams, playwright

Evita is lovely to look at—tall, svelte, brunette, alabaster-skinned. —*Time*, June 1944, her first mention in the foreign press

Perón achieves; Evita dignifies. —Political slogan chanted by their supporters

✦ First Sexual Experience

Probably lost her virginity to José Armani, a minor-league tango singer, when she was about fourteen.

✦ Husbands

Juan Perón, president-dictator of Argentina

✦ Did You Know?

Evita posed, early in her career, for some cheesecake photos. In 1947, at a society event, copies of one of those photos—Evita posed in a swimsuit, sucking an orange—were distributed as a party favor. Within an hour police swarmed in and closed the event, and the perpetrators were soon forced into exile.

When Porfirio Rubirosa, during a visit to Argentina, gave Evita money for one of her charities, other diplomats complained, being afraid that she would now start "shaking them down" for dubious contributions; one even said it was the *"only time a pimp had given money to a harlot."*

Lovers, Flings, or Just Friends?

- Eloy Borrás, Argentinean actor
- Raphael Firtuoso, theater owner
- Errol Flynn, actor
- José Franco, Argentinean actor
- Emilio Kastulovic, publisher
- Aristotle Onassis, millionaire shipping owner
- Tyrone Power, actor
- Porfirio Rubirosa, Dominican playboy-diplomat
- Pablo Suero, theatrical director

Lovers, Flings, or Just Friends?

Audie Murphy, actor–soldier hero

Robert Wagner, actor (costar in *Broken Lance,* '54)

Jean Peters 1926–

✦ She Said

I just didn't understand Hollywood. If a girl isn't married, everyone tries to get her married, and if she is, everyone tries to get her divorced.

✦ They Said

While Jean was pretty, she was not particularly chic. . . . Some of the studio personnel called her Miss Hairy-Legs, but not to her face. —Sheilah Graham, gossip columnist

A greenish-grey-eyed girl of twenty-one, much like an average coed in appearance. —Louella Parsons, gossip columnist

✦ First Sexual Experience

Unknown.

✦ Husbands

Stuart Warren Cramer III, assistant director (they separated after thirty-three days)

Howard Hughes, aviation-cinema mogul

Stanley Hough, director

✦ Did You Know?

Lover Audie Murphy once claimed to a friend that he had "laid" Peters nine times one night during their affair.

Michelle Pfeiffer 1957–

✦ She Said

Hollywood is filled with beautiful, unhappy women who have shut down.

I don't know that I've ever felt I was extraordinary looking. In fact, I know I'm not.

I have a very addictive personality.

I think I look like a duck.

✦ They Said

She's a lot stronger than even she *knows sometimes. It's not possible to mess with her and come out on top.* —Cher, actress and costar in *The Witches of Eastwick* ('87)

✦ First Sexual Experience

Unknown.

✦ Husbands

Peter Horton, actor
David Kelley, producer

✦ Did You Know?

Pfeiffer belonged to a religious cult, whose philosophy she has described as "bizarre," for several years before pulling free from them. She's also said that the cult brainwashed her into giving them "an enormous amount of money."

Lovers, Flings, or Just Friends?

- Eric Clapton, rock musician
- Kevin Costner, actor
- Michael Keaton, actor (costar in *Batman Returns,* '92)
- John Malkovich, actor (costar in *Dangerous Liaisons,* '88)
- Al Pacino, actor (costar in *Frankie and Johnny,* '91)
- Fisher Stevens
- Kiefer Sutherland, actor

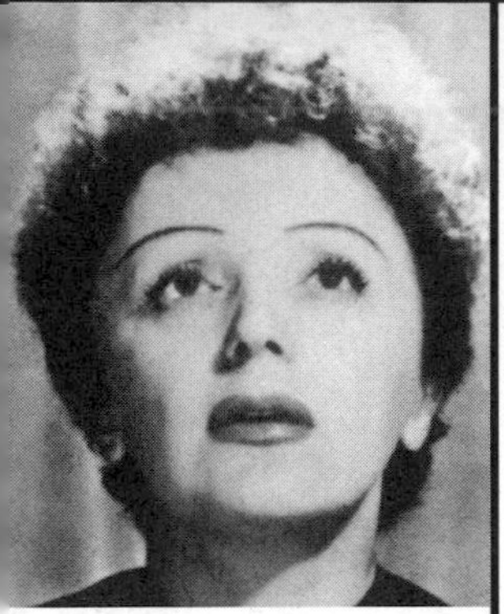

Lovers, Flings, or Just Friends?

Raymond Asso, songwriter
Pierre Brasseur, actor (costar in *Les Amants de demain,* '48)
Marcel Cerdan, boxer
Jean Cocteau, writer
Eddie Constantine, actor
Henri Contet, film publicist
Douglas Davis, American painter
Marlene Dietrich, singer-actress
Louis Dupont, errand boy
Claude Figus, secretary (who was sent to prison for frying eggs over the eternal flame at the Arc de Triomphe)
John Garfield, actor
Louis "Toto" Gérardin, professional cyclist
Felix Marten, singer
Paul Meurisse, singer
Yves Montand, singer-actor
Georges Moustaki, songwriter-guitarist
André Pousse, professional cyclist
André Schoeller, art-gallery director

Edith Piaf 1915–1963

✦ She Said

I thought that when a boy summoned a girl, the girl must never say no. I thought this was what women should do.

These men make many demands on a woman, but at the same time they protect her. —Telling why she preferred very masculine men

✦ They Said

Men had done her so much harm when she was young I think she was taking her revenge by seducing all possible men. —Eddie Constantine, American actor working in French films

Who is that plain little woman with a voice too big for her body? —Mistinguette, French chanteuse

✦ First Sexual Experience

Unknown.

✦ Husbands

Jacques Pills, singer
Théo Sarapo, hairdresser-singer

✦ Did You Know?

Piaf twice resided in a whorehouse. As a child of about six, she lived with her grandmother in a whorehouse in Bernay, Normandy, where the old lady was a cook. The whores loved having Piaf around because they thought having a child in the establishment brought them luck. Then, during the German occupation of Paris, Piaf paid to move into a whorehouse because it was heated. Most private residences and apartments were denied heat during the occupation, but whorehouses—to keep the German troops using them comfortable—were not.

Mary Pickford 1893–1979

✦ She Said

I only want to be one man's sweetheart, and I'm not going to let him go. —Even though she was billed as "America's sweetheart"

✦ They Said

You're too little and too fat, but I may give you a chance. —D. W. Griffith, director, assessing Mary for a role in one of his films

She was the most feminine female I've ever met in my life. —Anita Loos, author

Say anything you like about me, but don't say I "like" to work. That sounds too much like Mary Pickford, that prissy bitch. —Mabel Normand, fellow silent star, to reporters

✦ First Sexual Experience

Unknown, but possibly Owen Moore, whom she married at age nineteen.

✦ Husbands

Owen Moore, actor
Douglas Fairbanks Sr., actor
Charles "Buddy" Rogers, actor

✦ Did You Know?

While married to Owen Moore, Pickford went horseback riding while she was pregnant, deliberately causing herself to abort. She didn't want to disrupt her career at that time by having a child.

When they were married, Fairbanks specifically asked Pickford never to dance with another man.

Lovers, Flings, or Just Friends?

- Johnny Mack Brown, actor (costar in *Coquette,* '29)
- Leslie Howard, actor (costar in *Secrets,* '33)
- James Kirkwood, director
- Eddie Mannix, studio executive

Lovers, Flings, or Just Friends?

Paul Clemens, businessman

Gene Nelson, actor (costar in *Three Sailors and a Girl*, '53)

Jane Powell 1928–

✦She Said

I was very frightened of sex. I didn't know what sex was. I didn't understand the feelings.

I didn't quit movies. They quit me.

✦They Said

Nobody wants you. —James Fitzgerald, second husband, zinging her about both his and Hollywood's lack of interest in her

✦First Sexual Experience

Lost her virginity to her first husband, although when she was eight, several older girls used to pull her panties down and insert things like a Coke bottle and a candle into her. Powell says she didn't understand what they were doing, but she knew it was something awful and was afraid to tell anyone.

✦Husbands

Geary Anthony Steffen Jr., ice-skater (one of Sonja Henie's ex-partners)

Patrick W. Nerney, automobile magnate (who was a former Mr. Mona Freeman)

James (Jim) Fitzgerald, publicist-producer

David Parlour, writer-producer

Dick (Dickie) Moore, ex–child star

✦Did You Know?

Powell says her mother almost never educated her about femininity. For example, she had no idea that women shaved their underarms or legs until she was rehearsing a dance number for *Nancy Goes to Rio* ('50). When she raised her arms above her head, choreographer Nick Castle asked, "Don't you think you should shave?" Poor embarrassed Powell was about twenty at the time.

Stephanie Powers 1942–

✦ She Said

I've always been attracted to older men, even as a teenager.

I tried it all, even smoking heroin—though, thank God, I had a guardian angel and got out of it."

✦ They Said

She has a lovely bust. It's the right shape—it doesn't sag, it doesn't droop, it isn't all distorted. She's a very attainable type of beauty and yet someone to look up to. —Richard Christian, stylist

Most of my life I've had to take care of people, but with her I haven't had to do anything. How many women would accompany a man upriver in northern New Guinea, wind up with dengue fever, and not complain? Not many. —William Holden

✦ First Sexual Experience

Unknown for certain, but Powers has said that first hubby Lockwood was only the second sexual partner she'd ever had.

✦ Husbands

Gary Lockwood, actor
Patrick de la Chesnais, French biologist

✦ Did You Know?

When Powers learned to bullfight during her late teens in Mexico, the natives called her *La Pecosa* (the freckled one) because of her skin.

Lovers, Flings, or Just Friends?

Michael Brockman, race driver
Timothy Dalton, actor
Eddie Fisher, singer-actor
William Holden, actor
David Janssen, actor
Tom Mankiewicz, producer and son of screenwriter-director Joseph
Robert Wagner, actor

Lovers, Flings, or Just Friends?

- Peter de Donato
- George Gershwin, composer
- Howard Hughes, aviation-cinema mogul
- Jean Negulesco, director
- Erich Marie Remarque, novelist
- Rudy Vallee, singer-actor

Luise Rainer 1909–

✦ She Said

I became an actress only because I had quickly to find some vent for the emotion that inside of me went around and around, never stopping.

In my day, making films was like working in a factory. You were a piece of machinery with no rights.

All my dreams are dreams of fear.

✦ They Said

Why don't you come sit on my lap when we're discussing your contract the way the other girls do, and *Luise, we've made you and now we're going to kill you.* —Louis B. Mayer, head of MGM, who didn't appreciate what he perceived as her "leftish" views, which he thought were aggravated by her marriage to Clifford Odets

Luise Rainer has a look of perpetual surprise, as though she has been unexpectedly, but not unpleasantly, goosed. —Harold J. Kennedy, theatrical producer

Everything a temperamental European actress is supposed to be. —Robert Ryan, actor

✦ First Sexual Experience

Unknown.

✦ Husbands

Clifford Odets, playwright
Robert Knittel, publisher

✦ Did You Know?

Rainer loved and had an affair with an aviator who was killed during an expedition to Africa in the middle thirties; shortly thereafter, she made a patchwork dress from the covering on the sofa where they had made love for the last time.

Martha Raye 1916–1994

✦ She Said

I have the face of a vulture and the voice of a crow. If you threw a rock at me, you could kill two birds with one stone!

I don't think I could ever become marriage shy. Cowards give up the search for happiness because they're afraid of getting hurt.

✦ They Said

She was very pretty, and the studio decided to make a mugging clown out of her. She could have gone one way or the other. If they had handled her differently, she would have been a Rita Hayworth type. —Neel Bate, artist

Anybody who can make Martha Raye look that good can't be all bad. —William Goetz, president of Universal-International on hiring Raye's ex-husband Bud Westmore

✦ First Sexual Experience

Unknown.

✦ Husbands

Bud Westmore, makeup specialist
David Rose, conductor-arranger (who was also the first Mr. Judy Garland)
Neal Lang, hotelier
Nick Condos, dancer
Thomas Edward Begley, dancer
Robert O'Shea, her bodyguard
Mark Harris, hairdresser

✦ Did You Know?

Martha's married life, from her first husband to her last, was usually controversial. She lasted only three months with her first, and slept with a pistol under her pillow during much of that period. Her final one was much, much younger. She never published an autobiography while alive, but rumors of one having been written surfaced after her death. It's supposed to detail all the facts behind her affair with Joan Crawford—and undoubtedly some other ladies, given her lack of matrimonial success. Will it ever appear? Who knows.

Lovers, Flings, or Just Friends?

Joan Crawford, actress
Jackie Gleason, comedian-actor

Lovers, Flings, or Just Friends?

Warren Beatty, actor

Fidel Castro, dictator of Cuba

Timothy Dalton, actor (costar of *Mary, Queen of Scots,* '71)

George Hamilton, actor

Hakim Jamal, black nationalist (who was also involved with Jean Seberg)

Bernard Levin, drama critic

Franco Nero, Italian actor, (costar in *Camelot,* '67)

Vanessa Redgrave 1937–

✦ She Said

I don't believe marriage would make me a very nice person to live with. I had to make too many plans to get out of my first marriage to get into marriage again. —Comment made when pregnant with the child of Franco Nero

I have a tremendous use for passionate statement.

✦ They Said

Some Trotskyite. She travels by Rolls-Royce. —Robert Duvall, sneering at her radicalism while she enjoys the "fruits" of the labor of the oppressed masses

She can't act, but I think she should be a professional protester. She's so tall it would give her lots of opportunity to sit down. —Noel Coward

She is the kind of woman every man would be pleased to tell his wife he has had an affair with. —Sammy Davis Jr.

✦ First Sexual Experience

Unknown.

✦ Husbands

Tony Richardson, director

✦ Did You Know?

Why is Vanessa perceived as "rebellious"? One friend has speculated that it's because she apparently discovered in 1961—from her friends—that her father was bisexual, and that her mother had been having affairs with other men.

Donna Reed 1921–1986

✦ She Said

Most movie directors are a bunch of hackneyed craftsmen. They're scared to death of actors and even more scared of actresses. And they hate women, which is why they make the female characters in their pictures as unpleasant as possible.

Forty pictures I was in, and all I remember is, "What kind of bra will be you be wearing, honey?"

Everything they say about Hollywood is true. It's a walled-in city bounded on all sides by arrogance.

✦ They Said

On the surface, Donna was sweet and demure. Inside, she was a tough dame. She had to be. I never met a successful Hollywood actress who wasn't. —Mickey Rooney, who costarred with her in *The Courtship of Andy Hardy* ('42)

Sort of a cold fish. Personally, I was never able to warm up to her. —Montgomery Clift

Donna Reed looks like the girl with the novocained face. —Sonja Henie

✦ First Sexual Experience

Unknown.

✦ Husbands

William Tuttle, makeup artist
Tony Owen, agent-producer
Grover Asmus, colonel

✦ Did You Know?

One evening during World War II, Reed slept soundly in a bed with fashion designer Oleg Cassini and a fellow actress on the USO tour while the two had sex.

Lovers, Flings, or Just Friends?

If Reed ever engaged in extramarital or "between-marital" affairs, she certainly kept it discreet. Her name was never linked romantically to anyone except her spouses.

Lovers, Flings, or Just Friends?

Bob Fallon, producer
Glenn Ford, actor (costar in *It Started With a Kiss,* '59)
Bob Neal, businessman
Walter Trautman, businessman
Robert Wagner, actor

Debbie Reynolds 1932–

✦ She Said

I stopped making movies because I don't like taking my clothes off. Maybe it's realism, but in my opinion, it's utter filth.

It's painful to read about your private life in the papers, knowing that strangers are reading about it, too. —Expressing her feeling about press coverage of the breakup of her marriage to Eddie Fisher

I grew up thinking that sex and "making love" and "that thing" were all disgusting. —Remarking about hearing her parents arguing in bed about having sex

✦ They Said

She just smiles that impish smile, but you know those wheels are turning, scheming, pushing her forward to the next step. She's the last person we'll ever have to worry about. —Louis B. Mayer, head of her studio, MGM

✦ First Sexual Experience

Lost her virginity, shortly before their marriage, to singer Eddie Fisher.

✦ Husbands

Eddie Fisher, singer
Harry Karl, shoe manufacturer (who was also the third Mr. Marie McDonald)
Richard Hamlett, real-estate developer

✦ Did You Know?

When Reynolds was six, two neighborhood teenage boys conned her into getting into a car and taking a drive with them. One of them pulled out his penis and convinced her to "lick it." In all innocence, she did, and they returned her home. Months later she overheard that the same boys had used another little girl in a similar manner and seriously injured the child.

Leni Riefenstahl 1902–

✦ She Said

They say I was Hitler's mistress. I deny this.

Hitler fascinated me.

I filmed the truth as it was then. Nothing more.

✦ They Said

Alongside her contributions to the art of filmmaking, our efforts, if I may say so, appear very puny. —Peter Sellers, actor

She lent her name, her fame, her talent, to the Nazi murderers. —Julius Schatz, director of the American Jewish Congress

There is something fascinating about her. She has a cold sensuality that attracts me. She is also the most ambitious woman I have ever known. —Adolf Hitler

✦ First Sexual Experience

Lost her virginity at twenty-one to Otto Froitzheim, who was eighteen years older and the lover of actress Pola Negri at the time.

✦ Husbands

Peter Jacob, Wehrmacht major

✦ Did You Know?

Actress Pola Negri once beat Leni on the head with her parasol because Riefenstahl had become engaged to the tennis player with whom Negri was having an affair.

After World War II, Riefenstahl sued in court over stories that she had often danced nude in her apartment for Hitler's enjoyment.

Lovers, Flings, or Just Friends?

Anatole, Greek runner

Arnold Franck, director

Otto Froitzheim, German tennis player

Adolf Hitler, *der Führer*

Guzzi Lantschner, skier-actor (costar and directed by her in *Das blaue Licht* [*The Blue Light*], '32)

Glenn Morris, Olympic champion

Walter Prager, skier

Max Reinhardt, director-producer

Hans Schneeberger, cameraman

Harry Sokal, financier

Luis Trenker, German actor (costar in *Der heilige Berg* [*The Holy Mountain*], '30)

Ernst Udet, World War I flying ace

Josef von Sternberg, director

Lovers, Flings, or Just Friends?

- Daniel Day-Lewis, actor
- Dave Evans, rock musician
- Ethan Hawke, actor
- Dylan McDermott, actor (costar in *Steel Magnolias*, '89)
- Liam Neeson, actor (costar in *Satisfaction*, '88)
- Jason Patric, actor and grandson of comedian-actor Jackie Gleason
- Kiefer Sutherland, actor (costar in *Flatliners*, '90)

Julia Roberts 1967–

✦ She Said

I'm too tall to be a girl, I never had enough dresses to be a lady, I wouldn't call myself a woman. I'd say I'm somewhere between a chick and a broad.

I'm really against nudity in movies. When you act with your clothes on, it's a performance. When you act with your clothes off, it's a documentary. I don't do documentaries.

I did not have a lip implant. My lips are the way they were when I was born.

I want to thank my beautiful blue-eyed, green-eyed boy, who does everything for me. —Accepting an award and referring to Kiefer Sutherland, whom she dumped two days before they were to be married

✦ They Said

In real life, she doesn't hold anything back emotionally. —Joseph Ruben, director, who directed her in *Sleeping With the Enemy* ('91)

She got a big break [referring to Pretty Woman, *'90] and was exposed to more stress than she could handle.* —Anonymous family friend

Her time limit seems to be twelve to eighteen months. As soon as the romance gets serious, she can't handle it. She can't seem to handle the reality of commitment. —Liz Smith, columnist, on Roberts's love affairs

✦ First Sexual Experience

Supposedly lost her virginity to Keith Leeper, a high school friend, at age sixteen. Leeper said in a national tabloid, "We were always naked."

✦ Husbands

Lyle Lovett, musician

✦ Did You Know?

While engaged, Roberts and Kiefer Sutherland were both tattooed with identical Chinese symbols to show their undying love. Two years later Kiefer was gone and so was the tattoo.

Rachel Roberts 1927–1980

✦ She Said

I'm a clean middle-class slut.

All they need is a cock up their cunt or arse. —Replying, during an interview on British TV, to the question, "What do you think of women's lib?"

My idea of heaven is to be surrounded by pussycats, a glass of wine in my hand, someone playing a piano, and me singing.

✦ They Said

Rachel was, let's say, "neurotic," but then we have a lot of people like that in the acting profession. —Douglas Fairbanks Jr.

"Put pure and simple: Rachel was an absolute bitch and pure hell to live with." —Rex Harrison, actor-spouse

✦ First Sexual Experience

Unknown.

✦ Husbands

Alan Dobie, actor
Rex Harrison, actor (who was also the first Mr. Kay Kendall)

✦ Did You Know?

Drunk at a studio premiere party for a film starring husband Harrison, Roberts got annoyed at photographers who were clamoring over his costars Richard Burton and Elizabeth Taylor. She climbed up on a table, pulled her dress up, and shouted, "Here's my pussy! Take some pictures of it!" When hubby Rex chided her behavior, she cut him off quickly, saying, "Don't you talk to me. You can't get it up, you old fart!"

Roberts filled her personal journals with bizarre fantasies of personal degradation, such as being auctioned off to slave drivers, who fondled her breasts, making them grow larger and larger.

Lovers, Flings, or Just Friends?

Joss Ackland, actor

Peter Copley, actor

Albert Finney, actor (costar in *Saturday Night and Sunday Morning*, '60)

Richard Gere, actor

Gene Hackman, actor (costar in *Doctors' Wives*, '71)

Richard Harris, actor (costar in *This Sporting Life*, '63)

Val Mayer, actor

Darren Ramirez, Mexican businessman

and Paul, a black hustler

Ginger Rogers 1911–1995

✦ She Said

I was never at ease wearing too little. The ways things are on the screen today, with nothing left to the imagination, I don't think I'd be making movies.

✦ They Said

When Ginger Rogers danced with Fred Astaire, it was the only time in the movies when you looked at the man, not the woman. —Gene Kelly

She has a little love for a lot of people, but not a lot for anybody. —George Gershwin

We'd give her a new scene and she couldn't remember the lines. She couldn't sing, and surprisingly, she couldn't do the dances. And all through the horror of it all, she was smiling and grinning and unreal. She almost smiled me into bankruptcy. —Paul Gregory

✦ First Sexual Experience

Lost her virginity at age seventeen to Jack Culpepper, her first husband.

✦ Husbands

Jack Culpepper, singer
Lew Ayres, actor (costar in *Don't Bet on Love,* '33)
PFC Jack Briggs, U.S. Marine Corps
Jacques Bergerac, French lawyer-actor (costar in *Twist of Fate,* '54) (who later married actress Dorothy Malone)
G. William Marshall, actor (who was also the first Mr. Michéle Morgan)

✦ Did You Know?

While on a visit to France, Rogers engaged a well-known artist to paint her portrait. The completed picture left the ultraconservative Rogers in a rage; the artist had painted her with an exposed left breast. Although she hated the work, she bought it anyway, to keep anyone else from seeing it. She wasn't entirely successful, as a photo of it—taken by the artist, probably—soon turned up in a French magazine.

Lovers, Flings, or Just Friends?

Desi Arnaz, actor-singer
Fred Astaire, actor-dancer (costar in *The Barkleys of Broadway,* '49)
Greg Bautzer, attorney–Hollywood escort
Jean Gabin, French actor
George Gershwin, composer
Cary Grant, actor (costar in *Monkey Business,* '52)
Howard Hughes, aviation-cinema mogul
Mervyn LeRoy, director
Burgess Meredith, actor (costar in *Tom, Dick and Harry,* '41)
George Montgomery, actor
David Niven, actor (costar in *Bachelor Mother,* '39)
Dick Powell, actor-director (costar in *20 Million Sweethearts,* '34)
Robert Riskin, writer
Robert Ryan, actor (costar in *Tender Comrade,* '43)
George Stevens, director
Jimmy Stewart, actor (costar in *Vivacious Lady,* '38)
Rudy Vallee, singer-actor
Alfred Gwynne Vanderbilt, socialite

Diana Ross 1944–

Lovers, Flings, or Just Friends?

Richard Gere, actor

Berry Gordy, head of Motown Records

Brian Holland, songwriter

Julio Iglesias, singer

Ryan O'Neal, actor

Smokey Robinson, singer

Gene Simmons, rock singer and possessor of an extra-long tongue

✦ She Said

I know that my fans want to know who I'm sleeping with, but it isn't really any of their business.

I'd never dated a white man before so I couldn't believe this thing we had would last. Frankly, I expected there would be a problem marrying a white man. —On marrying her first husband; her second husband is also white

✦ They Said

Diana Ross doesn't want to show her body, doesn't want to do sex scenes on the screen, and doesn't want to be black. —Ryan O'Neal, remarking on why a costarring venture between the two fell through

"She's too damn skinny and ugly for me." —Elvis Presley, singer

She's a delicately boned, gentle, intelligent, trembling, electric wire of a girl. —Rona Jaffe, *Cosmopolitan*

These broads don't even understand how they make this music we fellows love so much! —George Harrison, amazed at the basic lack of technical musical knowledge displayed by Ross and her fellow Supremes when he attempted to talk music with them

✦ First Sexual Experience

Unknown.

✦ Husbands

Robert Silberstein, public relations
Arne Naess, Norwegian shipping magnate

✦ Did You Know?

When Ross heard the phrase *You have nothing to fear except fear itself,* she asked where it came from. On being told Franklin Roosevelt had said it, she asked who he was. After being told he'd been president of the United States, she said she'd never heard of him. Ross was about thirty-three when the incident occurred in 1977.

Lovers, Flings, or Just Friends?

Mikhail Baryshnikov, actor–ballet dancer (costar in *White Nights,* '85)

David Lynch, director (directed her in *Blue Velvet,* '86)

Isabella Rossellini 1952–

✦ She Said

When I see myself on film, I find it kind of disturbing. She [her mother, Ingrid Bergman] *is so much in me. It's a genetic thing.*

David Lynch came out of it a genius and I came out of it a fat girl. I'm sorry that the only comment I get about the part is the way I look. —Referring to what many critics said about her in *Blue Velvet* ('86)

✦ They Said

With those thick lips of hers, she looks like a Ubangi. —Marlene Dietrich, who didn't like Isabella's mommy either, calling her "a Swedish horse"

The first time I saw her was like ascending to heaven. —Francesco Scavullo, photographer

Her bottom droops a bit, and you can discern incipient cellulite on her thighs. —One reviewer, assessing her physical appearance in *Blue Velvet* ('86)

✦ First Sexual Experience

Unknown.

✦ Husbands

Martin Scorsese, director
Jonathan Wiedemann, model
Gary Oldman, actor (costar in *Immortal Beloved,* '95)

✦ Did You Know?

Isabella, daughter of Ingrid Bergman and Italian director Roberto Rossellini, was born after the adulterous couple married. Ingrid and Roberto were both known for their shenanigans while filming. She had numerous affairs and so did he. In fact, he dumped her for Sonali, a woman he met while making a movie in India. Isabella's younger half-sister, Raffaella, claimed that a costar raped her while they were making *The Witches' Black Sabbath,* a horror film. According to her, actor Daniel Ezralov, "dragged me into the pond. And in the water, he went all the way." She sued over the incident, but it all came to naught. Isabella hasn't had such indignities performed on her body in the course of her career.

Gail Russell 1921–1961

✦She Said

I was a sad character. I was sad because of myself. I didn't have any self-confidence.

Get me a drink! —Her plaintive cry whenever she had a "tough" scene to film

✦They Said

A lovely girl who didn't belong in the movie industry. —Milton Lewis, studio executive

Gail Russell died of alcoholism because she was deathly frightened of acting, but she had the makings of a great star. —Joseph Losey, director, who directed her in *The Lawless* ('50)

✦First Sexual Experience

Unknown.

✦Husbands

Guy Madison, actor

✦Did You Know?

Russell, while drinking and driving, lost control of her car and careened it through the front window of Jan's Coffee Shop in Los Angeles. The night janitor of the restaurant ended up pinned under the car's front wheels. She was fortunate that he survived: she got a thirty-day jail sentence, a fine under $500, and a three-year probation. Had he died, she might have spent the rest of her life in prison—sober.

Lovers, Flings, or Just Friends?

- John Farrow, director and father of actress Mia (he directed Russell in *Calcutta,* '47)
- William Holden, actor
- Howard Hughes, aviation-cinema mogul
- Dorothy Shay, actress
- John Wayne, actor (costar in *Angel and the Badman,* '47)

Lovers, Flings, or Just Friends?

Dan Darby, businessman

Robert Mitchum, actor (costar in *Macao,* '51)

John Payne, actor

Bobby Preston, football player

Jane Russell 1921–

✦ She Said

The Lord is a living doll.

Christians can have big tits, too. —Remarking about her devout faith

✦ They Said

That woman terrified me. I knew if I didn't run from her, she'd end up owning the studio. —Howard Hughes, who was both obsessed with and frightened of Russell

There are two good reasons why men will go to see her. —Howard Hughes on why she'd succeed as a film star

✦ First Sexual Experience

Unknown for certain, but probably lost it to sweetheart Robert Waterfield.

✦ Husbands

Robert Waterfield, UCLA and LA Rams football star
Roger Barrett, actor
John Peoples, businessman

✦ Did You Know?

Much has been made of the "special" brassiere that Howard Hughes designed for Russell to wear in his film *The Outlaw.* Yes, he designed it; no, she didn't wear it. Russell tried it on, out of Hughes' sight, then decided to take matters into her own hands. She put on one of her regular bras, smoothed out the seams, hid the straps and proceeded to the set. Hughes never knew the difference.

Russell got pregnant in 1942, before she and Waterfield married, and had an abortion, which he paid for. She's said that she supposes that was because he "thought it was his. I wasn't that sure." Her comment suggests some hanky-panky on her part while they were engaged.

Jean Seberg 1938–1979

✦ She Said

I used to be a little princess. They'd come and get me in black limousines. They don't come anymore. —Comment made one year before her suicide

I have it in my contract that I'll never play a scene in the nude, even if my husband demands it.

✦ They Said

It was important to her to feel, well, excuse the term, "fuckable." In her depression, she'd turn to men for reassurance. Jean could have sex in an elevator, between the third and fourth floors. —Yves Boisset, French director, on the last years of her life

She was either unhappy because she was making a movie or unhappy because she wasn't making one. It was always a drama with her. —François Moreuil

She was the most unlikely person to be a film star. —Patrick O'Neal, costar in *A Fine Madness* ('66)

✦ First Sexual Experience

Lost her virginity when she was seventeen or eighteen to a high school date at a local drive-in movie.

✦ Husbands

François Moreuil, French lawyer-director (directed her in *La Récréation* [*Playtime*], '61)
Romain Gary, French author-diplomat-director (directed her in *Birds in Peru,* '68)
Dennis Berry, director (directed her in *Le Grand Délire,* '75)

✦ Did You Know?

Although they were living in France at the time, Seberg and her third husband married in Las Vegas. He persuaded her to go there by saying, "Ever since I was twelve years old, I've had this mad desire to marry a movie star in Las Vegas." Seberg paid for the entire trip—including the ring—with her credit cards because neither one had any American currency. Their ceremony, at one of Las Vegas' ubiquitous wedding "chapels," was almost drowned out by the minister's children, who were yelling and screaming while watching *Frankenstein* ('31) on television in the next room.

Lovers, Flings, or Just Friends?

- Warren Beatty, actor (costar in *Lilith,* '64)
- Sammy Davis Jr., singer-dancer-actor
- Paul Desmond, musician
- Clint Eastwood, actor (costar in *Paint Your Wagon,* '69)
- Philippe Garrel, French director
- Kader Hamadi, Algerian restaurant owner
- Ahmed Hasni, Algerian actor–soccer player
- Raymond "Masai" Hewitt, Black Panther leader
- Dennis Hopper, actor
- Hakim Abdullah Jamal, black nationalist
- Jean-Claude Killy, French skier
- John Maddox, actor (who later disappeared in the Bermuda Triangle)
- Mohammed, Moroccan medical student
- Carlos Navarra, Mexican "revolutionary"
- Ricardo Nero, Spanish director
- Franco Testi, Italian actor
- *plus* lots of musicians, students, outright bums, hippies, and an assortment of blacks and Algerians

Lovers, Flings, or Just Friends?

- Monta Bell, director
- Johnny Mack Brown, actor (costar in *A Lady of Chance,* '28)
- Lew Cody, actor (costar in *A Slave of Fashion,* '25)
- Harry d'Abbadie d'Arrast, director
- Victor Fleming, director
- Ralph Forbes, actor (costar in *The Actress,* '28)
- John (Jack) Marion Fox, businessman (who was also the first Mr. Joan Bennett)
- Clark Gable, actor
- John Gilbert, actor (costar in *The Wolf Man,* '24)
- William "Billy" Haines, homosexual actor-decorator (who said, "She really got a *rise* out of me")
- Howard Hughes, aviation-cinema mogul
- Alexander Kirkland, actor (costar in *Strange Interlude,* '32)
- Burgess Meredith, actor (costar in *Idiot's Delight,* '39)
- Robert Montgomery, actor (costar in *The Divorcee,* '30)
- Conrad Nagel, actor (costar in *Excuse Me,* '25)
- David Niven, actor
- John Pickford, actor and Mary's younger brother (costar in *Waking Up the Town,* '25)
- James Quirk, magazine editor
- George Raft, actor
- Mickey Rooney, actor (who was only sixteen, some twenty years younger than her)
- Jimmy Stewart, actor

Norma Shearer 1900–1983

✦ She Said

It is impossible to get anything major accomplished without stepping on some toes; enemies are inevitable when one is a doer.

An actress must never lose her ego—without it she has no talent.

✦ They Said

She was hotter than a half-fucked fox in a forest fire. —Mickey Rooney, who had his fiery affair with Shearer extinguished by MGM studio head Louis B. Mayer

Damn, the dame doesn't wear any underwear in her scenes. Is she doing that in the interests of realism or what? —Clark Gable, while filming *A Free Soul* ('31) with her

And you can tell Miss Shearer I didn't get where I am on my ass! —Joan Crawford, Shearer's rival at MGM, who felt that Shearer often got the better parts because she was married to Irving Thalberg, second-in-command at the studio

A face unclouded by thought. —Lillian Hellman, who thought Shearer somewhat vapid and ignorant

✦ First Sexual Experience

Possibly lost her virginity to Victor Fleming, with whom she had an affair when she was about nineteen or twenty.

✦ Husbands

Irving Thalberg, producer–MGM whiz kid
Martin Jacques (Marti) Arrougé, ski instructor

✦ Did You Know?

Shearer avidly pursued many of her costars, but occasionally one of them eluded her. Actor Tyrone Power—known for being had by one and all, male and female—was one who wasn't taken by Shearer's sexual charms. She wanted him badly, as did so many others, and had him cast as the love interest in her film *Marie Antoinette* ('38) hoping to weave her magic during shooting. Power didn't rise to Norma's bait. He made the film with her but didn't grace her dressing room couch. He felt that she was too aggressive in her pursuit of him.

Cybill Shepherd 1949–

✦ She Said

They're all so frightened of being sexy or voluptuous in case they offend the feminist movement. There isn't a decent breast or bottom among them. —Delivering her opinion of the current "sex goddesses"

When you finally catch on to the fact that most men aren't interested in what you have to say—and are only looking at you because you're pretty—it's a shock.

Men! I thank God every morning I don't have a man in my house.

I'm not saying I don't like men as lovers. It's just that I never met a man I wanted forever.

✦ They Said

She's tall, but not top-heavy. —Mr. Blackwell, Hollywood designer

✦ First Sexual Experience

Unknown.

✦ Husbands

David Ford, car dealer
Bruce Oppenheim, chiropractor

✦ Did You Know?

Elvis and his buddies weren't too impressed with Cybill and what they perceived as her "attitude." They felt that she had too much of the Tennessee beauty queen about her (she was Miss Memphis once). Maybe she gave them the same beauty tip she's been known to give others: put cucumbers on your face. That would have probably turned the King and his minions against her, since they expected more from their girls.

Lovers, Flings, or Just Friends?

Peter Bogdanovich, director (directed her in *Daisy Miller,* '74)
Jeff Bridges, actor
Larry McMurtry, writer
Elvis Presley, singer-actor
Burt Reynolds, actor (costar of *At Long Last Love,* '75)
Frank Smith, attorney
Michael Wolff, bandleader

Ann Sheridan 1915–1967

✦ She Said

Oomph is the noise a fat man makes when he bends over to tie his shoelace in a telephone booth. Honey, don't ask me about Oomph! —Commenting on the word *Oomph* used in her appellation the Oomph Girl

I've seen parties in New York that make Hollywood look like the A&P.

✦ They Said

They made her a star in spite of the bad pictures. —Howard Hawks, director

Annie was just a plain, simple girl. She liked her sex simple and her liquor plain. And, she liked both of them a lot. —Jack Benny, comedian-actor

✦ First Sexual Experience

Unknown.

✦ Husbands

Edward Norris, actor
George Brent, actor (costar in *Honeymoon for Three,* '41)
Scott McKay, actor

✦ Did You Know?

Columnist Walter Winchell started Sheridan with her "Oomph" nickname when he wrote that she has "plenty of Umph!" Her studio, Warner Bros., saw a good promotional gimmick and slightly changed the appellation. Despite all the hype about being The Oomph Girl, and posing for plenty of pictures to tout it, Sheridan had a body like a skinny, young man. She was so devoid of "figure" that the studio made a chest harness, with rubber size-38 breasts, for her to wear. Whenever she got annoyed with wearing it, she would take it off and fling it at someone nearby saying, "Here, hold my tits for me, willya?"

Lovers, Flings, or Just Friends?

Donald "Red" Barry, actor
Jack Benny, actor (costar in *George Washington Slept Here,* '42)
Milton Berle, comedian-actor
Oscar Brooks, head of Warner Bros. office in Mexico
Pat DeCiccio, playboy
Errol Flynn, actor
John Garfield, actor (costar in *They Made Me a Criminal,* '39)
Jackie Gleason, comedian-actor
Steve Hannagan, publicist
Allan Jones, singer (and father of singer Jack Jones)
Anatole Litvak, director
Gene Markey, writer-producer
Dean Martin, singer-actor
Jean Negulesco, director
David Niven, actor
George Raft, actor (costar in *They Drive by Night,* '40)
Cesar Romero, actor
Dr. Charles M. Taylor, physician
Perc Westmore, makeup specialist

Sylvia Sidney 1910–

✦ She Said

I never knew much about it and I never lived there much. —Referring to Hollywood

I was inclined to be impatient with some of the trimmings surrounding stardom. I liked my independence and wanted to live my own life and not be at the mercy of fan magazines, columnists, and studio press agents.

Women who try to hide their age just call attention to it. Why lie about it?

✦ They Said

One should never legalize a hot romance. —Bennett Cerf, whose marriage to Sidney ended quickly; they separated after three months and divorced after eight

✦ First Sexual Experience

Unknown.

✦ Husbands

Bennett Cerf, publisher and longtime panelist on TV's *What's My Line*
Luther Adler, actor
Carleton Alsop, producer

✦ Did You Know?

In the middle 1930s, all over Asia, condoms bearing a photograph of Sidney, then a reigning Paramount queen, were extremely popular. The package bore a retouched photograph (slanted eyes and larger breasts) of the actress as she appeared in *Merrily We Roll Along*. Director Walter Wanger once told Sidney, "You go into any drugstore in the Far East and ask for a S.S., and you get a condom with your picture on it." Sidney has bemoaned the fact that she received no royalties for the items.

One year Sidney and her husband, Carleton Alsop, asked their close friend Judy Garland what she wanted for her birthday present. "Ronald Colman," announced the singer, who said that she'd never met the actor. At Garland's party Sidney and Alsop carried Colman in—wrapped in cellophane. He agreed to the stunt because he was just as anxious to meet Garland as she was him.

Lovers, Flings, or Just Friends?

B. P. Schulberg, producer and head of production at Paramount

Lovers, Flings, or Just Friends?

Marcel Duhamel, translator-publisher

Daniel Gélin, French actor

Claude Jaeger, wealthy heir of a Swiss family

Simone Signoret 1921–1985

✦ She Said

Between 1940 and 1942 I had all the prerequisites—extenuating circumstances included—for becoming a prostitute. I was good-looking, poor, and half-Jewish. —Remarking on what could have happened to her during the German occupation of Paris

We're engaged, but we're not getting married. —On her long association with the French Communist Party and espousal of its causes, but her reluctance to actually become a Party member

Three chins, or is it four? —Joking about her aged looks near the time of her death

When you tell a story, you usurp other people's memory.

✦ They Said

This is one aging actress who will never ask an audience to mourn her ruined beauty. —David Denby

✦ First Sexual Experience

Possibly lost her virginity to Claude Jaeger, a rich, young man who picked her up at the theater one evening in 1941, when she was twenty, and ended up introducing her to Paris's bohemian intellectuals.

✦ Husbands

Yves Allégret, French director (directed her in *Manèges,* '49)
Yves Montand, singer-actor

✦ Did You Know?

Signoret was to have played the role that won Lila Kedrova an Oscar in *Zorba the Greek* ('64), but a perception about her sexuality got in the way. Her husband Yves Montand had, only a few years before, ended an affair with Marilyn Monroe. After two days of filming, Signoret confessed in tears to the director that she simply couldn't play the role. Her reason: She had a young husband and she couldn't have him seeing her look old and haggard.

Jean Simmons 1929–

✦ She Said

It takes a great deal to make me angry, and I don't say a lot of things I should be saying—I keep it all bottled up.

✦ They Said

One wonders why she didn't become the great star she could have been. —Joseph L. Mankiewicz, director

✦ First Sexual Experience

Unknown.

✦ Husbands

Stewart Granger, actor
Richard Brooks, writer-director

✦ Did You Know?

Howard Hughes was so obsessed with "having" Simmons that his pursuit of her really began to grate on the nerves of her then-husband Stewart Granger. So much, in fact, that he admitted in his autobiography that he "planned how to murder the bastard" if he'd been forced to do so.

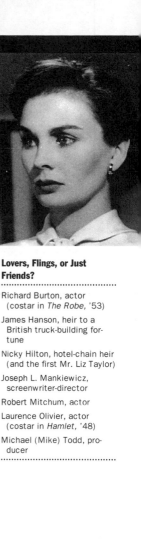

Lovers, Flings, or Just Friends?

- Richard Burton, actor (costar in *The Robe,* '53)
- James Hanson, heir to a British truck-building fortune
- Nicky Hilton, hotel-chain heir (and the first Mr. Liz Taylor)
- Joseph L. Mankiewicz, screenwriter-director
- Robert Mitchum, actor
- Laurence Olivier, actor (costar in *Hamlet,* '48)
- Michael (Mike) Todd, producer

Lovers, Flings, or Just Friends?

- Marc Allegret, director (directed her in *Lac aux Dames,* '34)
- Fred De Cordova, producer-director
- Francis Louis Dreyfus, French publisher
- Jean Gabin, actor (costar in *The Human Beast,* '38)
- George Gershwin, composer
- Raymond Hakim, businessman
- David Niven, actor
- Aristotle Onassis, Greek shipping mogul
- Tyrone Power, actor
- Gilbert Roland, actor
- James (Jimmy) Stewart, actor (costar in *Seventh Heaven,* '37)
- Darryl F. Zanuck, studio head

Simone Simon 1910–

✦ She Said

They didn't know how to pronounce it. See-moan See-moan, indeed! If you're going to pronounce it phonetically, it should be See-mun See-mown.

If you do not do as they say, they treat you like dirt. They try to break your spirit. —Reflecting on Hollywood's studio system of the 1940s

✦ They Said

A stocky little girl with small eyes and a square chin and freckles. —Dorothy Kilgallen, columnist, who was famed for having no chin

She had achieved some success in her homeland and had been brought to Hollywood, where she became considerably more famous for her boudoir activities than her appearances on the screen. —Fred De Cordova, producer-director

Simone looked like a peach blossom, and everybody knew what a tramp she was. —Mary Loos, MGM story editor

✦ First Sexual Experience

Unknown.

✦ Husbands

Simon has never been married.

✦ Did You Know?

When Simon sued a former private secretary for fraud, it was revealed in court that the actress had a penchant for giving her current amour a gold doorkey to her house in Hollywood.

It was once rumored that Simon was the illegitimate daughter of Marion Davies and William Randolph Hearst. That seems unlikely, given that Davies would have been about thirteen years old at the time of Simon's birth.

Barbara Stanwyck 1907–1990

✦ She Said

Come on, Bob. You know you'd like to fuck me. Admit it. —Teasing costar Robert Cummings, right before a shot on the set of *The Bride Wore Boots* ('46)

If there's anything I hate, it's a goddamned phony, and Hollywood's filled with 'em, pretending to be what they're not and some of them never were.

What I had, it worked, didn't it? —Comment to Rex Reed on her appeal to audiences

✦ They Said

I certainly agree with all those who find more sex appeal in Barbara Stanwyck and her ankle bracelet in Double Indemnity *['44] than in all these naked bodies rolling around on the screen today.* —Bette Davis

There was a trait I admired in Barbara. She turned off anyone who crossed her just once. —Robert Taylor, the love of her life, from whom she kept taking alimony long, long after their divorce

✦ First Sexual Experience

Unknown.

✦ Husbands

Frank Fay, actor
Robert Taylor, actor (costar in *This Is My Affair,* '37)

✦ Did You Know?

Although madly in love with husband Robert Taylor, Stanwyck bossed him around so roughly, even hounding him about being a homosexual, which was partially true, that he finally became impotent—but only with her. Taylor even told another actor, "Ah, that woman, she always wants to run the fuck."

Lovers, Flings, or Just Friends?

- Jean-Pierre Aumont, French actor
- Frank Capra, director (directed her in *Ladies of Leisure,* '30)
- Rex Cherryman, actor
- Gary Cooper, actor (costar in *Meet John Doe,* '41)
- Joan Crawford, actress
- Marlene Dietrich, singer-actress
- Helen Ferguson, personal publicist
- Glenn Ford, actor
- Moss Hart, theatrical director (who later became Mr. Kitty Carlisle)
- William Holden, actor (costar in *Golden Boy,* '39)
- Al Jolson, entertainer
- Edward Kennedy, actor (*not* the carousing senator)
- Robert Wagner, actor (costar in *Titanic,* '53)
- *and* some much, much younger men with beautiful faces and athletic bodies as she got older and indulged in brief flings

Lovers, Flings, or Just Friends?

Bill MacDonald, film producer

Christopher Peters, musician and son of hairdresser-producer Jon Peters, onetime playmate of Barbra Streisand

Bob Wagner, production assistant

Dwight Yoakum, country singer

Sharon Stone 1958–

✦ She Said

I'm not a bombshell. I don't have the breasts for it.

If you have a vagina and a point of view, you're suspect.

My films have enabled me to torture more formidable men.

✦ They Said

I really wanted to sue the pants off her, but she doesn't wear any. —Ron Winston, whose firm lent Stone a diamond necklace and then disputed its return with her

So goddamned mean—when she's angry, she knows how to say things that hurt. —Paul Verhoeven, director, who directed her in *Basic Instinct* ('92)

✦ First Sexual Experience

Unknown.

✦ Husbands

None yet.

✦ Did You Know?

Such are the tangled "swapping relationships" of Hollywood: After the producer of Stone's film *Sliver* ('93), Bill MacDonald, left his wife of five months for the actress, his wife, Baka, became involved with Joe Eszterhas, the screenwriter of both *Sliver* and Stone's previous film, *Basic Instinct* ('92). MacDonald and Stone became engaged, but didn't marry. They soon parted company and the actress became involved with someone else.

Susan Strasberg 1938–

✦ She Said

People expect too much of me as Lee Strasberg's daughter. It wasn't fair to him or me. —Pondering on the drawback of being the daughter of the famed founder of the Actors Studio, where Method acting was born

✦ They Said

If I could be anyone, *I would want to be* you. —Marilyn Monroe, actress and close friend, plus student of Strasberg's father, Lee

Hookers pose for Playboy!" —Christopher Jones, angered to find out that Strasberg had posed for the magazine before they became involved

✦ First Sexual Experience

Probably lost her virginity to Richard Adler, whom she has dubbed her "first love affair." She's also said that friends told her that she would never forget when she lost her virginity. "They lied, I have forgotten," she's written.

✦ Husbands

Christopher Jones, actor

✦ Did You Know?

Strasberg's affair with Richard Burton developed while she was appearing with him and Helen Hayes on Broadway. Her dressing room, where much of their affair was conducted, was next to Miss Hayes's. Since the rooms had thin walls, Hayes heard almost every sexual encounter of the duo, but was much too ladylike to mention it—except in a book she later wrote.

Lovers, Flings, or Just Friends?

Richard Adler, Broadway lyricist

Warren Beatty, actor

Richard Burton, actor

James Dean, actor

Jerry, businessman

Cary Grant, actor

Arthur Loew Jr., cinema-chain heir

Marcello Mastroianni, actor

William, musician-farmer

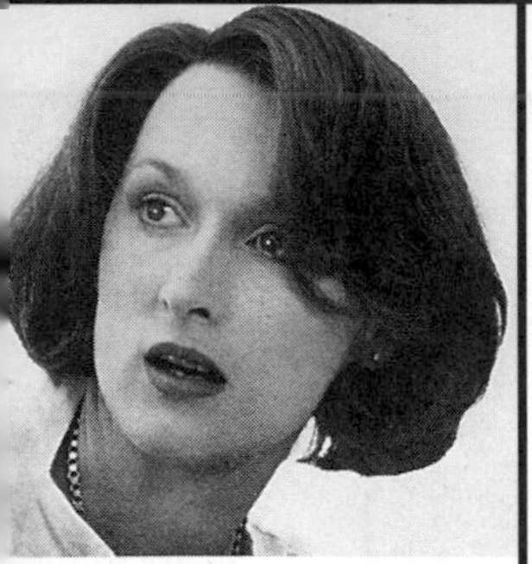

Lovers, Flings, or Just Friends?

John Cazale, actor (costar in *The Deer Hunter,* '78)

Meryl Streep 1949–

✦ She Said

Everybody can make out, but not everybody can feel the real thing.

Why do famous people only want to meet other famous people? —Comment after turning down Canadian prime minister Pierre Trudeau's request to meet her

✦ They Said

Her nose. That red, thin, sharp snout—it reminds you of an anteater. And those eyes. If they were any smaller, or closer, you'd think she was a hen, and *Oh, God, she looks like a chicken.* —Truman Capote

She's one of the most sensible, well-adjusted people I've ever met. —Robert Benton, writer-director, who directed her in *Kramer vs. Kramer* ('79)

Who would I like to fuck the most? Meryl Streep . . . even if I wasn't good, she would fake it the best. —Keanu Reeves, actor

✦ First Sexual Experience

Unknown. Possibly lost her virginity to high school sweetheart Bruce Thompson.

✦ Husbands

Donald Gummer, sculptor

✦ Did You Know?

Streep and costar Dustin Hoffman's arguments while filming *Kramer vs. Kramer* ('79) seem to be the stuff of which legends are made. The intense Hoffman was afraid that Streep was going to upstage him. Streep, dissatisfied with her lines as written, rewrote much of her part. At one point, Hoffman threw a wine glass against a wall during one of their arguments. Soon after he said, "I hated her guts," but he's since modified that to say, "Yes, I hated her guts, but I respected her." Perhaps all the anger between the two stars resulted from an encounter at their first meeting, an audition for the roles in the film. According to Streep, "He [Hoffman] came up to me and said, 'I'm Dustin—burp—Hoffman,' and he put his hand on my breast. 'What an obnoxious pig,' I thought."

Barbra Streisand 1942–

✦She Said

I am a bit coarse, a bit low, a bit vulgar, and a bit ignorant. I am also part princess, sophisticated, elegant, and controlled. I appeal to everyone. —Stated to *Life*, 1966

It's my *look. I don't copy* fake *Jews.* —Replying to being complimented on an Elizabeth Taylor Cleopatra-ish eye makeup she wore

In my family sex was taboo. You don't screw anybody until you get married, you don't hold hands, you don't kiss, because you'll get a disease. It was all so awful I had to develop a fantasy.

✦They Said

My nose is not one of my favorite things and her *nose is not one of my favorite things either.* —Cher, replying to columnist Earl Wilson's question about how she felt about remarks that she had a Barbra Streisand nose

She's got the balls of a Russian infantryman. —Martin Ritt, director

She's a monster. But she's a fascinating monster. I think her biggest problem is that she wants to be a woman and she wants to be beautiful and she is neither. —Omar Sharif, who knew her intimately, confiding in Rex Reed

✦First Sexual Experience

Lost her virginity to Barry Dennen, a young actor, when she was eighteen.

✦Husbands

Elliott Gould, actor

✦Did You Know?

Have filmgoers ever seen Barbra's tits? Surprisingly, some claim they have—at least a very few of them. When *The Owl and the Pussycat* ('70) was first released it contained a scene of her topless, which, according to them, played briefly in a very few theatres. She quickly got word of her exposure and had the film yanked for re-cutting, possible since she held the right of "final cut" approval. Photos from the flick later appeared in *High Society,* but she forced most of the issue to be "recalled" by threatening a lawsuit. Barbra's made it clear that she'll sue again if either the photos or the film scene ever reappear.

Lovers, Flings, or Just Friends?

- Andre Agassi, tennis player
- Richard Baskin, ice cream heir
- Warren Beatty, actor
- Richard Burton, actor
- Gary Busey, actor
- Sydney Chaplin, actor and son of Charlie
- Richard Cohen, businessman
- Barry Dennen, actor
- Anthony Michael DeToth, son of actress Veronica Lake
- Clint Eastwood, actor
- Sam Elliott, actor
- Charles Evans, businessman
- Richard Gere, actor
- Richard Greyson, businessman
- James Newton Howard, composer
- Don Johnson, actor
- Kris Kristofferson, singer-actor
- Liam Neeson, actor
- Anthony Newley, British actor-singer
- Ryan O'Neal, actor (costar in *What's Up, Doc?* '72)
- Jon Peters, hairdresser-producer
- Elvis Presley, singer-actor
- Robert Redford, actor
- Omar Sharif, actor
- Tommy Smothers, comedian
- Pierre Trudeau, prime minister of Canada
- Peter Weller, actor
- Neil Wolfe, pianist

Lovers, Flings, or Just Friends?

- John Boles, actor (costar in *Only Yesterday,* '33)
- Humphrey Bogart, actor
- Johnny Downs, actor
- Philip Dunne, screenwriter
- Glenn Ford, actor, (costar in *So Ends Our Night,* '40)
- Alan Hale, actor (costar in *Little Man, What Now?* '34)
- Jed Harris, producer
- Charles Leatherbee, producer
- Randolph Scott, actor (costar in *So Red the Rose,* '35)
- Charles Starrett, actor
- James (Jimmy) Stewart, actor (costar in *The Shop Around the Corner,* '39)
- *and* lots of young, handsome actors in both New York and London, where she'd attend their plays, then follow them home and "offer" herself to them, *plus* lots of pickups on the street from her car

Margaret Sullavan 1909–1960

✦She Said

There was so much prissy propriety and sexual prudery and emotional repression among the people who inhabited my early life that I suppose I went to the other extreme.

The wonder of men is that no two of them are alike, especially when making love.

If there's one type I can't stand, it's a tame man.

In Hollywood the only thing that matters is the hullabaloo of fame.

✦They Said

I couldn't believe my wife and that son of a bitch were in bed together. But I knew they were. . . . Never in my life have I felt so betrayed, so rejected, so alone. —Henry Fonda, remembering how he felt about Sullavan's affair with Jed Harris

She's a rude, contrary, spiteful bitch sometimes. —Louella Parsons, gossip columnist

This wonderful voice of hers—strange, fey, mysterious—like a voice singing in the snow. —Louise Brooks, silent-screen star, calling Sullavan her favorite actress

✦First Sexual Experience

Unknown, but probably lost her virginity in high school or college.

✦Husbands

Henry Fonda, actor (she said Fonda, a premature ejaculator who never satisfied her, was a "fast starter and a lousy finisher")
William Wyler, director (directed her in *The Good Fairy,* '35)
Leland Hayward, agent
Kenneth Wagg, British businessman

✦Did You Know?

Hayward's marriage to Sullavan wasn't all roses; he said, "She castrates a guy—she makes him feel like two cents—and two inches," and "Hell, Maggie knew all about highway pickups before they became fashionable—or rather infamous."

Gloria Swanson 1899–1983

✦ She Said

I'm sure you don't have a baby every *time you kiss someone. Only when you kiss a certain person a certain way at a certain time of the month.* —Displaying her ignorance of sex, at fifteen, when telling a close girlfriend about kissing her first boy

✦ They Said

Damned if she didn't keep on getting married. I got her into an awful habit. —Wallace Beery, actor

Gloria, how you wear me out! Where do you get all this energy? —Greta Garbo, actress

✦ First Sexual Experience

Lost her virginity to Wallace Beery on their wedding night. Swanson expected that her license to marry would be her "ticket to heaven." She said, instead, she was "brutalized in pitch blackness by a man who whispered filth in my ear while he ripped me almost in two." After Beery went to sleep, Swanson spent the remainder of her wedding night huddled on the bathroom floor, swathed in towels to soak her bleeding and ease the pain.

✦ Husbands

Wallace Beery, actor

Herbert Somborn, president of the Equity Picture Corp.

James Henri Le Bailly de la Falaise, Marquis de la Coudraye, French nobleman (and also the third Mr. Constance Bennett)

Michael Farmer, Irish playboy

William Davey, socialite

William Dufty, author

✦ Did You Know?

Swanson became pregnant within the first few weeks of her marriage to Beery. When she began suffering severe stomach cramps, he kindly provided some medicine to ease them. After taking it, she awoke to find herself hospitalized, having suffered a miscarriage. Later she learned Beery's "medicine" was a poison, which had caused her miscarriage.

Lovers, Flings, or Just Friends?

- James Conway, director (directed her in *You Can't Believe Everything,* '18)
- Craney Gartz, wealthy playboy
- Joseph P. Kennedy, businessman and JFK's father
- Rod La Rocque, actor (costar in *A Society Scandal,* '24)
- Gene Markey, screenwriter
- Herbert Marshall, actor
- Joel McCrea, actor
- Marshall "Mickey" Neilan, director
- Aristotle Onassis, shipping magnate
- Albert Parker, director (directed her in *Secret Code,* '18)
- Gustave Schirmer, music-publishing heir
- Raoul Walsh, director-actor (costar in *Sadie Thompson,* '28)

Lovers, Flings, or Just Friends?

- Richard Barthelmess, actor
- Irving Berlin, composer
- Johnny Considine, writer-producer
- George Gershwin, composer
- Martin Herman, socialite
- Howard Hughes, aviation-cinema mogul
- Myron Selznick, agent and brother of producer David O.
- Irving Thalberg, MGM wunderkind

Constance Talmadge 1898–1973

✦ She Said

Are you kidding? Why, I couldn't even act when I was a movie star. —Answering why she never appeared on the stage after she quit making films

Leave 'em while you're looking good and thank God for the trust funds Mama had set up. —Commenting on why she retired from films

Every time I open my mouth, something silly comes out.

✦ They Said

Heaven protect my kid from any guy who can't make up his mind. —Peg Talmadge, her mother, referring to Howard Hughes's on-again, off-again pursuit of her daughter

Norma was the beauty, but a snob, while Constance, her sister, was a darling with a great sense of humor. —Lina Basquette, silent-film star

The deft princess of lingerie and love. —F. Scott Fitzgerald, writer

✦ First Sexual Experience

Unknown.

✦ Husbands

John Pialogiou, tobacco importer
Capt. Allaster MacIntosh, British socialite
Townsend Nechter, scion of Chicago department-store tycoon
Walter Giblin, stock broker

✦ Did You Know?

Constance liked to party in Los Angeles–area gay bars with MGM actor, later turned interior decorator, William (Billy) Haines and his lover, Frank. On one of their forays into a gay bar, in one of LA's seedier neighborhoods, a fight broke out, forcing the trio to run out the back door and up the alley with the cops in close pursuit. Why was the actress hanging out in gay bars with Haines? She was acting as "bait" for her friend, helping him pick up his favorites—sailors.

Norma Talmadge 1893–1957

✦ She Said

Get away, dear. I don't need you anymore. Snapping at a fan pestering for her autograph, after she had retired

✦ They Said

Norma's got a pretty face, but faces don't mean nothing to a box office. I wouldn't touch Norma Talmadge with a ten-foot pole. —Samuel Goldwyn, producer

Don't even let him hold your hand. —Peg Talmadge, her mother, cautioning her against letting the men she was dating go "too far" with her

✦ First Sexual Experience

Unknown.

✦ Husbands

Joseph Schenck, studio executive
George Jessel, actor-comedian
Dr. Carvel James, physician

✦ Did You Know?

Norma was the first person to have her feet in the cement at Graumann's Chinese Theater in Hollywood. She accidentally stepped into some freshly poured cement there in 1927, which gave owner Sid Graumann the idea for having stars regularly commemorated in the same manner.

While her sister Constance became a lifelong devotee to alcohol, Norma became a drug addict. Anita Loos has said she probably married her last husband so he could supply her with drugs on a regular basis.

Lovers, Flings, or Just Friends?

- Maurice Costello, silent star
- William S. Hart, silent cowboy star
- Edwin J. Mayer, studio exec at MGM and relative of Louis B.
- James Morrison, silent star
- Eugene O'Brien, actor (costar in *Poppy*, '17)
- Gilbert Roland, actor

Sharon Tate 1943–1969

✦ She Said

My whole life has been decided by fate. . . . I've never planned anything that ever happened to me.

✦ They Said

She had hopes and dreams and was a thoughtful member of society until a crazy man decided for no reason that she shouldn't be around anymore. —Doris Gwen Tate, her mother

She was incredibly beautiful. I'd never seen anyone like her, before or since. —Hal Gefsky, agent

✦ First Sexual Experience

Unknown.

✦ Husbands

Roman Polanski, director (directed her in *The Fearless Vampire Killers*, '67)

✦ Did You Know?

After Tate and several of her friends were slaughtered by the Manson family of killers, lots of Hollywood folks claimed that they were supposed to have been present that night partying with Tate's crew. Among the people who "claimed" that they were supposed to have been visiting were Cary Grant, Steve McQueen, Jacqueline Susann, and "Mama" Cass Elliott, among others. For a while, it seemed almost the trendy thing in Hollywood to have spread the rumor that one was "supposed" to have been at the house that evening but had fortunately canceled the plans.

Lovers, Flings, or Just Friends?

- Richard Beymer, actor
- Philippe Forquet, French actor
- Steve McQueen, actor
- Jay Sebring, hair stylist

Dorothy Dentice Taylor, Countess di Frasso 1888–1954

✦ She Said

I say it depends on who's between the sheets. —Answering when asked to describe paradise

✦ They Said

She was the first outsider to become a social member and to give parties in the magnificent homes she rented that surpassed in lavishness and originality any that Hollywood had known before. —Adela Rogers St. Johns, author

She mixed titles with prizefighters, and motion-picture stars with babes of the evening. Her food and liquor were of top quality, even though some of her guests weren't. —Hedda Hopper, Hollywood gossip columnist

It was hard to tell whether the countess threw one party that lasted all summer or a series of weekend parties that lasted all week. —Anonymous society wit

I always wanted to go to Europe on the Countess di Frasso. —Robert Benchley, author, mocking the countess's reputation for being both well-traveled and well-ridden by those in her circle of acquaintances

✦ First Sexual Experience

Unknown.

✦ Husbands

Claude Graham White, British aviator (she divorced him when she caught him in bed with her best friend)

Count Carlo di Frasso, impoverished Italian nobleman

✦ Did You Know?

Tallulah Bankhead, who'd sampled the charms of Gary Cooper, endlessly needled Cooper and Taylor during their affair. She was quite fond of referring to the much older woman as "Gary's mother." Once when she was asked about Cooper, Tallulah referred to him as having been sexually "worn down to a di Frasso."

Lovers, Flings, or Just Friends?

- Gary Cooper, actor
- Ben Hecht, author
- Fred McAvoy, playboy and close friend of Errol Flynn
- Benjamin "Bugsy" Siegel, mobster

Lovers, Flings, or Just Friends?

- Carl Bernstein, investigative reporter–author
- Richard Brooks, director (directed her in *The Last Time I Saw Paris,* '55)
- Zev Buffman, producer
- Montgomery Clift, actor (costar in *A Place in the Sun,* '51)
- Vic Damone, singer
- Peter Darmanin, advertising executive
- Stanley Donen, director (directed her in *Love Is Better Than Ever,* '51)
- Malcolm Forbes, millionaire magazine publisher
- Anthony Geary, actor
- George Hamilton, actor
- Ingemar Johansson, Swedish boxer
- Peter Lawford, actor
- Max Lerner, columnist
- Arthur Loew Jr., cinema-chain heir
- Victor Luna, Mexican attorney
- Joseph Mankiewicz, director (directed her in *Suddenly, Last Summer,* '59)
- Kevin McClory, production assistant
- Sir Gordon Reece, public relations consultant
- Frank Sinatra, singer-actor
- Dennis Stein, entrepreneur
- Henry Wynberg, car salesman (Liz said, "He fucks me beautifully")
- Ardeshir Zahedi, Iranian ambassador to the United States

Elizabeth Taylor 1932–

✦ She Said

I guess the world thinks of me as such a scarlet woman; I'm almost purple.

I don't pretend to be an ordinary housewife.

All I can say is I dig sex.

✦ They Said

Always a bride, never a bridesmaid. —Oscar Levant, pianist-composer

Every man should have the opportunity of sleeping with Elizabeth Taylor—and at the rate she's going, every man will. —Howard Hughes, whom Liz said she didn't get to, despite his offering her mother $1 million to marry her

Lemme tell ya, any minute that this little dame spends out of bed is totally wasted. —Mike Todd, the third Mr. Elizabeth Taylor

✦ First Sexual Experience

Lost her virginity to first husband Nicky Hilton.

✦ Husbands

Nicky Hilton, hotel-chain heir
Michael Wilding, actor
Michael Todd, showman-producer (and the third Mr. Joan Blondell)
Eddie Fisher, singer (and the first Mr. Debbie Reynolds)
Richard Burton, actor (costar in *The Sandpiper,* '65)
Richard Burton, actor (costar in *Boom!* '68)
John Warner, U.S. senator
Larry Fortensky, trucker

✦ Did You Know?

Besides her unusually colored eyes—a strange shade of violet—Taylor's best known assets are her breasts. Richard Burton said that they were "apocalyptic, they would topple empires down before they withered."

At one of her weddings when the justice of the peace asked for the names of her former husbands, Liz snapped, "What is this, a memory test?"

Shirley Temple 1928–

✦ She Said

The studio didn't control my life, but I went to work every *day. I thought every child worked because I was born into it.*

I stopped believing in Santa Claus at an early age. Mother took me to see Santa Claus in a Hollywood department store and he asked for my autograph.

✦ They Said

Sparkle, Shirley, sparkle! —The final words her mother, Gertrude, said to her each time right before she stepped in front of the camera to film a scene

Shirley Temple had charisma as a child, but it cleared up as an adult. —Totie Fields, comedienne

I suppose for her range of roles, her career span, and her age, the most talented actress in movies was probably Shirley Temple. —Eve Arden

A swaggering, tough little slut. —Louise Brooks, silent-screen star

✦ First Sexual Experience

Unknown for certain, but probably with John Agar, in view of both the high moral standards with which the Temples raised Shirley and the young age at which she married him.

✦ Husbands

John Agar, actor (costar in *Fort Apache,* '48, who later appeared as Mr. Clean in some commercials on television)

Charles Black, businessman

✦ Did You Know?

Shirley once shot First Lady Eleanor Roosevelt in the butt with her slingshot.

While Temple was being interviewed by MGM producer Arthur Freed in his office, he exposed his penis to her.

Dickie Moore, himself an ex–child star, gave Shirley her first on-screen kiss in *Miss Annie Rooney* ('42). How did he feel about the experience? Moore was afraid he was going to get an erection in front of the camera while kissing her.

Lovers, Flings, or Just Friends?

Since her name has never been sexually connected with that of any man other than those of her two husbands, Shirley Temple is hereby awarded the *Croix de Crossed Ankles with a Banner of Tightly-held Knees,* the supreme accolade of Hollywood purity.

Gene Tierney 1920–1991

✦ She Said

I had heard in New York that the casting couch was a way of life in Hollywood; it posed no threat to me.

Everyone should see Hollywood once, I think, through the eyes of a teenage girl who has just passed a screen test.

Men are wonderful. I adore them. They always give you the benefit of the doubt.

✦ They Said

Although she was beautiful in her films, they couldn't quite capture all of her. Fortunately I did, even if it was late in my life. —Spencer Tracy, actor

You're like a red, red rose. —Robert Morley, actor

✦ First Sexual Experience

Unknown for certain, but she once stated that she was raised to believe that a woman "only went to bed with the man you married."

✦ Husbands

Oleg Cassini, fashion designer

W. Howard Lee, oil businessman (and also the fifth Mr. Hedy Lamarr)

✦ Did You Know?

The plot for the 1980 film *The Mirror Crack'd,* from an Agatha Christie novel, is loosely based on an awful episode in Tierney's life. The actress's first child was born deaf and hopelessly retarded, due to Tierney's exposure to German measles during her pregnancy. A year later Tierney discovered she had caught the disease from a young female Marine she'd met while working at the Hollywood Canteen entertaining World War II GIs. The starstruck woman had risen from her sickbed—with measles—and come to the Canteen specifically to meet film stars. Tierney learned of this horrid coincidence from the woman herself, who approached the actress at a tennis match, saying, "Everyone told me I shouldn't go, but I just had to go. And you were my favorite."

Lovers, Flings, or Just Friends?

- Kirk Douglas, actor (he's said she'd leave the window open so he could sneak in)
- Howard Hughes, aviation-cinema mogul
- John F. Kennedy, lieutenant U.S. Navy and later president
- Prince Aly Khan, playboy
- Joseph L. Mankiewicz, screenwriter-director
- Victor Mature, actor
- Tyrone Power, actor (costar in *The Razor's Edge,* '46)
- Mickey Rooney, actor
- George Sanders, actor
- Robert Sterling, actor
- Spencer Tracy, actor (costar in *Plymouth Adventure,* '52)
- Rudy Vallee, singer-actor
- Henry J. Van Dyke II, socialite
- Darryl F. Zanuck, studio head

Ann Todd 1909–1993

✦ She Said

I don't think people realize what an enormous difference it makes if two personalities in a play or film have rapport and understanding and like each other. . . . In fact, I think that when filming, it is rather important for the director to be in love with one for the duration of the film. It makes one feel good, more confident.

✦ They Said

I presume you have a bust—show it. —David O. Selznick, producer, sending Todd a memo while she was working on his film *The Paradine Case* ('48)

What a pity, because when you die, you won't have Shakespeare mentioned in your obituary and that's a shame for a serious actress. —Anonymous friend, decrying Todd's reluctance to play Shakespearean roles on the stage

✦ First Sexual Experience

Unknown.

✦ Husbands

Victor Malcolm, grandson of actress Lillie Langtry
Nigel Tangye, author–BBC air correspondent
David Lean, director (directed her in *One Woman's Story,* '49)

✦ Did You Know?

Todd's English sexuality didn't always show best on-screen, but one friend certainly used it to his own advantage. David Niven, a close friend of Todd's, carried a picture of her as a young girl with braids with him in his wallet. Whenever one of his many amorous conquests grew maritally minded, Niven would extract Todd's photo saying, "Oh, sorry, I forgot to tell you—this is my fiancée." Todd didn't mind her friend's deception. After all, they'd been extremely "close" at one time and she was flattered that he chose to use her picture.

Lovers, Flings, or Just Friends?

- Sir Alexander Korda, producer
- James Mason, actor (costar in *The Seventh Veil,* '45)
- David Niven, actor
- Gregory Peck, actor (costar in *The Paradine Case,* '48)

Thelma Todd 1905–1935

✦ She Said

It's really wild out here. The men are something, wolves. A girl's gotta watch her britches. Remark about Hollywood to a friend back home

I've fallen in love with a tough bunch of characters. I'm not sure what I'm going to do about it. I'm really frightened for the first time in my life.

✦ They Said

She was a favorite with everybody on the lot from the lowest employee to the highest. —Hal Roach, for whom Todd made most of her films, speaking about her after her mysterious murder

✦ First Sexual Experience

Unknown.

✦ Husbands

Pasquale (Pat) DiCiccio (DiCicco), playboy–studio executive with mob connections

✦ Did You Know?

Todd had been overly dependent on alcohol and diet pills for several years before she met "Lucky" Luciano. He got her hooked on pills of pure speed. He also apparently was the one who ordered her murdered several years later, probably over a dispute about his introducing illegal gambling into her popular oceanside restaurant.

Lovers, Flings, or Just Friends?

- Charley Chase, actor (costar in *The Real McCoy*, '30)
- Charles "Lucky" Luciano, mobster
- Harvey Priester, insurance counselor
- Roland West, director–business partner
- Perc Westmore, makeup specialist

Sophie Tucker 1884–1966

✦ She Said

The trouble with TV is that it gives too much for nothing. You can't give the people too much for nothing. It makes them disrespectful to the artist, makes everybody a critic.

I didn't learn my English at Harvard.

✦ They Said

She was always so good. A little bit fat, but very attractive. —Maurice Chevalier, singer-actor

Sophie was wearing a dress with feather highlights. In her hand she had a big feather fan, and on her head a band with a feather in it. She looked like she'd fucked a chicken on the way to the stage. —Julian Eltinge, drag performer, making fun of the way Tucker always dressed for her performances

✦ First Sexual Experience

Probably lost her virginity to first husband Tuck, since she married him at age sixteen.

✦ Husbands

Louis Tuck, horse driver for a brewery
Frank Westphal, vaudeville piano player
Al Lacky, gambler–clothing manufacturer

✦ Did You Know?

In 1934 when a newspaper asked the Last of the Red-Hot Mamas for her opinion on who were the eight handsomest men in the world, Tucker included Mussolini, George Bernard Shaw, and Albert Einstein.

Lovers, Flings, or Just Friends?

John Ellsmere, an undertaker and her second cousin

Benjamin "Bugsy" Siegel, mobster–casino owner

Lovers, Flings, or Just Friends?

Desi Arnaz, singer-actor
Leonard Bernstein, conductor-composer
Turhan Bey, Turkish actor
Richard Burton, actor
Sean Connery, actor
Billy Daniels, singer
Tommy Dorsey, bandleader
Kirk Douglas, actor (costar of *The Bad and the Beautiful,* '52)
Robert Evans, producer
Clark Gable, actor
John Garfield, actor (costar in *The Postman Always Rings Twice,* '45)
John Hodiak, actor (costar in *Marriage Is a Private Affair,* '44)
Howard Hughes, aviator-cinema mogul
John F. Kennedy, U.S. president
Fernando Lamas, actor (costar in *The Merry Widow,* '52)
Peter Lawford, actor
Dean Martin, singer
Tony Martin, singer (costar in *Betrayed,* '54)
Victor Mature, actor
George Montgomery, actor
Tyrone Power, actor
Mickey Rooney, actor
Frank Sinatra, singer-actor
Robert Stack, actor
Robert Taylor, actor (costar in *Johnny Eager,* '41)
Mel Torme, singer
Robert Wagner, actor

Lana Turner 1920–1995

✦ She Said

I expected to have one husband and seven babies.

Sex was never important to me.

Don't worry, honey. Who's gonna believe it? —Retort to an MGM executive who was chastising her about picking up a gas station attendant

If they're clever and give me the right story, I take the bait.

✦ They Said

She was not even an actress . . . only a trollop. —Gloria Swanson

She was the type of woman a guy would risk five years in jail for rape. —Robert Taylor, on Lana's special allure

She was amoral. If she saw a stagehand with tight pants and a muscular build, she'd invite him into her dressing room. —MGM executive

✦ First Sexual Experience

Lost her virginity to Greg Bautzer, Hollywood attorney and perennial escort of beautiful women. Lana said that "I didn't enjoy it at all."

✦ Husbands

Artie Shaw, musician (who was also the second Mr. Ava Gardner and the fourth Mr. Evelyn Keyes)
Josef Stephen Crane, restaurateur
Bob Topping, millionaire
Lex Barker, actor (who was also the first Mr. Arlene Dahl)
Fred May, rancher sportsman
Robert Eaton, businessman
Ronald Dante, nightclub hypnotist

✦ Did You Know?

Real name: Julia Jean Mildred Turner

Did Frank Sinatra catch Lana and Ava Gardner in bed together? Or were they merely sitting around, skimpily dressed, and talking as they claimed? Whichever, it certainly created a stir when it happened.

Lana got pregnant by Mickey Rooney, but didn't tell him about it until after she had an abortion—or so Mickey says. Lana denied his accusation, but Mickey says he didn't "dream it up."

Liv Ullmann 1939–

✦ She Said

Something has to be kept for the person I'm with. My breasts aren't actresses.

The older one gets in this profession, the more people there are with whom one would never work again.

Why do Americans think I should be depressing just because I was in a lot of Bergman films?

✦ They Said

To the women, she is the woman they think they are or would be; to the men, she is all the women they have known or would like to know. —A. Alvarez

I never miss a Liv Ullmann musical. —Bette Midler, mocking *Lost Horizon* ('73), which she also called *Lost Her Reason,* Ullman's big-budget film that turned into the ultraflop of the midseventies.

✦ First Sexual Experience

Unknown.

✦ Husbands

Dr. Hans Jacob (Gappe) Stang, psychiatrist
Donald Richard Saunders, real-estate broker

✦ Did You Know?

Liv is that rarity of rarities: a Norwegian born in Tokyo, Japan.

Lovers, Flings, or Just Friends?

Edward Albert Jr., actor (costar in *40 Carats,* '73)

"Axel," Czech interviewer

Warren Beatty, actor

Ingmar Bergman, Swedish director (directed her in *Autumn Sonata,* '78)

Robert Evans, producer

Henry Kissinger, U.S. secretary of state

Gloria Vanderbilt 1924–

✦ She Said

Women in the past have thought of money as part of masculine power, a male perogative.

✦ They Said

Gloria Vanderbilt. You know, that lady that took her good family name and put it all over everybody's ass in America. —Gilda Radner, comedienne

She was a nasty little girl. She lied about her mother during her custody trial and she was terrible to her until shortly before she died. —Truman Capote, author and gossipmonger

✦ First Sexual Experience

Unknown.

✦ Husbands

Pasquale (Pat) DiCiccio, playboy–studio exec with mob connections (and the ex–Mr. Thelma Todd)
Leopold Stokowski, conductor
Sidney Lumet, director
Wyatt Cooper, actor-writer-editor

✦ Did You Know?

Truman Capote claimed that whenever Gloria had sex with husband Wyatt Cooper, she'd scream, "Daddy! Daddy! Daddy!" How did Tru get the intimate details? He said Cooper himself spilled the beans.

Lovers, Flings, or Just Friends?

- Bruce Cabot, actor
- Roald Dahl, author (and Mr. Patricia Neal)
- Peter Donat, actor
- Errol Flynn, actor
- Van Heflin, actor
- Howard Hughes, aviation-cinema mogul
- George Montgomery, actor
- Nelson Rockefeller, governor of New York
- Frank Sinatra, singer-actor
- Bobby Short, singer-entertainer
- Franchot Tone, actor
- Orson Welles, director-actor

Mamie Van Doren 1933–

✦ She Said

Hollywood is full of these watching, waiting helpers, who look for pretty girls in distress. Mostly what they want is to help you take your clothes off.

I don't wear panties anymore—this startles the Hollywood wolves so much they don't know what to pull at, so they leave me alone.

The casting couch did exist, and I did occasionally find myself on it. Many of us who made a career out of the movies did. Many, many more than want to admit it.

✦ They Said

Do your best, Mamie, not to fall in love with anybody in government. Because after they fuck you—they fuck *you.* —Marilyn Monroe, passing along some advice at their last meeting

Mamie was a hot number. She knew how to make a man feel like a man. —Nicky Hilton, hotel chain heir

✦ First Sexual Experience

Lost her virginity to Jack Newman, her first husband.

✦ Husbands

Jack Newman, men's sportswear manufacturer
Ray Anthony, bandleader-musician
Lee Meyers, baseball player
Ross McClintock, executive, Fluor Corporation
Thomas Dixon, local (Florida) actor

✦ Did You Know?

Mamie tried, but she couldn't always make a man feel like the perfect man. Her encounter with Rock Hudson must have been somewhat frustrating for her. He prematurely ejaculated as she tried to guide him inside her.

Lovers, Flings, or Just Friends?

- Warren Beatty, actor
- Bo Belinsky, baseball player
- Johnny Carson, entertainer–television personality
- Antonio Cifariello, Italian actor (costar in *The Beautiful Legs of Sabrina,* '72)
- Steve Cochran, actor
- Tony Curtis, actor
- Major "Dan," U.S. Air Force
- Jack Dempsey, fighter
- Robert (Bob) Evans, producer
- Charlie Fischetti, mobster
- Nicky Hilton, hotel chain heir (and first Mr. Liz Taylor)
- Rock Hudson, actor
- Maj. William Kilgore, U.S. Army
- Steve McQueen, actor
- Joe Namath, NY Jets football player
- Elvis Presley, singer-actor
- Dwayne Ratliff, dance teacher
- Burt Reynolds, actor
- Johnny Rivers, singer

Lovers, Flings, or Just Friends?

- Bruce Cabot, actor
- Charlie Chaplin, actor
- Russ Columbo, singer-actor (costar in *Wolf Song,* '29)
- Gary Cooper, actor (costar in *Wolf Song,* '29)
- Arturo de Cordova, actor (costar in *La Zandunga,* '38)
- Jack Dempsey, heavyweight boxing champion
- Douglas Fairbanks Jr. actor
- Douglas Fairbanks Sr. (costar in *The Gaucho,* '27)
- Victor Fleming, director (directed her in *Wolf Song,* 29)
- Errol Flynn, actor
- Clark Gable, actor
- John Gilbert, actor
- Jack Johnson, black heavyweight boxing champion
- Bert Lahr, comedian-actor
- Rod La Rocque, actor (costar in *Stand and Deliver,* '28)
- Tom Mix, actor in silent westerns
- Clayton Moore, actor (who was better known as the Lone Ranger)
- Erich Maria Remarque, author (and later the last Mr. Paulette Goddard)
- Edward G. Robinson, actor (costar in *East Is West,* '30)
- Gilbert Roland, actor
- Randolph Scott, actor and one of Cary Grant's homosexual lovers
- Red Skelton, comedian-actor
- Lawrence Tibbet, actor
- Henry Wilcoxon, actor
- Alvin "Big Boy" Williams, cowboy actor

Lupe Velez 1908–1944

✦ She Said

The first time you buy a house you think how pretty it is and sign the check. The second time you look to see if the basement has termites. It's the same with men.

I am a woman who tells of her love for a man to the whole world.

You did not want us. Now we will never be disgraced. —From her suicide note. Velez, a Catholic, was pregnant by Harald Ramond, who refused to marry her, and she refused to have an abortion

✦ They Said

In the legends of Hollywood there has never been another like her, so stormy, so merry, so warmhearted. —Adela Rogers St. Johns, author

She was the Zsa Zsa Gabor of the thirties. —Douglas Fairbanks Jr.

She was the twistiest, most sensuous-looking thing I've ever seen. —Leon Ames, character actor

✦ First Sexual Experience

Unknown.

✦ Husbands

Johnny Weissmuller, actor-swimmer

✦ Did You Know?

To put it mildly, Velez came from unsavory beginnings. Her mother was a streetwalker, and she herself began her career in some of the raunchiest burlesque houses of Mexico City when she was in her early teens. When the men who attended those performances sought her favors, Mama Velez willingly peddled Lupe to the highest bidder.

Velez was known as a notorious de facto nymphomaniac in the Hollywood of the 1930s, with the comment being made that she "never met a man she didn't like." When she was filming, Velez loved to lounge around the set minus her underpants. She'd sit with her legs spread apart, thoroughly enjoying the parade of males who stopped to admire the view.

Lupe could rotate her left breast in one direction, then rotate it easily in the opposite direction.

Raquel Welch 1940–

✦ She Said

There aren't any hard women, only soft men.

I can't say the mini [skirt] *made me an actress, but it sure helped make me a star.*

If everybody knows what my toes, knees, thighs, and belly button look like, it is as okay by me as I hope it is by them.

I've never found a man who can satisfy me. No one partner has ever fulfilled my needs.

What I do on the screen is not to be equated with what I do in my private life. Privately, I am understated and dislike any hoopla.

✦ They Said

She has a good heart, which she hides under beautiful boobs. —Burt Reynolds, actor

She's silicone from the knees up. —George Masters, makeup man and hairdresser to the stars

The art of Raquel Welch is her flair for looking nude with clothes on. —Donald Zee, British author

I have never met anyone so badly behaved. —James Mason

✦ First Sexual Experience

Probably lost her virginity to first husband James Welch, since he was a high school classmate and she married him at age eighteen.

✦ Husbands

James W. Welch, high school classmate
Pat Curtis, press agent and personal manager
Andre Weinfeld

✦ Did You Know?

Welch recently blabbed that she likes for her lovers to limit their visits to the weekend so she could send them away on Sunday.

Lovers, Flings, or Just Friends?

Richard Burton, actor (costar in *Bluebeard,* '72)

Ron Talsky, costume designer

Lovers, Flings, or Just Friends?

- John (Drew) Barrymore Jr., actor
- Raymond Burr, actor
- Edd Byrnes, actor
- Fabian Forte, actor-singer
- Richard Gere, actor
- Dennis Hopper, actor
- John Ireland, actor
- Gary Lockwood, actor (and the first Mr. Stefanie Powers)
- Tom Mankiewicz, youngest son of screenwriter-director Joseph L. Mankiewicz
- Sal Mineo, actor
- Ryan O'Neal, actor
- Al Pacino, actor (costar of *Author! Author!* '82)
- Elvis Presley, singer-actor (costar in *Wild in the Country*, '61)
- Frank Sinatra, singer-actor
- David Steinberg, comedian
- Patrick Wayne, actor

Tuesday Weld 1943–

✦ She Said

As a teenager I was a wreck. I drank so much I can't remember anything.

I'm too easily influenced by negative things. If I'm with a bunch of dopers, I'll follow them right into the opium den.

It seems the brighter you are, the deeper the hole you get into.

✦ They Said

Tuesday's done some wild, wild things and screwed up many, many guys. She's highly sexual. —Ryan O'Neal

What turns me on? Tuesday Weld in a dirty slip, drinking a can of beer. I could use up a case of Trojans on that one. She gets me really hot." —Alice Cooper, rock musician

No actress was ever so good in so many bad films. —Roddy McDowall, costar of *Lord Love a Duck* ('66)

✦ First Sexual Experience

Lost her virginity at age twelve to a guy who, as she's said, "turned out to be a homosexual."

✦ Husbands

Claude Harz, writer
Dudley Moore, actor
Pinchas Zukerman, violinist

✦ Did You Know?

Weld is truly a survivor: she had her first nervous breakdown at age nine, began drinking heavily at ten, made her first suicide attempt at twelve, and debuted on-screen at thirteen.

Mae West 1892–1980

✦ She Said

I'm not a little girl from a little town makin' good in a big town. I'm a big girl from a big town makin' good in a little town. —Assessing Hollywood after having already been a star on the New York stage

I ached for it, the spotlight, which was like the strongest man's arms around me.

I didn't have to take my clothes off. Men imagined what was under them.

Sex with love is the greatest thing in life. But sex without love—that's not so bad either.

✦ They Said

I've seen Mae West without a stitch and she's all woman. No hermaphrodite could have bosoms . . . well, like two large melons. —Edith Head, famed Hollywood costume designer, debunking theories that West was really a man or something else

When I look at that dame's tits, I know what lusty *means.* —Adolph Zukor, head of Paramount Studios

Sex for her is an animated cartoon. —John Mason Brown

She was just plain and simply a sweet old lady who told me marvelous stories about her life. —Rock Hudson, describing the rehearsal sessions he held with West prior to their performing a song on the Oscar show

✦ First Sexual Experience

Lost her virginity at age thirteen to her twenty-one-year-old music teacher on the stairs in her parents' home. Mae kept her fur coat on throughout the encounter.

✦ Husbands

Frank Wallace, a vaudevillian she married at about age seventeen

✦ Did You Know?

Mae West and Marlene Dietrich developed a friendship—of sorts, since West was never really close to any woman—when they shared adjoining dressing rooms at Paramount during the 1930s. Mae said she had to curtail their relationship because Dietrich kept wanting to wash her hair. According to Mae, she was afraid the hair Dietrich meant "wasn't all on my head."

Lovers, Flings, or Just Friends?

- Max Baer, boxer
- Steve Cochran, actor
- Gary Cooper, actor
- Jack Dempsey, boxer
- Richard DuBois, Mr. America 1954
- Duke Ellington, bandleader
- Joe Gold, bodybuilder (who later founded Gold's Gym)
- Cary Grant, actor (costar of *She Done Him Wrong,* '33)
- Oscar Hammerstein II, composer
- Mickey Hargitay, Mr. Universe
- Harry Houdini, magician
- Jack Johnson, boxer
- Jack LaRue, actor
- Joe Louis, boxer
- Owney Madden, gangster
- Mike Mazurki, wrestler-actor
- Victor McLaglen, actor (costar in *Klondike Annie,* '36)
- David Niven, actor
- Paul Novak, bodybuilder
- Anthony Quinn, actor (he says they didn't, and Mae said they did)
- George Raft, actor
- Steve Rossi, singer
- Joseph Schenck, MGM producer
- Benjamin "Bugsy" Siegel, mobster
- Sri Deva Ram Sukul, Indian holy man
- James Timony, attorney-manager
- *plus* lots of boxers, wrestlers, and other men with well-built physiques and endowments

Carol White 1942–1991

✦ She Said

My intention was to leave every man I met with a broken heart, but any suffering I gave out was to return ten times over.

Pimps, pushers, and ex-husbands brought me crashing down.

The only escape [from Hollywood] *was the unlimited supply of drink and drugs that combined to make the plastic seem like glitter.*

✦ They Said

The poor man's Julie Christie. —Rona Barrett, gossip columnist

Carol has ears pretty and soft as camellia petals. —Rex Reed, journalist

✦ First Sexual Experience

White lost her virginity when she was raped at age sixteen by seventeen-year-old Alain Rentz, a Frenchman.

✦ Husbands

Michael (Mike) King, singer (who also had a fling with model Christine Keeler, of the Profumo Affair scandal)

Stuart Lerner, psychiatrist

Michael Arnold, office designer

✦ Did You Know?

At one point White's friends got so concerned that she only seemed to date or get involved with married men that they tried fixing her up with a single one. They chose actor James Caan, who was unattached at the time; he liked White well enough to pursue her, banging on her door, begging to be permitted to enjoy some of her favors, but she declined to share any with him.

Lovers, Flings, or Just Friends?

- John Barry, composer
- Warren Beatty, actor
- Paul Burke, actor (costar in *Daddy's Gone A-Hunting,* '69)
- Tony (Little Tony) Ciacci, Italian rock star
- John Davis, amateur golfer
- Adam Faith, singer-actor (costar in *Never Let Go,* '60)
- David Hemmings, actor
- Ian Hendry, actor
- Brian Jones, musician
- Peter Jones, journalist
- Eden Kane, musician
- John Lennon, musician-composer
- Irv Levin, producer
- Si Litvinoff, producer
- Ian McShane, actor
- Keith Moon, musician
- Richard O'Sullivan, actor
- Cliff Potts, actor (costar in *The Groundstar Conspiracy,* '72)
- P. J. Proby, rock singer
- Oliver Reed, actor (costar in *I'll Never Forget What's 'is Name,* '68)
- Peter Sellers, actor (costar in *Never Let Go,* '60)
- Frank Sinatra, actor
- Chris Stamp, brother of actor Terence
- Terence Stamp, actor (costar in *Poor Cow,* '67)
- Freddie Starr, actor (costar in *The Squeeze,* '76)
- Richard Todd, actor (costar in *Never Let Go,* '60)
- Chaim Topol, actor

Esther Williams 1923–

✦She Said

All they ever did for me at MGM was change my leading men and the water in my swimming pool.

I can't act. I can't sing. I can't dance. My pictures are put together out of scraps they find in the producer's wastebasket.

✦They Said

Wet she's a star, dry she ain't. —Joe Pasternak, Hollywood producer

Producers were forever chasing her all around because she was considered one of the sexiest actresses on the lot. —Ann Miller, dancer-actress

Another rumor is that I made Esther give up her career when we got married. That is a lie! She was already washed up when we got married. —Fernando Lamas, actor and former spouse

✦First Sexual Experience

Unknown.

✦Husbands

Leonard Kovner, premed student
Ben Gage, personal manager
Fernando Lamas, actor and costar in *Dangerous When Wet* ('53) (and also the second Mr. Arlene Dahl)

✦Did You Know?

Esther's first screen kiss was from none other than short-stuff Mickey Rooney in *Andy Hardy's Double Life* ('42).

Williams evidently had a good sense of humor about her stardom. One day, after she and two male friends had stopped at an isolated roadside bar for a drink, she encountered a fan as the trio was leaving. "Esther! Esther Williams! Nobody will believe me!" her fan cried out. She graciously gave him an autograph, then lowered the top of her dress and exposed her breasts. When her friends later asked why she'd done it, the aquatic actress replied, "The guy said nobody would believe him. I just wanted to help the guy out. I made sure that nobody would."

Lovers, Flings, or Just Friends?

Jeff Chandler, actor (costar in *Raw Wind in Eden*, '57)

Lovers, Flings, or Just Friends?

Stedman Graham, public relations

Lloyd Kramer, television reporter

William "Bubba" Taylor, television coworker

Trent Winfrey, paternal uncle

and her cousin, another cousin's boyfriend, *plus* assorted teenage boys during her "wild" years

Oprah Winfrey 1954–

✦ She Said

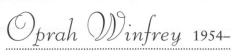

We were so poor we couldn't afford a dog or a cat, so I made pets of two cockroaches. —Oprah's sister has refuted this assertion about the cockroaches

I sold my silence for an ice-cream cone and a trip to the zoo. —Referring to being molested by several of her male relatives

I spent a lot of time trying to be Diana Ross.

I will never, never—as long as I'm black!—give up my power to another person.

✦ They Said

She's Fat City, Dr. Ruth, Mr. Rogers, and Mrs. Olson all rolled into one. —*The Washington Post*

She had big dreams when she was little. She told me many times, "I'm going to be a star." —Patricia Lee, her younger sister

She has genuine fear of sin and sincerely delights in goodness. —Maya Angelou, poet

✦ First Sexual Experience

Lost her virginity when she was nine years old to a nineteen-year-old cousin. She's said, "I had no idea it was a sexual thing because I didn't have a name for it."

✦ Husbands

Has never yet been married.

✦ Did You Know?

Oprah isn't named for Harpo (spelled backwards) Marx. She's named for Ruth's sister-in-law in the Bible; someone in her family just misspelled the name on her birth certificate.

Oprah received the ultimate insult in August 1979 when *TV Guide* (after she had refused to pose) placed her head on an upper-body photo of singer-actress Ann-Margret, then used the doctored picture on their cover. The resulting furor angered the singer, infuriated Oprah, and damaged the publication's reputation.

Debra Winger 1955–

✦ She Said

Women often shy away from intensity.

People collect money [in Hollywood] *without doing anything, and I'm politically opposed to it.*

I certainly tried to live like a movie star. But it didn't work for me.

✦ They Said

She's a lot like me. —Jack Nicholson, actor

You worry too much. You remind me of Simone Signoret. —Costa-Garvas, director, who directed her in *Betrayed* ('88)

I see a lot in Debra Winger. I think if she wants it, she could go a very long way. And she's been called very difficult. Until you're called difficult in Hollywood, you're really nobody at all. —Bette Davis, actress

✦ First Sexual Experience

Unknown.

✦ Husbands

Timothy Hutton, actor

✦ Did You Know?

Long before she became an actress, Winger worked on a kibbutz in Israel, served three months in the Israeli army, and even applied for permanent Israeli citizenship before changing her mind and returning to the US.

Winger once claimed in an interview that she seduced a professor in college because he resembled news anchor Tom Brokaw, on whom she'd had a crush on for a long time. According to her, "I closed my eyes and pretended I was fucking Tom Brokaw."

Lovers, Flings, or Just Friends?

- Bob Kerrey, U.S. senator from Nebraska
- Nick Nolte, actor (costar in *Cannery Row*, '82)
- Al Pacino, actor
- John Travolta, actor

Shelley Winters 1922–

✦ She Said

I'm not too fat at all—I'm just short for my weight.

I desperately needed to get fucked. —Explaining why she flew cross-country one weekend while she was on location for a film

Honey, every girl ought to be married to an Italian once. —Comparing notes with actress Elizabeth Ashley on their Italian husbands

I was drowned by Monty Clift, run over by James Mason, crushed to death by Robert Mitchum—been strangled, raped, and otherwise done away with. I think I am just about due for incineration.

✦ They Said

Shelley was like a fine prime specimen of a woman. Then she got fat. —Burt Lancaster, actor

It is surprisingly what some people will let happen to themselves. Shelley Winters is a prime example. —Marlene Dietrich, singer-actress

✦ First Sexual Experience

Lost her virginity to a young actor she seduced—with Southern Comfort and potato chips—when she was fifteen.

✦ Husbands

Mack Paul Mayer, whom she's described as a "handsome, Jewish, intelligent" Chicago salesman

Vittorio Gassman, Italian actor

Anthony Franciosa, actor

✦ Did You Know?

During the making of *Meet Danny Wilson* ('52), Winters and Frank Sinatra got into a yelling match as only they could. Sinatra pronounced Shelley a "bowlegged bitch of a Brooklyn blonde," while she retorted that Sinatra was a "skinny, no-talent, stupid Hoboken bastard." They later made up.

Seated at a dinner party next to author Dylan Thomas, who was visiting Hollywood at the time, Winters asked why he had come to visit the movie colony. The Welshman replied, "To touch the titties of a beautiful blonde starlet and to meet Charlie Chaplin." To satisfy his dream, Shelley let him touch hers.

Lovers, Flings, or Just Friends?

- Marlon Brando, actor
- Ronald Colman, actor (costar in *A Double Life,* '48)
- Sean Connery, actor
- Alex Cord, actor
- Robert De Niro, actor
- Albert Finney, actor
- Errol Flynn, actor
- Clark Gable, actor
- John Garfield, actor (costar in *He Ran All the Way,* '51)
- Farley Granger, actor
- John Gregson, British actor
- Sterling Hayden, actor
- William Holden, actor
- Howard Hughes, aviation-cinema mogul
- John Ireland, actor
- Burt Lancaster, actor
- Raymond Pelligrin, French actor
- Anthony Quinn, actor
- Paul Schutzer, British photographer
- Lawrence Tierney, actor

Natalie Wood 1938–1981

✦ She Said

I didn't know who the hell I was. I was whoever they *wanted me to be,* they *being agents, producers, directors, or whoever I was trying to please at the time.*

I didn't want to live anymore. —Comment when she was revived after taking sleeping pills after an argument with ex-lover Warren Beatty over starring with him in *Bonnie and Clyde* ('67)

✦ They Said

I never saw what was so great about Natalie. She was short and lousy in bed. —Steve McQueen, actor

Natalie was very unwilling to be told that she was wrong. —Richard Gregson, her second husband

✦ First Sexual Experience

Lost her virginity to her boyfriend, fellow actor Nick Adams, when she was fourteen. According to Adams, Natalie's mother asked him to teach her daughter "the ways of the world." She supposedly said that she preferred that it be Adams who deflowered her daughter because she trusted him, rather than some of the other men around Natalie.

✦ Husbands

Robert J. Wagner, actor (costar in *All the Fine Young Cannibals,* '60)
Richard Gregson, British producer-agent
Robert J. Wagner, actor (and the fourth Mr. Jill St. John)

✦ Did You Know?

One of Natalie's contract clauses provided that the producer always had to provide bracelets, of an appropriate design, to cover her deformed left wrist.

What caused the Beatty-Wood affair to break up? It seems the couple was dining in Chasen's when Warren excused himself to go to the rest room. On the way, he propositioned the checkroom attendant into walking off the job. They left, through the back door, and disappeared together for several days, and Warren didn't even say goodbye or pay the check.

Lovers, Flings, or Just Friends?

Nick Adams, actor

Warren Beatty, actor (costar in *Splendor in the Grass,* '61)

Raymond Burr, actor

Tom Courtenay, British actor

James Dean, actor (costar in *Rebel Without a Cause,* '55)

Robert Evans, producer-actor

Nicky Hilton, hotel-chain heir (and the first Mr. Liz Taylor)

Dennis Hopper, actor (costar in *Rebel Without a Cause,* '55)

Tab Hunter, actor

John Ireland, actor

Richard Johnson, British actor

Arthur Loew Jr., cinema-chain heir

Perry Lopez, actor

Scott Marlowe, actor

Steve McQueen, actor (costar in *Love with the Proper Stranger,* '63)

Audie Murphy, actor–soldier hero

David Niven Jr., agent, son of David Niven

Elvis Presley, singer-actor

Nicholas Ray, director (he directed her in *Rebel Without a Cause,* '55)

Lance Reventlow, wealthy heir son of Barbara Hutton

Frank Sinatra, actor-singer (costar in *Kings Go Forth,* '58)

Tommy Thompson, writer

Robert Vaughn, actor

Christopher Walken, actor costar in *Brainstorm,* '83)

Stuart Whitman, actor

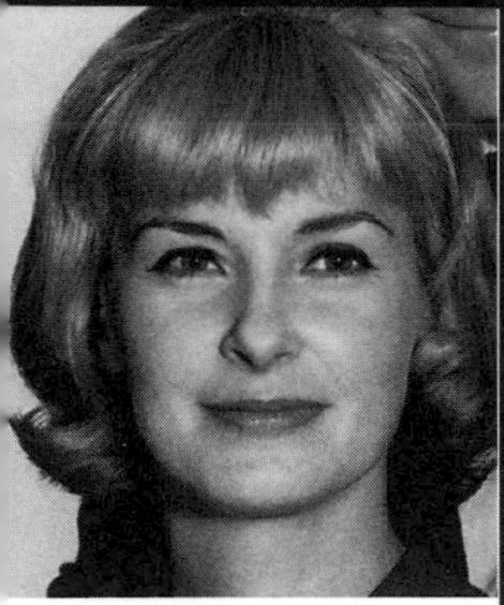

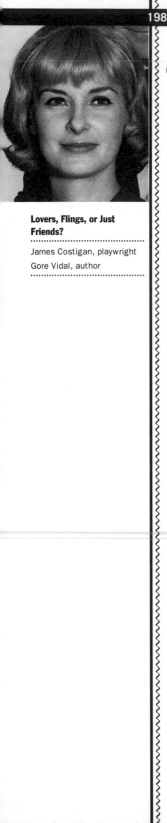

Lovers, Flings, or Just Friends?

James Costigan, playwright
Gore Vidal, author

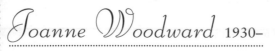

Joanne Woodward 1930–

✦ She Said

Acting is like sex. You should do it and not talk about it.

All Southern girls like to get engaged even when they aren't ready for marriage. —Referring to her three engagements before she married Newman

As you get older and the wrinkles come, you realize the tragedy of the worship of the young in films.

Conservatively, I think people have at most two or three generations left. And I'm certainly raising my children not to have any children.

✦ They Said

I don't like to discuss my marriage, but I will tell you something which may sound corny, but which happens to be true. I have steak at home. Why should I go out for hamburger? —Paul Newman, actor and spouse

✦ First Sexual Experience

Unknown.

✦ Husbands

Paul Newman, actor (costar in *WUSA,* '70)

✦ Did You Know?

In *Rachel, Rachel* ('68) Woodward played one of the first women to masturbate on-screen in a feature film.

Fay Wray 1907–

✦ She Said

"You will have the tallest, darkest leading man in Hollywood." *Those were the first words I heard about King Kong* ['33].

What does it matter that many people think King Kong ['33] *was my only film?*

✦ They Said

The most womanly woman I have ever known. —Clifford Odets, playwright-screenwriter

You're the kind of girl a man would want to have for a wife. —George Raft

Never let a man enter your dressing room. I know. I've been in dressing rooms. —John Monk Saunders, cautioning his wife against "misbehavior" on film sets

✦ First Sexual Experience

Lost her virginity to her first husband, John Monk Saunders, at age twenty.

✦ Husbands

John Monk Saunders, author
Robert Riskin, screenwriter
Dr. Sanford Rothenberg, physician

✦ Did You Know?

Erich von Stroheim almost seduced Wray and claimed her virginity, but she decided at the last minute not to meet him at their trysting place, a noted Hollywood costume company.

Lovers, Flings, or Just Friends?

- George Gershwin, composer
- Cary Grant, actor
- Leland Hayward, agent-producer
- Howard Hughes, aviation-cinema mogul
- Sinclair Lewis, novelist
- Clifford Odets, playwright-screenwriter

Jane Wyman 1914–

✦ She Said

I've been pushed around by experts. I don't have to take it anymore.

I just had to go dancing and dining at the Troc or the Grove or some nightspot every night to be happy.

✦ They Said

That Wyman woman, unlike the genuine cream of the cinema crop whose names are box-office magic, seems to consider the approach of a reporter as an irksome intrusion upon the privacy of a high-priced public goldfish. —Hy Gardner, columnist, reflecting on Wyman's aversion to some members of the press

She was a most vital and arresting presence, really born for the movies. I always thought her most vivid. —Cole Porter, commenting on her role in the film about him (*Night and Day*, '46)

Miss Wyman looks like a mystery nobody has bothered to solve. —Marlene Dietrich

✦ First Sexual Experience

Unknown.

✦ Husbands

Eugene Wyman, rumored marriage to a fellow high school student that ended in divorce after about a month

Myron Futterman, dress manufacturer

Ronald Reagan, actor-politician (his pet name for her was "Little Miss Button Nose")

Fred Karger, bandleader-musician

Fred Karger, bandleader-musician

✦ Did You Know?

While never thought of as a particularly sexy woman, Wyman does hold a record in the kissing book. Her kiss with Regis Toomey in *You're in the Army Now* ('41) lasts three minutes five seconds—an astounding 4 percent of the film's total running time.

Lovers, Flings, or Just Friends?

- Milo Anderson, costume designer
- Lew Ayres, actor (costar in *Johnny Belinda*, '48)
- Greg Bautzer, attorney–Hollywood escort
- Curtis Bernhardt, director (directed her in *The Blue Veil*, '51)
- Bing Crosby, actor-singer (costar in *Here Comes the Groom*, '51)
- Cedric Hardwicke, actor
- Clark Hardwicke, golfer
- Travis Kleefeid, building contractor
- Peter Lawford, actor
- John Payne, actor
- Manny Sachs, record executive
- Gail Smith, business executive
- Tony Trabert, tennis player

Loretta Young 1913–

✦She Said

I never think about the characters I play. I just try to do what the director tells me.

I don't enjoy the groping, grabby kind of love scenes. I don't like to play rough. It's no fun being mauled.

If you want a place in the sun, you have to expect a few blisters.

✦They Said

Every time she 'sins', she builds a church. That's why there are so many Catholic churches in Hollywood. —Marlene Dietrich, who abhorred Loretta

She was sickeningly sweet, a pure phoney. Her two faces sent me home angry and crying several times. —Virginia Field, costar in *Eternally Yours* ('39)

Whatever it is this actress never had, she still hasn't got it. —Bosley Crowther, *New York Times* critic panning one of her film performances

✦First Sexual Experience

Lost her virginity to first husband Grant Withers, whom she married only days after her seventeenth birthday.

✦Husbands

Grant Withers, actor
Thomas Lewis, advertising executive
Jean Louis, costume designer
Ricardo Montalban, actor, brother-in-law

✦Did You Know?

Young was known for her religious devotion. During one of Joan Crawford's parties, a friend was about to sit in a chair from which Loretta had just risen. Joan rushed over and grabbed her friend just in time, saying, "You can't sit there! Loretta Young just got up and it still has the mark of the cross on it."

Lovers, Flings, or Just Friends?

- Irving Asher, studio executive
- George Brent, actor (costar in *They Call It Sin,* '32)
- William Buckner, lawyer
- Louis Calhern, actor (costar in *They Call It Sin,* '32)
- Ricardo Cortez, actor
- Douglas Fairbanks, Jr., actor
- Norman Foster, actor (costar in *Play Girl,* '32)
- Clark Gable, actor (costar in *Call of the Wild,* '35)
- Richard Greene, actor
- Joseph Mankiewicz, writer-director
- John McClain, newspaperman
- Wayne Morris, actor
- David Niven, actor (costar in *The Bishop's Wife,* '47)
- Fred Perry, tennis star
- Tyrone Power, actor (costar in *Love Is News,* '37)
- Gregory Ratoff, director
- Robert Riskin, screenwriter (and the second Mr. Fay Wray)
- Gilbert Roland, actor
- Herbert Somborn, restaurateur (and the second Mr. Gloria Swanson)
- James (Jimmy) Stewart, actor
- Edward Sutherland, director
- Spencer Tracy, actor (costar in *A Man's Castle,* '33)
- John Hay "Jock" Whitney, businessman-socialite
- Darryl F. Zanuck, studio head

Bibliography

Autobiographies, Biographies, Memoirs, Reminiscences, and Anecdotes

Aadland, Florence, as told to Tedd Thomey. *The Big Love.* Lancer Books, 1961.

Adams, Edie and Robert Windeler. *Sing a Pretty Song. . . .* William Morrow, 1990.

Agan, Patrick. *The Decline and Fall of the Love Goddesses.* Pinnacle Books, 1979.

Aherne, Brian. *A Proper Job.* Houghton-Mifflin, 1969.

Alexander, Paul. *Boulevard of Broken Dreams: The Life, Times and Legend of James Dean.* Viking, 1994.

Allyson, June and Frances Spatz Leighton. *June Allyson.* G. P. Putnam's, 1982.

Altman, Diana. *Hollywood East.* Hawthorn Books, 1992.

Amburn, Ellis. *Pearl: The Obsessions and Passions of Janis Joplin.* Warner Books, 1993.

Andersen, Christopher. *A Star, Is a Star, Is a Star.* Doubleday, 1980.

———. *Citizen Jane: The Turbulent Life of Jane Fonda.* Henry Holt, 1990.

———. *Jagger Unauthorized.* Delacorte, 1993.

———. *Madonna Unauthorized.* Simon and Schuster, 1991.

———. *Michael Jackson: Unauthorized.* Simon and Schuster, 1994.

Anger, Kenneth. *Hollywood Babylon.* Associated Press Professional Services, 1965.

———. *Hollywood Babylon: II.* E. P. Dutton, 1984.

Ankerich, Michael C. *Broken Silence: Conversations with Twenty-five Silent Film Stars.* MacFarland, 1993.

Ann-Margret. *Ann-Margret: My Story.* G. P. Putnam's, 1994.

Arce, Hector. *Gary Cooper: An Intimate Biography.* William Morrow, 1979.

———. *The Secret Life of Tyrone Power.* William Morrow, 1979.

Arnaz, Desi. *A Book.* William Morrow, 1976.

Arnold, William. *Shadowland.* McGraw-Hill, 1978.

Ashley, Elizabeth. *Actress: Postcards From the Road.* M. Evans, 1978.

Astor, Mary. *A Life on Film.* Delacorte, 1971.

———. *Mary Astor: My Story.* Doubleday, 1959.

Aumont, Jean-Pierre. *Sun and Shadow.* W. W. Norton, 1977.

Bacall, Lauren. *Lauren Bacall by Myself.* Knopf, 1978.

———. *Now.* Knopf, 1994.

Bach, Steven. *Marlene Dietrich: Life and Legend.* William Morrow, 1992.

Bacon, James. *Hollywood is a Four-Letter Word.* Regnery, 1976.

———. *Made in Hollywood.* Contemporary Books, 1977.

Baker, Carroll. *Baby Doll.* Arbor Books, 1983.
Baker, Jean-Claude and Chris Chase. *Josephine: The Hungry Heart.* Random House, 1993.
Barker, Malcolm J., with T. C. Sobey. *Living With the Queen.* Barricade Books, 1991.
Barlett, Donald L. and James B. Steele. *Empire: The Life, Legend and Madness of Howard Hughes.* W. W. Norton, 1979.
Barrymore, Diana. *Too Much, Too Soon.* Henry Holt, 1957.
Baxter, Anne. *Intermission.* G. P. Putnam's, 1976.
Beck, Marilyn. *Marilyn Beck's Hollywood.* 1973.
Bego, Mark. *The Best of Modern Screen.* St. Martin's, 1986.
Behlmer, Rudy. *Memo from Darryl F. Zanuck: The Golden Years at Twentieth Century-Fox.* Grove, 1993.
———. *Inside Warner Bros.* Viking, 1985.
Behr, Edward. *The Good Frenchman: The True Story of the Life and Times of Maurice Chevalier.* Villard Books, 1993.
Bennett, Joan and Lois Kibbee. *The Bennett Playbill.* Holt, Rinehart and Winston, 1970.
Benson, Ross. *Charles: The Untold Story.* St. Martin's, 1993.
Berg, A. Scott. *Goldwyn.* Knopf, 1989.
Bergen, Candice. *Knock Wood.* G. K. Hall, 1984.
Bergman, Ingmar. *The Magic Lantern.* Viking, 1988.
Bergman, Ingrid and Alan Burgess. *Ingrid Bergman: My Story.* Delacorte, 1980.
Berle, Milton. *B.S. I Love You.* McGraw-Hill, 1988.
Berle, Milton, with Haskel Frankal. *Milton Berle: An Autobiography.* Delacorte, 1974.
Bernard, Matt. *Mario Lanza.* Macfadden-Bartell, 1971.
Bibb, Porter. *It Ain't As Easy As It Looks.* Crown Publishers, 1993.
Black, Jonathan. *Streisand.* Leisure Books/Norden, 1980.
Blair, Clay Jr., and Joan Blair. *The Search for JFK.* Berkley Publishing, 1976.
Blake, Michael F. *Lon Chaney: The Man Behind the Thousand Faces.* Vestal Press, 1990.
Bloom, Claire. *Limelight and After.* Harper and Row, 1982.
Bly, Nellie. *Barbra Streisand: The Untold Story.* Pinnacle Books, 1994.
———. *Marlon Brando: Larger Than Life.* Pinnacle Books, 1994.
———. *Oprah! Up Close and Down Home.* Zebra Books, 1993.
Bona, Damien. *Opening Shots.* Workman, 1994.
Bonderoff, Jason. *Tom Selleck: An Unauthorized Biography.* Signet/NAL, 1983.
Bosworth, Patricia. *Montgomery Clift.* Harcourt, Brace, 1978.
Bova, Joyce. *Don't Ask Forever.* Kensington Books, 1994.
Bowie, Angela. *Backstage Passes.* G. P. Putnam's, 1993.
Bradshaw, Jon. *Dreams Money Can Buy.* William Morrow, 1985.
Brady, Frank. *Citizen Welles.* Scribner's, 1989.
———. *Onassis: An Extravagant Life.* Prentice-Hall, 1977.
Brady, Kathleen. *Lucille.* Hyperion, 1994.
Bragg, Melvyn. *Richard Burton: A Life.* Little, Brown, 1988.

Brando, Anna Kashfi, and E. P. Stein. *Brando for Breakfast*. Crown, 1979.

Brando, Marlon. *Songs My Mother Taught Me*. Random House, 1994.

Braun, Eric. *Deborah Kerr*. W. H. Allen, 1977.

Brenman-Gibson, Margaret. *Clifford Odets: American Playwright—The Years From 1906–1940*. Atheneum, 1981.

Brian, Denis. *Tallulah Darling: A Biography of Tallulah Bankhead*. Pyramid, 1972.

Brooks, Louise. *Lulu in Hollywood*. Knopf, 1982.

Brown, David. *Star Billing*. Weidenfeld and Nicolson, London, 1985.

Brown, Peter H. *Marilyn: The Last Take*. Dutton, 1992.

Brown, Peter Harry. *Kim Novak: The Reluctant Goddess*. St. Martin's, 1986.

———. *Such Devoted Sisters: Those Fabulous Gabors*. St. Martin's, 1985.

Brown, Peter Henry, and Pamela Ann Brown. *The MGM Girls: Behind the Velvet Curtain*. St. Martin's, 1983.

Brownlow, Kevin. *The Parade's Gone By. . . .* University of California, 1968.

Brunette, Peter. *Roberto Rossellini*. Oxford University, 1987.

Bruno, Michael. *Venus in Hollywood*. Lyle Stuart, 1970.

Brynner, Rock. *Yul: The Man Who Would Be King*. Simon and Shuster, 1989.

Burton, Humphrey. *Leonard Bernstein*. Doubleday, 1994.

Cafarakis, Christian. *The Fabulous Onassis: His Life and Loves*. William Morrow, 1972.

Callow, Simon. *Charles Laughton: A Difficult Actor*. Grove, 1987.

Calvet, Corinne. *Has Corinne Been a Good Girl*. St. Martin's, 1983.

Callan, Michael Feeney. *Julie Christie*. St. Martin's, 1984.

———. *Richard Harris*. Sidgwick & Jackson, 1990.

Canales, Luis. *Imperial Gina*. Branden, 1990.

Capote, Truman. *Music for Chameleons*. Random House, 1980.

Carey, Gary. *All the Stars in Heaven: Louis B. Mayer's MGM*. E. P. Dutton, 1981.

———. *Anita Loos*. Knopf, 1988.

———. *Judy Holliday: An Intimate Life Story*. Seaview, 1982.

Cary, Diana Serra. *Hollywood's Children*. Houghton Mifflin, 1979.

Carne, Judy. *Laughing on the Outside, Crying on the Inside*. Rawson Associates, 1985.

Caserta, Peggy. *Going Down With Janis*. Dell, 1974.

Cassini, Oleg. *In My Own Fashion*. Simon and Schuster, 1987.

Castle, William. *Step Right Up: I'm Going to Scare the Pants Off America*. G. P. Putnam's, 1976.

Celebrity Research Group. *Beside Book of Celebrity Gossip*. Crown, 1984.

Celebrity Service International, Inc. *Earl Blackwell's Entertainment Celebrity Register*. Visible Ink, 1991.

Chandler, Charlotte. *The Ultimate Seduction*. Doubleday, 1984.

Chaplin, Charles. *My Autobiography*. Simon and Schuster, 1964.

Chaplin, Saul. *The Golden Age of Movie Musicals and Me*. University of Oklahoma Press, 1994.

Christian, Linda. *Linda: My Own Story*. Crown, 1962.

Citron, Stephen. *Noel and Cole: The Sophisticates.* Oxford University, 1993.
Clarke, Donald. *Wishing on the Moon: The Life and Times of Billie Holliday.* Viking, 1994.
Clarke, Gerald. *Capote: A Biography.* Simon and Schuster, 1988.
Clayson, Alan. *Ringo Starr.* Paragon House, 1991.
Coe, Jonathan. *Humphrey Bogart: Take It and Like It.* Grove Weidenfeld, 1991.
Cole, Gerald, and Wes Farrell. *The Fondas.* W. H. Allen, 1984.
Collier, James Lincoln. *Duke Ellington.* Oxford University, 1987.
Collins, Joan. *Joan Collins: Past Imperfect.* W. H. Allen, 1978.
Colman, Juliet Benita. *Ronald Colman: A Very Private Man.* William Morrow, 1975.
Conner, Floyd. *Lupe Velez and Her Lovers.* Barricade Books, 1993.
Conover, David. *Finding Marilyn: A Romance.* Grosset and Dunlap, 1981.
Conrad, Earl. *Billy Rose: Manhattan Primitive.* World Publishing, 1968.
Considine, Shaun. *Barbra Streisand.* Delacorte, 1985
———. *Bette and Joan: The Divine Feud.* E. P. Dutton, 1989.
———. *Mad as Hell: The Life and Work of Paddy Chayefsky,* Random House, 1994.
Cooper, Jackie, and Dick Kleiner. *Please Don't Shoot My Dog.* William Morrow, 1981.
Crane, Cheryl. *Detour: A Hollywood Story.* William Morrow, 1988.
Crawford, Joan, with Jane Kerner Ardmore. *A Portrait of Joan.* Doubleday, 1962.
Crawley, Tony. *Bébé: The Films of Brigitte Bardot.* Citadel Press, 1977.
Crivello, Kirk. *Fallen Angels.* Citadel Press, 1988.
Curcio, Vincent. *Suicide Blonde: The Life of Gloria Grahame.* William Morrow, 1989.
Curtis, James. *Between Flops.* Harcourt Brace, 1982.
Curtis, Tony, and Barry Paris. *Tony Curtis: The Autobiography.* William Morrow, 1993.
Curtiss, Thomas Quinn. *Erich von Stroheim.* Farrar, Straus and Giroux, 1971.
Daly, Marsha. *Steve Martin. An Unauthorized Biography Well Excuuuuse Us!*. Signet/NAL, 1980.
Dandridge, Dorothy, and Earl Conrad. *Everything and Nothing: The Dorothy Dandridge Tragedy.* Abelard-Schuman, 1970.
Dardis, Tom. *Keaton: The Man Who Wouldn't Lie Down.* Scribner's, 1979.
———. *Some Time in the Sun.* Scribner's, 1976.
David, Catherine. *Simone Signoret.* Overlook Press, 1993.
David, Lester. *Jacqueline Kennedy Onassis: A Portrait of Her Private Years.* Birch Lane, 1994.
David, Lester, and Jhan Robbins. *Richard and Elizabeth.* Funk and Wagnalls, 1977.
Davidson, Bill. *Spencer Tracy: Tragic Idol.* E. P. Dutton, 1987.
Davis, Bette. *The Lonely Life.* G. P. Putnam's, 1962.
———. *This 'n That.* G. P. Putnam's, 1987.

Davis, John H. *The Kennedys: Dynasty and Disaster 1848–1984.* McGraw-Hill, 1984.

Davis, Judith. *Richard Gere: An Unauthorized Biography.* NAL/Signet, 1983.

Davis Jr., Sammy, and Burt Boyar with Jane Boyer. *Why Me: The Sammy Davis, Jr. Story.* Farrar, Straus and Giroux, 1989.

Davis Jr., Sammy. *Hollywood in a Suitcase.* William Morrow, 1980.

Davis, Ronald L. *Hollywood Beauty: Linda Darnell and the American Dream.* University of Oklahoma Press, 1991.

Davis, Ronald L. *The Glamour Factory.* Southern Methodist University, 1993.

De Havilland, Olivia. *Every Frenchman Has One.* Random House, 1961.

De Carlo, Yvonne, and Doug Warren. *Yvonne: An Autobiography.* St. Martin's, 1987.

De Cordova, Fred. *Johnny Came Lately.* Simon and Schuster, 1988.

Dent, Alan. *Mrs. Patrick Campbell.* Museum Press, 1961.

Des Barres, Pamela. *I'm With the Band: Confessions of a Groupie.* Beech Tree Books, 1987.

———. *Take Another Little Piece of My Heart.* William Morrow, 1992.

Deutsch, Armand. *Bogie and Me.* G. P. Putnam's, 1991.

Dewey, Donald. *Marcello Mastroianni.* Birch Lane, 1993.

Diane, Jacobs. *Christmas in July: The Life and Art of Preston Sturges.* University of California Press, 1992.

Dick, Bernard. *The Merchant Prince of Poverty Row.* University of Kentucky Press, 1993.

Dick, Bernard F. *Hellman in Hollywood.* Fairleigh-Dickinson University, 1982.

Dickens, Norman. *Jack Nicholson: The Search for a Superstar.* New American Library, 1975.

DiOrio, Al. *Barbara Stanwyck.* Coward-McCann, 1983.

———. *Borrowed Time.* Running Press, 1981.

———. *Little Girl Lost: The Life and Hard Times of Judy Garland.* Arlington, 1973.

Dodd, Darin. *Dream Lovers.* Warner Books, 1994.

Douglas, Kirk. *The Ragman's Son.* Simon and Schuster, 1988.

Downing, David. *Jack Nicholson.* Stein and Day, 1983, 1984.

Duberman, Martin Bauml. *Paul Robeson.* Knopf, 1988.

Du Bois, Diana. *In Her Sister's Shadow.* Little, Brown, 1995.

Duke, Patty and Kenneth Turan. *Call Me Anna: The Autobiography of Patty Duke.* Bantam, 1987.

Dunaway, David King. *Huxley in Hollywood.* Harper and Row, 1989.

Durgnat, Raymond and Scott Simmon. *King Vidor: American.* University of California Press, 1988.

Edmonds, Andy. *Bugsy's Baby.* Birch Lane, 1993.

———. *Hot Toddy.* William Morrow, 1989.

Edwards, Anne. *Early Reagan.* William Morrow, 1987.

———. *Judy Garland: A Biography.* Simon and Schuster, 1974.

———. *Shirley Temple: American Princess.* William Morrow, 1988.

———. *Vivien Leigh.* Simon and Schuster, 1977.

Edwards, Michael. *In the Shadow of the King: Priscilla, Elvis and Me.* St. Martin's, 1988.
Eells, George. *Final Gig.* Harcourt, Brace, 1991.
———. *Hedda and Louella.* G. P. Putnam's, 1972.
———. *Ginger, Loretta and Irene Who?.* G. P. Putnam's, 1976.
———. *The Life That Late He Led.* G. P. Putnam's, 1967.
———. *Robert Mitchum: A Biography.* Franklin Watts, 1984.
———, and Stanley Musgrove. *Mae West.* William Morrow, 1982.
Eisenschitz, Bernard. *Nicholas Ray.* Faber and Faber, 1993.
Ekland, Britt. *True Britt.* Prentice-Hall, 1980.
Eliot, Marc. *Burt! The Unauthorized Biography.* Dell, 1982.
———. *Walt Disney: Hollywood's Dark Prince.* Birch Lane, 1993.
Epstein, Edward Z. *Portrait of Jennifer.* Simon and Schuster, 1995.
Esposito, Joe, and Elena Cumans. *Good Rockin' Tonight.* Simon and Schuster, 1994.
Evans, Peter. *Ari: The Life and Times of Aristotle Socrates Onassis.* Summit, 1986.
———. *Bardot: Eternal Sex Goddess.* Leslie Frewin, 1972.
———. *The Kid Stays in the Picture.* Hyperion, 1994.
———. *Peter Sellers: The Mask Behind the Mask.* New English Library, 1980.
Eyeles, Allen. *James Stewart.* Stein and Day, 1984.
Eyman, Scott. *Ernst Lubitsch: Laughter in Paradise.* Simon and Schuster, 1993.
———. *Mary Pickford: America's Sweetheart.* Donald I. Fine, 1990.
Fairbanks, Douglas, Jr. *A Hell of a War.* St. Martin's, 1993.
———. *The Salad Days.* Doubleday, 1988.
Fairey, Wendy W. *One of the Family.* W. W. Norton, 1992.
Farber, Stephen, and Marc Green. *Hollywood Dynasties.* Delilah Communications, 1984.
Faulkner, Trader. *Peter Finch.* Taplinger, 1979.
Feibleman, Peter. *Lilly.* William Morrow, 1988.
Feinman, Jeffrey. *Hollywood Confidential.* Playboy Press, 1976.
Ferris, Paul. *Richard Burton.* Coward, McCann and Geoghegan, 1981.
Fine, Marshall. *Bloody Sam.* Donald I. Fine, 1991.
Fisher, Clive. *Noel Coward.* St. Martin's, 1992.
Fisher, Eddie. *Eddie: My Life and Loves.* Harper and Row, 1981.
Flamini, Roland. *Ava.* Coward, McCann and Geoghegan, 1983.
———. *Scarlett, Rhett, and a Cast of Thousands.* Macmillan, 1975.
———. *Thalberg.* Crown, 1994.
Fleming, Karl, and Ann Taylor Fleming. *The First Time.* Simon and Schuster, 1975.
Fonda, Henry, and Howard Teichmann. *Fonda: My Life.* New American Library, 1981.
Fontaine, Joan. *No Bed of Roses: An Autobiography.* William Morrow, 1978.
Fountain, Leatrice Gilbert. *Dark Star.* St. Martin's, 1985.
Francisco, Charles. *Gentleman: The William Powell Story.* St. Martin's, 1985.
Frank, Gerold. *Judy.* Harper and Row, 1975.

Freedland, Michael. *Cagney*. Stein and Day, 1975.

———. *Gregory Peck*. William Morrow, 1980.

———. *Jolson*. Stein and Day, 1972.

———. *Maurice Chevalier*. William Morrow, 1981.

———. *Peter O'Toole*. St. Martin's, 1982.

———. *The Secret Life of Danny Kaye*. St. Martin's, 1985.

———. *Sophie: The Sophie Tucker Story*. Woburn, 1978.

———. *The Two Lives of Errol Flynn*. William Morrow, 1978.

Frewin, Leslie. *The Late Mrs. Dorothy Parker*. Macmillan, 1986.

Frischauer, Willi. *Bardot: An Intimate Biography*. Michael Joseph, 1978.

———. *Behind the Scenes of Otto Preminger*. William Morrow, 1974.

Fussell, Betty Harper. *Mabel*. Tichnor and Fields, 1982.

Gabler, Neal. *Winchell: Gossip, Power and the Culture of Celebrity*. Knopf, 1995.

Gabor, Eva. *Orchids and Salami*. Doubleday, 1954.

Gabor, Zsa Zsa, and Gerold Frank. *Zsa Zsa Gabor: My Story*. World, 1960.

———, and Wendy Leigh. *One Lifetime Is Not Enough*. Delacorte, 1991.

Gaines, Steven, and Sharon Churcher. *Obsession: The Life and Times of Calvin Klein*. Birch Lane, 1994.

Galante, Pierre. *Mademoiselle Chanel*. Regnery, 1973.

Gardner, Ava. *Ava: My Story*. Bantam Books, 1990.

Geist, Kenneth L. *Pictures Will Talk*. Scribner's, 1978.

George, Don. *Sweet Man: The Real Duke Ellington*. G. P. Putnam's, 1981.

Gibson, Barbara. *The Kennedys: The Third Generation*. Thunder's Mouth Press, 1993.

Gil-Montero, Martha. *Brazilian Bombshell*. Donald I. Fine, 1989.

Goldman, Albert. *Elvis*. McGraw-Hill, 1981.

———. *Ladies and Gentlemen—Lenny Bruce!!*. Random House, 1974.

———. *The Lives of John Lennon*. William Morrow, 1988.

Goldman, Herbert G. *Fanny Brice: The Original Funny Girl*. Oxford University, 1992.

———. *Jolson: The Legend Comes to Life*. Oxford University, 1988.

Goldsmith, Barbara. *Little Gloria . . . Happy at Last*. Knopf, 1980.

Goldstein, Toby. *Sally Field*. PaperJacks, 1988.

Gottfried, Martin. *All His Jazz: The Life and Death of Bob Fosse*. Bantam, 1990.

———. *Jed Harris: The Curse of Genius*. Little, Brown, 1984.

———. *Nobody's Fool: The Lives of Danny Kaye*. Simon and Schuster, 1994.

Gottlieb, Polly Rose. *The Nine Lives of Billy Rose*. Crown, 1968.

Govoni, Albert. *Cary Grant: An Unauthorized Biography*. Regnery, 1971.

Graham, Don. *No Name on the Bullet*. Viking Penguin, 1989.

Graham, Sheilah. *Confessions of a Hollywood Columnist*. William Morrow, 1969.

———. *Garden of Allah*. Crown, 1970.

———. *Hollywood Revisited*. St. Martin's, 1985.

———. *How to Marry Super Rich*. Grosset and Dunlap, 1974.

Granger, Stewart. *Sparks Fly Upward.* Granada, 1981.
Greenwood, Earl. *The Boy Who Would Be King.* E. P. Dutton, 1990.
Gregory, Adela and Milo Speriglio. *Crypt 33: The Saga of Marilyn Monroe—The Final Word.* Birch Lane, 1993.
Grobel, Laurence. *Conversations With Capote.* New American Library, 1985.
Grobel, Lawrence. *The Hustons.* Scribner's, 1989.
Gronowicz, Antoni. *Garbo: Her Story.* Simon and Schuster, 1990.
Grosland, Margaret. *Piaf.* G. P. Putnam's, 1985.
Grossman, Barbara W. *Funny Woman.* Indiana University Press, 1991.
Gross, Michael. *Model.* William Morrow, 1995.
Groteke, Kristi and Majorie Rosen. *Mia and Woody: Love and Betrayal.* Carroll and Graf, 1994.
Gubernick, Lisa Rebecca. *Squandered Fortune: The Life and Times of Huntington Hartford.* G. P. Putnam's, 1991.
Guiles, Fred Lawrence. *Joan Crawford: The Last Word.* Birch Lane, 1995.
———. *Marion Davies.* McGraw-Hill, 1972.
———. *Norma Jean: The Life of Marilyn Monroe.* McGraw-Hill, 1979.
———. *Stan: The Life of Stan Laurel.* Stein and Day, 1980.
Gussow, Mel. *Don't Say Yes Until I Finish Talking: A Biography of Darryl Zanuck.* Doubleday, 1971.
Guthrie, Lee. *The Lives and Loves of Cary Grant.* Drake, 1977.
Hadleigh, Boze. *Conversations With My Elders.* St. Martin's, 1976.
———. *Hollywood Babble On.* Birch Lane, 1994.
———. *Hollywood Lesbians.* Barricade, 1994.
Hall, Elaine Blake. *Burt and Me: My Days and Nights With Burt Reynolds.* Pinnacle, 1994.
Hall, William. *Raising Caine.* Prentice-Hall, 1981.
Hamblett, Charles. *Who Killed Marilyn Monroe?* Leslie Frewin, 1966.
Hamilton, Nigel. *JFK: Reckless Youth.* Random House, 1992.
Haney, Lynn. *Naked at the Feast.* Dodd, Mead, 1981.
Hanna, David. *Come Up and See Me Sometime: A Confidential Biography of Mae West.* Tower, 1976.
Hanna, Robert. *Robert Redford.* Nordon Publications, 1978.
Harmetz, Aljean. *Rolling Thunder and Other Movie Business.* Knopf, 1983.
Harris, Marlys J. *The Zanucks of Hollywood.* Crown, 1989.
Harris, Radie. *Radie's World.* G. P. Putnam's, 1975.
Harris, Warren G. *Audrey Hepburn.* Simon and Schuster, 1994.
———. *Lucy and Desi.* Simon and Schuster, 1991.
———. *Natalie and R.J.: Hollywood's Star-Crossed Lovers.* Doubleday, 1988.
———. *The Other Marilyn.* Arbor House, 1985.
Harrison, Elizabeth. *Love, Honor and Dismay.* Doubleday, 1977.
Harrison, Rex. *Rex: An Autobiography.* William Morrow, 1975.
Hart, Kitty Carlisle. *Kitty.* Doubleday, 1988.
Haskins, James, and Kathleen Benson. *Lena.* Stein and Day, 1984.
Hayman, Ronald. *Tennessee Williams: Everyone Else Is an Audience.* Yale University, 1993.

Hayward, Brooke. *Haywire*. Knopf, 1977.
Head, Edith, and Paddy Calistro. *Edith Head's Hollywood*. E. P. Dutton, 1983.
Henner, Marilu, with Jim Jerome. *By All Means Keep On Moving*. Pocket Books, 1994.
Henreid, Paul and Julius Fast. *Ladies' Man*. St. Martin's, 1984.
Henry III, William A. *The Great One: The Life and Legend of Jackie Gleason*. Doubleday, 1992.
Herndon, Venable. *James Dean: A Short Life*. Doubleday, 1974.
Heymann, C. David. *Liz*. Birch Lane, 1995.
———. *Poor Little Rich Girl*. Lyle Stuart, 1983.
———. *A Woman Named Jackie*, Lyle Stuart, 1989.
Hickey, Des, and Gus Smith. *The Prince: The Public and Private Life of Laurence Harvey*. Leslie Frewin Publisher, Ltd., 1975.
Higham, Charles. *Audrey: The Life of Audrey Hepburn*. Macmillan, 1984.
———. *Ava: A Life Story*. Delacorte, 1974.
———. *Bette*. Macmillan, 1981.
———. *Brando*. New American Library, 1987.
———. *Charles Laughton*. Doubleday, 1976.
———. *Errol Flynn: The Untold Story*. Doubleday, 1980.
———. *Howard Hughes: The Secret Life*. G. P. Putnam's, 1993.
———. *Kate: The Life of Katherine Hepburn*. W. W. Norton, 1975.
———. *The Life of Marlene Dietrich*. W. W. Norton, 1988.
———. *Lucy: The Real Life of Lucille Ball*. St. Martin's, 1986.
———. *Merchant of Dreams: L. B. Mayer, MGM and the Secret Hollywood*. Donald I. Fine, 1993.
———. *Orson Welles: The Rise and Fall of an American Genius*. St. Martin's, 1985.
———. *Rose*. Pocket Books, 1995.
———. *Sisters*. Coward-McCann, 1984.
———. *Ziegfeld*. Regnery, 1972.
———, and Roy Moseley. *Cary Grant: The Lonely Heart*. Harcourt, Brace, 1989.
———. *Princess Merle: The Romantic Life of Merle Oberon*. Coward-McCann, 1983.
Hirschhorn, Clive. *Gene Kelly*. St. Martin's, 1984.
Holtzman, Will. *Judy Holliday*. G. P. Putnam's, 1982.
Hopper, Hedda. *From Under My Hat*. Doubleday, 1952.
———. *The Whole Truth and Nothing But*. Doubleday, 1963.
Hoskyns, Barney. *Montgomery Clift: Beautiful Loser*. Bloomsbury, 1991.
Hotchner, A. E. *Doris Day: Her Own Story*. William Morrow, 1976.
———. *Sophia Living and Loving: Her Own Story*. William Morrow, 1979.
Houseman, Victoria. *Made in Heaven*. Bonus Books, 1991.
Howard, Ronald. *In Search of My Father*. St. Martin's, 1980.
Hudson, Rock, and Sara Davidson. *Rock Hudson: His Story*. Avon Books, 1986.
Hunter, Allan. *Faye Dunaway*. St. Martin's, 1986.

———. *Tony Curtis: The Man and His Movies*. St. Martin's, 1985.
Huston, John. *An Open Book: An Autobiography*. Knopf, 1980.
Hyams, Joe. *Bogie*. New American Library/Signet, 1966.
———, and Jay Hyams. *James Dean: Little Boy Lost*. Warner Books, 1992.
Infield, Glenn. *Leni Riefenstahl*. Thomas Y. Crowell, 1976.
Israel, Lee. *Miss Tallulah Bankhead*. G. P. Putnam's, 1972.
Jackson, Carlton. *Hattie*. Madison Books, 1990.
Jeffries, J. T. *Jessica Lange*. St. Martin's, 1986.
Jenkins, Garry. *Daniel Day-Lewis: The Fire Within*. St. Martin's, 1995.
Jennings, Dean. *We Only Kill Each Other*. Prentice-Hall, 1967.
Jerome, Stuart. *Those Crazy Wonderful Years When We Ran Warner Bros.*. Lyle Stuart, 1983.
Jordan, Rene. *The Greatest Star: The Barbra Streisand Story*. G. P. Putnam's, 1975.
Joyce, Aileen. *Julia: The Untold Story of America's Pretty Woman*. Pinnacle, 1993.
Kahn, E. J. *Jock: The Life and Times of John Hay Whitney*. Doubleday, 1981.
Kanin, Garson. *Hollywood*. Viking Press, 1974.
———. *Tracy and Hepburn: An Intimate Memoir*. Bantam, 1972.
Kashner, Sam, and Nancy Schoenberger. *A Talent for Genius: The Life and Times of Oscar Levant*. Villard Books, 1994.
Kazan, Elia. *A Life*. Knopf, 1988.
Keith, Slim, with Annette Tapert. *Slim: Memories of a Rich and Imperfect Life*. Simon and Schuster, 1990.
Kelley, Kitty. *Elizabeth Taylor: The Last Star*. Simon and Schuster, 1981.
———. *His Way: The Unauthorized Biography of Frank Sinatra*. Bantam, 1986.
———. *Jackie Oh!*. Ballantine, 1979.
———. *Nancy Reagan: The Unauthorized Biography*. Simon and Schuster, 1991.
Kendall, Alan. *George Gershwin*. Universe Books, 1987.
Kesting, Jürgen, translated by John Hunt. *Maria Callas*. Northeastern University Press, 1993.
Keyes, Evelyn. *I'll Think About That Tomorrow*. E. P. Dutton, 1991.
———. *Scarlett O'Hara's Younger Sister; or, My Lively Life In or Out of Hollywood*. Lyle Stuart, 1977.
Kiernan, Thomas. *Jane: An Intimate Biography of Jane Fonda*. G. P. Putnam's, 1973.
———. *Life and Times of Roman Polanski*. Grove, 1982.
———. *The Roman Polanski Story*. Grove, 1980.
———. *Sir Larry: The Life of Laurence Olivier*. Times Books, 1981.
Kirkpatrick, Sidney D. *A Cast of Killers*. E. P. Dutton, 1986.
Kissel, Howard. *David Merrick: The Abominable Showman*. Applause, 1993.
Kitt, Eartha. *Alone With Me*. Henry Regnery, 1976.
———. *Confessions of a Sex Kitten*. Barricade Books, 1991.
———. *Thursday's Child*. Duell, Sloan, & Pearce, 1956.

Klurfield, Herman. *Winchell: His Life and Times*. Praeger, 1976.
Kobal, John. *People Will Talk*. Knopf, 1985.
———. *Rita Hayworth: The Time, the Place and the Woman*. W. W. Norton, 1978.
Koch, Stephen. *Double Lives: Spies and Writers in the Secret Soviet War of Ideas Against the West*. Free Press, 1994.
Koffler, Kevin J. *The New Breed: Actors Coming of Age*. Henry Holt, 1988.
Konolige, Kit. *The Richest Women in the World*. Macmillan, 1985.
Korda, Michael. *Charmed Lives*. Random House, 1979.
Koszarski, Richard. *The Man You Loved to Hate*. Oxford University Press, 1983.
Kotsilibas-Davis, James. *The Barrymores: The Royal Family in Hollywood*. Crown, 1981.
———, and Myrna Loy. *Being and Becoming*. Knopf, 1987.
Kramer, Freda. *Jackie: A Truly Intimate Biography*. Grosset and Dunlap, 1979.
Kulik, Karol. *Alexander Korda: The Man Who Could Work Miracles*. Arlington House, 1975.
Lacey, Robert. *Grace*. G. P. Putnam's, 1994.
Laffey, Bruce. *Beatrice Lillie*. Wynwood Press, 1989.
LaGuardia, Robert. *Monty: A Biography of Montgomery Clift*. Arbor House, 1977.
———, and Gene Arceri. *Red: The Tempestuous Life of Susan Hayward*. MacMillan, 1985.
Lake, Veronica, with Donald Bain. *Veronica*. Citadel Press, 1971.
Lamarr, Hedy. *Ecstasy and Me: My Life as a Woman*. Bartholomew, 1966.
Lambert, Gavin. *Norma Shearer*. Knopf, 1990.
Lamour, Dorothy. *My Side of the Road,* as told to Dick McInnes. Prentice-Hall, 1980.
Lamparski, Richard. *Whatever Became of . . . ?* (Second series). Crown, 1968.
Landau, Deborah. *Janis Joplin: Her Life and Times*. Paperback Library, 1971.
Latham, Aaron. *Crazy Sundays: F. Scott Fitzgerald in Hollywood*. Viking, 1971.
Lawford, Patricia S. *The Peter Lawford Story*. Carroll and Graf, 1988.
Lawrence, Jerome. *Actor: The Life and Times of Paul Muni*. G. P. Putnam's, 1974.
Lax, Eric. *Woody Allen*. Knopf, 1991.
Leamer, Laurence. *The Kennedy Women*. Villard Books, 1994.
———. *The King of the Night*. William Morrow, 1989.
Leaming, Barbara. *Bette Davis: A Biography*. Summit Books, 1992.
———. *If This Was Happiness*. Viking, 1989.
———. *Katharine Hepburn*. Crown, 1995.
———. *Orson Welles*. Viking, 1985.
———. *Polanski, the Filmmaker as Voyeur*. Simon and Schuster, 1982.
Lee, Jennifer. *Tarnished Angel*. Thunder's Mouth Press, 1991.
Leigh, Janet. *There Really Was a Hollywood*. Doubleday, 1984.
Leigh, Wendy. *Arnold*. Congdon and Weed, 1990.

———. *Liza: Born a Star*. E. P. Dutton, 1993.
———. *Prince Charming: The John F. Kennedy, Jr. Story*. E. P. Dutton, 1993.
Lenburg, Jeff. *Dustin Hoffman: Hollywood's Antihero*. St. Martin's, 1983.
———. *Peekaboo: The Story of Veronica Lake*. St. Martin's, 1983.
———, Greg Lenburg, and Randy Skretvedt. *Steve Martin: The Unauthorized Biography*. St. Martin's, 1980.
Leonard, Maurice. *Mae West: Empress of Sex*. Birch Lane, 1992.
LeRoy, Mervyn. *Mervyn LeRoy: Take One*. Hawthorne Books, 1984.
Levy, Emanuel. *George Cukor: Master of Elegance*. William Morrow, 1994.
Lewis, Arthur H. *It Was Fun While It Lasted*. Trident Press, 1973.
Lewis, Judy. *Uncommon Knowledge*. Simon and Schuster, 1994.
Linet, Beverly. *Ladd*. Arbor House, 1979.
———. *Star-Crossed: The Story of Jennifer Jones and Robert Walker*. G. P. Putnam's, 1986.
———. *Susan Hayward: Portrait of a Survivor*. Atheneum, 1980.
Loos, Anita. *A Girl Like I*. Viking, 1966.
———. *The Talmadge Girls*. Viking, 1978.
Lovelace, Linda, and Mike McGrady. *Ordeal*. Berkley, 1980.
McAdams, William. *Ben Hecht*. Scribner's, 1990.
McBride, Mary Margaret. *The Life Story of Constance Bennett*. Star Library Publications, 1932.
McCabe, John. *Babe: The Life of Oliver Hardy*. Citadel Press, 1989.
McClelland, Doug. *Hollywood on Hollywood: Tinseltown Talks*. Faber and Faber, 1975.
———. *Star Speak: Hollywood on Everything*, Faber and Faber, 1987.
McGilligan, Patrick. *A Double Life: George Cukor*. St. Martin's, 1991.
———. *Jack's Life: A Biography of Jack Nicholson*. W. W. Norton, 1994.
McGovern, Dennis, and Deborah Grace Winer. *Sing Out, Louise!* Schirmer/Macmillan, 1993.
MacGraw, Ali. *Moving Pictures*. Bantam, 1991.
Machlin, Milt. *Libby*. Tower Publications, 1980.
McKay, Keith. *Robert DeNiro: The Hero Behind the Masks*. St. Martin's, 1986.
McKelway, Claire. *Gossip: The Life and Times of Walter Winchell*. Viking, 1940.
MacLaine, Shirley. *My Lucky Stars*. Bantam, 1995.
Madden, Nelson C. *The Real Howard Hughes Story*. Manor, 1976.
Madsen, Axel. *Chanel: A Woman of Her Own*. Henry Holt, 1990.
———. *Gloria and Joe*. Arbor House, 1988.
———. *John Huston: A Biography*. Doubleday, 1978.
———. *The Sewing Circle*. Birch Lane, 1995.
———. *Stanwyck*. HarperCollins, 1994.
———, and William Wyler. *William Wyler*. Thomas Y. Crowell, 1973.
Mailer, Norman. *Marilyn: A Biography*. Grosset and Dunlap, 1973.
Mair, George. *Oprah Winfrey: The Real Story*. Birch Lane, 1994.
Mannering, Derek. *Mario Lanza*. Robert Hale, 1991.

Mansfield, Stephanie. *The Richest Girl in the World.* G. P. Putnam's, 1992.
Manso, Peter. *Brando: The Biography.* Hyperion, 1994.
Martin, Mary. *My Heart Belongs.* Quill, 1984.
Martin, Pete. *Hollywood Without Make-Up.* J. B. Lippincott, 1948.
Marx, Arthur. *Everybody Loves Somebody Sometime (Especially Himself).* Hawthorne, 1974.
———. *The Nine Lives of Mickey Rooney.* Stein and Day, 1986.
———. *Red Skelton.* E. P. Dutton, 1979.
———. *The Secret Life of Bob Hope.* Barricade Books, 1993.
Marx, Samuel. *A Gaudy Spree: Literary Hollywood When the West Was Fun.* Franklin Watts, 1987.
———. *Mayer and Thalberg: The Make-Believe Saints.* Random House, 1975.
Maychick, Diana. *Audrey Hepburn: An Intimate Portrait.* Birch Lane, 1993.
———. *Meryl Streep.* St. Martin's, 1984.
———, and L. Avon Borgo. *Heart to Heart With Robert Wagner.* St. Martin's, 1986.
Meade, Marion. *Dorothy Parker: What Fresh Hell Is This?* Villard Books, 1988.
Meredith, Burgess. *So Far, So Good.* Little, Brown, 1994.
Merrill, Gary, and John Cole. *Bette, Rita and the Rest of My Life.* Lance Tapley, 1988.
Meyers, Jeffrey. *Scott Fitzgerald.* HarperCollins, 1994.
Milland, Ray. *Wide-Eyed in Babylon.* William Morrow, 1974.
Miller, Ann, with Norma Lee Browning. *Miller's High Life.* Doubleday, 1972.
Minnelli, Vincente, with Hector Arce. *I Remember It Well.* Doubleday, 1974.
Mix, Olive Stokes. *The Fabulous Tom Mix.* Prentice-Hall, 1975.
Mix, Paul E. *The Life and Legend of Tom Mix.* A. S. Barnes, 1972.
Moats, Alice-Leone. *The Million Dollar Studs.* Delacorte, 1977.
Montgomery, Paul L. *Eva, Evita.* Pocket Books, 1979.
Moore, Terry. *The Beauty and the Billionaire.* Pocket Books, 1984.
Mordden, Ethan. *Movie Star: A Look at the Women Who Made Hollywood.* St. Martin's, 1983.
Morella, Joe. *Paul and Joanne: A Biography of Paul Newman and Joanne Woodward.* Delacorte, 1988.
———. *The "It" Girl: The Incredible Story of Clara Bow.* Delacorte, 1976.
———. *Jane Wyman.* Delacorte, 1985.
———. *Lana: The Public and Private Lives of Miss Turner.* Citadel Press, 1971.
———. *Loretta Young: An Extraordinary Life.* Delacorte, 1986.
———. *Mia: The Life of Mia Farrow.* Delacorte, 1991.
———. *Paulette: The Adventurous Life of Paulette Goddard.* St. Martin's, 1985.
———, and Edward Z. Epstein. *Brando: The Unauthorized Biography.* Crown, 1973.
Morgan, Henry. *Here's Morgan.* Barricade Books, 1995.
Morley, Sheridan. *Gertrude Lawrence.* McGraw-Hill, 1981.

———. *James Mason: Odd Man Out.* Harper and Row, 1989.
———. *The Other Side of the Moon.* Harper and Row, 1983.
Morris, George. *John Garfield.* Jove, 1977.
Moseley, Leonard. *Zanuck.* Little, Brown, 1984.
Moseley, Roy. *Rex Harrison.* St. Martin's, 1987.
Mungo, Ray. *Palm Springs Babylon.* St. Martin's, 1993.
Munn, Michael. *Charlton Heston.* St. Martin's, 1986.
———. *The Hollywood Murder Casebook.* St. Martin's, 1987.
———. *The Kid From the Bronx: A Biography of Tony Curtis.* W. H. Allen, 1984.
———. *Kirk Douglas.* St. Martin's, 1985.
Munshower, Suzanne. *The Diane Keaton Scrapbook.* Grosset and Dunlap, 1979.
———. *Don Johnson: An Unauthorized Biography.* Signet/NAL 1986.
———. *John Travolta.* Grosset and Dunlap, 1976.
Naremore, James. *The Films of Vincente Minnelli.* Cambridge University Press, 1993.
Nash, Alana, with Billy Smith, Marty Lacker, and Lamar Fike. *Elvis Aaron Presley.* HarperCollins, 1995.
Neal, Patricia. *As I Am.* Simon and Schuster, 1988.
Negri, Pola. *Memoirs of a Star.* Doubleday, 1970.
Negulesco, Jean. *Things I Did and Things I Think I Did.* Simon and Schuster, 1984.
Newman, Phyllis. *Just in Time: Notes From My Life.* Simon and Schuster, 1988.
Niven, David. *Bring on the Empty Horses.* G. P. Putnam's, 1975.
———. *The Moon's a Balloon.* Coronet, 1971.
Norman, Barry. *The Film Greats.* Hodder and Staughton, 1985.
Odets, Clifford. *The Time Is Ripe: The 1940 Journal of Clifford Odets.* Grove, 1988.
Offen, Ron. *Cagney.* Regnery, 1972.
Ogdon, Christopher. *Life of the Party.* Little, Brown, 1994.
Onyx, Narda. *Water, World and Weissmuller.* Vion Publishing, 1964.
Oppenheimer, Jerry, and Jack Vitek. *Idol: Rock Hudson.* Villard Books, 1986.
Oremano, Elena. *Paul Newman.* St. Martin's, 1989.
Outerbridge, James. *Without Makeup, Liv Ullman: A Photobiography.* William Morrow, 1979.
Papich, Stephen. *Remembering Josephine.* Bobs-Merrill, 1976.
Paris, Barry. *Garbo.* Knopf, 1995.
———. *Louise Brooks.* Knopf, 1989.
Parish, James Robert. *The Fox Girls.* Arlington House, 1971.
———. *The Glamour Girls.* Rainbow Books, 1977.
———. *Great Western Stars.* Ace Books, 1976.
———. *The Hollywood Beauties.* Arlington House, 1978.
———. *The Hollywood Reliables.* Arlington House, 1980.
———. *The Jeanette MacDonald Story.* Mason/Charter, 1976.

———. *The Paramount Pretties.* Castle Books, 1972.
———. *The RKO Gals.* Rainbow Books, 1977.
———. *The Swashbucklers.* Arlington House, 1976.
———. *The Tough Guys.* Arlington House, 1976.
———, and Ronald L. Bowers. *The MGM Stock Company: The Golden Years.* Arlington House, 1973.
———, and Lennard DeCarl. *Hollywood Players: The Forties.* Arlington House, 1976.
———, and William T. Leonard. *The Funsters.* Arlington House, 1979.
———, and Don E. Stanke. *The Debonairs.* Arlington House, 1975.
———. *The Forties Gals.* Arlington House, 1980.
———. *The Leading Ladies.* Arlington House, 1977.
———, and Steven Whitney. *Vincent Price Unmasked.* Drake, 1974.
Parker, John. *Warren Beatty: The Last Great Lover of Hollywood.* Carroll and Graf, 1993.
Parton, Dolly. *Dolly: My Life and Other Unfinished Business.* HarperCollins, 1994.
Passingham, Kenneth. *Sean Connery.* St. Martin's, 1983.
Pastos, Spero. *Pin-Up: The Story of Betty Grable.* G. P. Putnam's, 1986.
Payn, Graham. *My Life With Noel Coward.* Applause, 1994
Peary, Danny. *Closeups.* Workman, 1978.
Pepitone, Lena, and William Stadiem. *Marilyn Monroe Confidential.* Simon and Schuster, 1979.
Peters, Margot. *The Barrymores.* Knopf, 1990.
Peyser, Joan. *Bernstein: A Biography.* Ballantine, 1988.
———. *The Memory of All That.* Simon and Schuster, 1993.
Pickard, Roy. *Jimmy Stewart: A Life in Film.* St. Martin's, 1992.
Pierce, Patrica Jobe. *The Ultimate Elvis: Day By Day.* Simon and Schuster, 1994.
Poitier, Sidney. *This Life.* Knopf, 1980.
Polanski, Roman. *Roman.* William Morrow, 1984.
Powell, Jane. *The Girl Next Door.* William Morrow, 1988.
Quinn, Anthony. *One Man Tango.* HarperCollins, 1995.
———. *The Original Sin.* Little, Brown, 1972.
Quirk, Lawrence J. *Claudette Colbert.* Crown, 1985.
———. *Fasten Your Seat Belts: The Passionate Life of Bette Davis.* William Morrow, 1990.
———. *The Films of Fredric March.* Citadel Press, 1971.
———. *Jane Wyman: The Actress and the Woman.* Dembner Books, 1986.
———. *Margaret Sullavan: Child of Fate.* St. Martin's, 1986.
———. *Norma.* St. Martin's, 1988.
———. *Totally Uninhibited: The Life and Wild Time of Cher.* William Morrow, 1991.
Ramer, Jean. *Duke: The Real Story of John Wayne.* Universal Award House, 1973.
Rasponi, Lanfranco. *International Nomads.* G. P. Putnam's, 1966.

Rathbone, Basil. *In and Out of Character*. Doubleday, 1962.
Reagan, Ronald, and Richard G. Hubler. *Where's the Rest of Me?*. Karz Publishers, 1981.
Redgrave, Deidre, with Danaë Brook. *To Be a Redgrave: Surviving Amidst the Glamour*. The Linden Press/Simon and Schuster, 1982.
Reed, Donald A. *Robert Redford*. Sherbourne Press, 1976.
Reed, Oliver. *Reed About Me*. W. H. Allen, 1979.
Reed, Rex. *Conversations in the Raw*. World Publishing Company, 1969.
———. *Do You Sleep in the Nude?* New American Library, 1968.
———. *People Are Crazy Here*. Delacorte, 1974.
———. *Travolta to Keaton*. William Morrow, 1979.
———. *Valentines and Vitriol*. Delacorte, 1977.
Reeves, Richard. *President Kennedy: Profile of Power*. Simon and Schuster, 1993.
Renay, Liz. *My First 2,000 Men*. Barricade Books, 1992.
Resnick, Sylvia S. *Burt Reynolds: An Unauthorized Biography*. St. Martin's, 1983.
Reynolds, Burt. *My Life*. Little, Brown, 1994.
Reynolds, Debbie, and David Patrick Columbia. *Debbie: My Life*. William Morrow, 1988.
Rich, Sharon. *Sweethearts*. Donald I. Fine, 1994.
Richards, David. *Played Out: The Jean Seberg Story*. Random House, 1981.
Richman, Harry. *A Hell of a Life*. Duell, Sloan and Pearce, 1966.
Riefenstahl, Leni. *A Memoir*. St. Martin's, 1992.
Riese, Randall. *Her Name Is Barbra*. Birch Lane, 1993.
———. *The Unabridged Marilyn: Her Life from A to Z*. Congdon and Weed, 1987.
Riley, Lee. *Teen Dreams; Tom Cruise*. Pinnacle, 1985.
———, and David Shumacher. *The Sheens: Martin, Charlie and Emilio*. St. Martin's, 1989.
Riva, Maria. *Marlene Dietrich*. Knopf, 1993.
Rivkin, Allen, and Laura Kerr. *Hello, Hollywood*. Doubleday, 1962.
Robbins, Jhan. *Yul Brynner: The Inscrutable King*. Dodd, Mead, 1987.
Robertson, James C. *The Casablanca Man: The Cinema of Michael Curtiz*. Routledge, 1993.
Robinson, Edward G., with Leonard Spigelgass. *All My Yesterdays,* Hawthorn Books, 1973.
Rodriguez, Elena. *Dennis Hopper: A Madness to His Method*. St. Martin's, 1988.
Rogers, Ginger. *Ginger: My Story*. HarperCollins, 1991.
Rollyson, Carl. *Lillian Hellman: Her Legend and Her Legacy*. St. Martin, 1989.
Rooney, Mickey. *Life Is Too Short*. Villard Books, 1991.
Rosen, Majorie. *Popcorn Venus*. Coward, McCann and Geoghegan, 1973.
Rovin, Jeff. *Stallone! A Hero's Story*. Pocket Books, 1985.
———. *TV Babylon*. Signet, 1987.
Rubin, Sam, and Richard Taylor. *Mia Farrow: Flower Child, Madonna, Muse*. St. Martin's, 1989.

Russell, Jane. *Jane Russell: My Path and Detours.* Franklin Watts, 1985.
Russell, Ken. *Altered States.* Bantam, 1982.
———. *A British Picture: An Autobiography.* William Heinemann, 1989.
Sanders, Coyne Steven. *Rainbow's End: The Judy Garland Show.* Zebra Books, 1992.
Sandford, Christopher. *Mick Jagger: Primitive Cool.* St. Martin's, 1993.
Saroyan, Aram. *Trio.* Linden Press/Simon and Schuster, 1985.
Satchell, Tim. *Astaire.* Hutchinson, 1987.
Saxton, Martha. *Jayne Mansfield and the American Fifties.* Houghton-Mifflin, 1975.
Schanke, Robert A. *Shattered Applause: The Lives of Eva Le Gallienne.* Southern Illinois University, 1992.
Scott, Michael. *Maria Meneghini Callas.* Northeastern University Press, 1991.
Seagrave, Kerry. *Politicans' Passions.* S.P.I. Books, 1992.
———, and Martin, Linda. *The Continental Actress.* McFarland, 1990.
Scaly, Shirley. *The Celebrity Sex Register.* Simon and Schuster, 1982.
Seay, Davin. *Mick Jagger: The Story Behind the Rolling Stone.* Birch Lane, 1993.
Segaloff, Nat. *Hurricane Billy.* William Morrow, 1990.
Segrest, Meryle. *Leonard Bernstein: A Life.* Knopf, 1994.
Sellers, Michael, with Sarah and Victoria Sellers. *P.S. I Love You.* Collins, 1981.
Selznick, Irene Mayer. *A Private View.* Knopf, 1983.
Servadio, Gaia. *Luchino Viscounti: A Biography.* Weidenfeld and Nicolson, 1982.
Seward, Ingrid. *Royal Children.* St. Martin's, 1993.
Sharif, Omar, and Marie-Thérèse Guinchard. *The Eternal Male: My Own Story.* Doubleday, 1977.
Shaw, Artie. *The Trouble With Cinderella.* Farrar Straus and Young, 1952.
Shevey, Sandra. *The Marilyn Scandal.* William Morrow, 1988.
Shepherd, Donald. *Duke: The Life and Times of John Wayne.* Doubleday, 1985.
———, and Robert F. Slatzer. *Bing Crosby: The Hollow Man.* St. Martin's, 1981.
Shepherd, Jack. *Jack Nicholson.* St. Martin's, 1991.
Shipman, David. *The Great Movie Stars: The Golden Years.* Bonanza Books, 1970.
———. *The Great Movie Stars: The International Years.* St. Martin's, 1972.
———. *Judy Garland: The Secret Life of an American Legend.* Hyperion, 1993.
———. *Movie Talk.* St. Martin's, 1988.
Shulman, Irving. *Harlow: An Intimate Biography.* Random House, 1964.
———. *Valentino.* Trident Press, 1967.
Siciliano, Enzo. *Pasolini.* Random House, 1982.
Simpson, Col. Harold B. *Audie Murphy: American Soldier.* Hill Junior College, 1975.

Sinclair, Andrew. *Spiegel: The Man Behind the Movies*. Little, Brown, 1987.
Singer, Kurt. *The Charles Laughton Story*. Winston, 1976.
Sklar, Robert. *City Boys*. Princeton University, 1992.
Skolsky, Sidney. *Don't Get Me Wrong, I Love Hollywood*. G. P. Putnam's, 1975.
Slater, Leonard. *Aly*. Random House, 1965.
Slide, Anthony. *Great Pretenders*. Wallace-Homestead, 1986.
Smith, Bruce. *Costly Performance—Tennessee Williams: The Last Stage*. Paragon House, 1990.
Smith, R. Dixon. *Ronald Colman, Gentleman of the Cinema*. McFarland, 1991.
Smith, Ronald L. *Johnny Carson*. St. Martin's, 1987.
Smith, Sally Bedell. *In All His Glory: The Life of William S. Paley*. Simon and Schuster, 1990.
Spada, James. *Grace: The Secret Lives of a Princess*. Doubleday, 1987.
———. *More Than a Woman*. Bantam Books, 1993.
———. *Peter Lawford: The Man Who Kept the Secrets*. Bantam, 1991.
———. *Streisand: The Woman and the Legend*. Doubleday, 1981.
Speigel, Penina. *McQueen: Untold Story of a Bad Boy in Hollywood*. Doubleday, 1986.
Sperling, Cass Warner, and Cork Millner with Jack Warner Jr. *Hollywood Be Thy Name*. Prima Publishing, 1994.
Spoto, Donald. *Blue Angel: The Life of Marlene Dietrich*. Doubleday, 1992.
———. *The Kindness of Strangers: The Life of Tennessee Williams*. Little, Brown, 1985.
———. *Laurence Olivier: A Biography*. HarperCollins, 1992.
———. *Madcap: The Life of Preston Sturges*. Little, Brown, 1990.
———. *Marilyn Monroe: A Biography*. HarperCollins, 1993.
———. *A Passion for Life*. HarperCollins, 1995.
Stack, Robert, with Mark Evans. *Strait Shooting*. Macmillan, 1980.
Stadiem, William. *Too Rich: The High Life and Tragic Death of King Farouk*. Carroll and Graf, 1991.
Stallings, Penny. *Flesh and Fantasy*. St. Martin's, 1978.
Stassinopoulos, Arianna. *Maria Callas: The Woman Behind the Legend*. Simon and Schuster, 1981.
Steel, Dawn. *They Can Kill You, But They Can't Eat You*. Pocket Books, 1993.
Stenn, David. *Bombshell: The Life and Death of Jean Harlow*. Doubleday, 1993.
———. *Clara Bow: Runnin' Wild*. Doubleday, 1988.
Stine, Whitney. *Stars and Star Handlers*. Roundtable, 1985.
Stirling, Monica. *A Screen of Time: A Study of Luchino Viscounti*. Harcourt, Brace, 1979.
St. Johns, Adela Rogers. *Love, Laughter and Tears: My Hollywood Story*. Doubleday, 1978.
Strait, Raymond. *The Tragic Secret Life of Jayne Mansfield*. Henry Regnery, 1974.

———, and Leif Henie. *Queen of Ice, Queen of Shadows: The Unsuspected Life of Sonja Henie*. Stein and Day, 1985.
———, and Terry Robinson. *Lanza: His Tragic Life*. Prentice-Hall, 1980.
Strasberg, Susan. *Bittersweet*. G. P. Putnam's, 1980.
———. *Marilyn and Me*. Warner Books, 1992.
Stuart, Otis. *Perpetual Motion: The Public and Private Lives of Rudolph Nureyev*. Simon and Schuster, 1995.
Swanson, Gloria. *Swanson on Swanson*. Random House, 1980.
Swindell, Larry. *Body and Soul: The Story of John Garfield*. William Morrow, 1975.
———. *Charles Boyer: The Reluctant Lover*. Doubleday, 1983.
———. *Screwball: The Life of Carole Lombard*. William Morrow, 1975.
Taraborrelli, Randy. *Call Her Miss Ross*. Carol Publishing, 1989.
———. *Michael Jackson: The Magic and the Madness*. Ballantine, 1991.
Taylor, Robert Lewis. *W. C. Fields: His Follies and Fortunes*. Doubleday, 1967.
Terrill, Marshall. *Steve McQueen*. Donald I. Fine, 1993.
Theodoracopulos, Taki. *Princes, Playboys and High-Class Tarts*. Karz-Cohl, 1984.
Thomas, Bob. *Clown Prince of Hollywood*. McGraw-Hill, 1990.
———. *Golden Boy: The Untold Story of William Holden*. St. Martin's, 1983.
———. *I Got Rhythm: The Ethel Merman Story*. G. P. Putnam's, 1985.
———. *Joan Crawford: A Biography*. Simon and Schuster, 1978.
———. *King Cohn*. G. P. Putnam's, 1967.
———. *Liberace*. St. Martin's, 1987.
———. *Marlon, Portrait of the Rebel as an Artist*. Random House, 1966.
———. *Thalberg: Life and Legend*. Doubleday, 1969.
———. *Winchell*. Doubleday, 1971.
Thomas, Tony. *The Dick Powell Story*. Riverwood Press, 1993.
Thompson, Douglas. *Clint Eastwood: Riding High*. Smith Gryphon, 1992.
Thompson, Verita, with Donald Shepherd. *Bogie and Me*. St. Martin's, 1982.
Thomson, David. *Showman*. Knopf, 1992.
———. *Warren Beatty and Desert Eyes: A Life and a Story*. Doubleday, 1987.
Thorson, Scott, with Alex Thorleifson. *Behind the Candelabra: My Life With Liberace*. E. P. Dutton, 1988.
Tierney, Gene. *Gene Tierney: Self-Portrait*. Wyden Books, 1979.
Todd, Ann. *The Eighth Veil*. G. P. Putnam's, 1981.
Todd Jr., Michael. *A Valuable Property*. Arbor House, 1983.
Toffel, Neile McQueen. *My Husband, My Friend*. Atheneum, 1986.
Tonetti, Claretta. *Luchino Viscounti*. Twayne Publishers, 1983.
Tormé, Mel. *It Wasn't All Velvet*. Viking Penguin, 1988.
Tornabene, Lyn. *Long Live the King: A Biography of Clark Gable*. G. P. Putnam's, 1975.
Toshes, Nick. *Dino: Living High in the Dirty Business*. Doubleday, 1992.
Turner, Lana. *Lana: The Lady, the Legend, the Truth*. E. P. Dutton, 1982.
Tynan, Kathleen. *Tynan*. William Morrow, 1987.
Ullman, Liv. *Changing*. Knopf, 1977.

———. *Choices*. Knopf, 1985.
Vadim, Roger. *Bardot, Deneuve, Fonda*. Simon and Schuster, 1986.
———. *Memoirs of the Devil*. Harcourt Brace, 1975.
Valentine, Tom, and Patrick Mahn. *Daddy's Duchess*. Lyle Stuart, 1987.
Vallée, Rudy. *Let the Chips Fall . . .* Stackpole Books, 1975.
———, and Gil McKean. *My Time Is Your Time*. Ivan Obolensky, 1962.
Van Doren, Mamie. *Playing the Field: My Story*. G. P. Putnam's, 1987.
Van Gelder, Peter. *That's Hollywood*. HarperCollins, 1990.
Van Rensselear, Philip. *Million Dollar Baby: An Intimate Portrait of Barbara Hutton*. G. P. Putnam's, 1979.
VanDerBeet, Richard. *George Sanders: An Exhausted Life*. Madison Books, 1990.
Vanderbilt, Gloria. *Black Knight, White Knight*. Knopf, 1987.
Vermilye, Jerry. *Ida Lupino*. Pyramid Publications, 1977.
Vickers, Hugo. *Cecil Beaton*. Little, Brown, 1985.
———. *Loving Garbo*. Random House, 1994.
———. *Vivien Leigh*, 1978.
Vidor, King. *King Vidor on Film Making*. David McKay, 1972.
———. *A Tree Is a Tree*. Harcourt, Brace, 1953.
Wagner, Walter. *You Must Remember This*. G. P. Putnam's, 1975.
Walker, Alexander. *Fatal Charm*. St. Martin's, 1992.
———. *Garbo: A Portrait*. Macmillan, 1980.
———. *Peter Sellers*. Macmillan, 1981.
———. *Rudolph Valentino*. Stein and Day, 1976.
———, ed. *No Bells on Sunday: The Rachel Roberts Journals*. Harper and Row, 1984.
Wallace, Irving, et. al. *Intimate Sex Lives of Famous People*. Delacorte, 1981.
Wallis, Hal, and Charles Higham. *Starmaker*. Macmillan, 1980.
Walsh, Raoul. *Every Man in His Time*. Farrar, Straus and Giroux, 1974.
Wansell, Geoffrey. *Haunted Idol: The Story of the Real Cary Grant*. William Morrow, 1983.
Wapshott, Nicholas. *Peter O'Toole*. Beaufort Books, 1983.
Warhol, Andy. *The Andy Warhol Diaries*. Warner Books, 1989.
Warner, Jack L., with Dean Jennings. *My First 100 Years in Hollywood*. Random House, 1965.
Warren, Doug. *Betty Grable: The Reluctant Movie Queen*. St. Martin's, 1981.
Waters, John. *Shock Value*. Dell, 1981.
Waterbury, Ruth. *Richard Burton: His Intimate Story*. Pyramid Books, 1965.
Wayne, Jane Ellen. *Ava's Men*. Prentice Hall, 1990.
———. *Clark Gable: Portrait of a Misfit*. St. Martin's, 1993.
———. *Cooper's Women*. Prentice Hall, 1988.
———. *Crawford's Men*. Prentice Hall, 1988.
———. *Gable's Women*. Prentice Hall, 1987.
———. *Grace Kelly's Men*. St. Martin's, 1991.
———. *Marilyn's Men*. St. Martin's, 1992.

———. *Robert Taylor: The Man With the Perfect Face.* St. Martin's, 1973, 1987.
———. *Stanwyck.* Arbor House, 1985.
Weddle, David. *If they Move . . . Kill 'Em!: The Life and Times of Sam Peckinpah.* Grove, 1994.
Weiss, Murray, and Bill Hoffman. *Palm Beach Babylon.* Birch Lane, 1992.
West, Mae. *Goodness Had Nothing to Do With It.* Bernarr McFadden, 1970.
Westmore, Frank, and Muriel Davidson. *The Westmores of Hollywood.* J. B. Lippincott, 1976.
White, Carol, with Clifford Harlow. *Carol Comes Home.* New English Library, 1982.
Wilk, Max, ed. *The Wit and Wisdom of Hollywood.* Atheneum, 1971.
Wilkie, Jane. *Confessions of an Ex-Fan Magazine Writer.* Doubleday, 1981.
Williams, John A., and Dennis A. Williams. *If I Stop I'll Die: The Comedy and Tragedy of Richard Pryor.* Thunder's Mouth Press, 1991.
Wilson, Earl. *I Am Gazing Into My 8-Ball.* Doubleday, 1945.
———. *Let 'Em Eat Cheesecake.* Doubleday, 1949.
———. *Show Business Laid Bare.* G. P. Putnam's, 1974.
———. *Sinatra: An Unauthorized Biography.* Macmillan, 1976.
Winchell, Walter. *Winchell Exclusive.* Prentice-Hall, 1975.
Windeler, Robert. *Julie Andrews.* St. Martin's, 1983.
———. *Burt Lancaster.* St. Martin's, 1984.
Winters, Shelley. *Shelley . . . Also Known as Shirley.* William Morrow, 1980.
———. *Shelley II: The Middle of My Century.* Simon and Schuster, 1989.
Wolfe, Jane. *Blood Rich: When Oil Billions, High Fashions and Royal Intimacies Are Not Enough.* Little, Brown, 1993.
Worrell, Denice. *Icons.* Atlantic Monthly Press, 1989.
Wray, Fay. *On the Other Hand.* St. Martin's, 1989.
Wright, William. *All the Pain That Money Can Buy.* Simon and Schuster, 1991.
———. *Heiress.* New Republic Books, 1978.
———. *Lillian Hellman: The Image, the Woman.* Simon and Schuster, 1986.
Yablonsky, Lewis. *George Raft.* McGraw-Hill, 1974.
Yule, Andrew. *Life on the Wire.* Donald I. Fine, 1991.
———. *Picture Shows.* Limelight Editions, 1992.
———. *Sean Connery.* Donald I. Fine, 1992.
Zec, Donald. *Marvin: The Story of Lee Marvin.* St. Martin's, 1980.
———. *Some Enchanted Egos.* Allison and Busby, 1972.
Zetterling, Mai. *All Those Tomorrows.* Grove, 1986.
Ziegfeld, Patricia. *The Ziegfelds' Girl: Confessions of an Abnormally Happy Childhood.* Little, Brown, 1964.
Zierold, Norman. *The Moguls: Hollywood's Merchants of Myth.* Silman-James Press, 1991.
———. *Sex Goddesses of the Silent Screen.* Regnery, 1973.
Zolotow, Maurice. *Shooting Star: A Biography of John Wayne.* Simon and Schuster, 1974.
Zorina, Vera. *Zorina.* Farrar, Straus and Giroux, 1986.

Film Genre, Film Reference, Miscellaneous

Balio, Tino. *United Artists: The Company That Changed the Film Industry*. University of Wisconsin Press, 1987.

Bell-Metereau, Rebecca. *Hollywood Androgyny*. Columbia University Press, 1985.

Bergan, Ronald. *Sports in the Movies*. Proteus Books, 1982.

Bova, Damien. *Opening Shots*. Workman Publishing, 1994.

Caine, Michael. *Michael Caine's Moving Picture Show*. St. Martin's, 1988.

Colombo, John Robert, ed. *Popcorn in Paradise*. Hall, Rinehart and Wilson, 1979.

Da, Lottie and Jan Alexander. *Bad Girls of the Silver Screen*. Carroll and Graf Publishers, 1989.

Dyer, Richard. *Heavenly Bodies: Film Stars and Society*. St. Martin's, 1986.

Eastman, John. *Retakes: Behind the Scenes of 500 Classic Movies*. Ballantine Books, 1989.

Elley, Derek. *The Epic Film: Myth and History*. Routledge and Kegan Paul, 1984.

Erens, Patricia. *The Jew in American Cinema*. Indiana University Press, 1984.

Farber, Stephen, and Marc Green. *Hollywood on the Couch*. William Morrow, 1993.

Gifford, Barry. *The Devil Thumbs a Ride*. Grove, 1988.

Gordon, William A. *The Ultimate Hollywood Tour Book*. NorthRidge Books, 1992.

Green, Abel, and Joe Laurie, Jr. *Show Biz: From Vaude to Video*. Kennikat Press, 1972.

Haberman, J., and Jonathan Rosenblum. *Midnight Movies*. Harper and Row, 1973.

Hadley-Garcia, George. *Hispanic Hollywood*. Citadel Press, 1993.

Hardy, Phil, ed. *The Encyclopedia of Horror Movies*. Harper and Row, 1986.

Harmetz, Aljean. *Rolling Breaks and Other Movie Business*. Knopf, 1983.

———. *Round Up the Usual Suspects*. Hyperion, 1992.

Haskell, Molly. *From Reverence to Rape*. Holt, Rinehart and Winston, 1973.

Katz, Ephraim. *The Film Encyclopedia*, 2d ed. HarperCollins, 1994.

Kessler, Judy. *Inside People*. Villard Books, 1994.

Koski, John, and Mitchell Symons. *Movielists*. Chapmans, 1992.

Lamparski, Richard. *Lamparski's Hidden Hollywood*. Simon and Schuster, 1981.

Lenne, Gerard. *Sex on the Screen: Eroticism in Film*. St. Martin's, 1975.

Malone, Michael. *Heroes of Eros*. E. P. Dutton, 1979.

Maltin, Leonard, ed. *Leonard Maltin's TV Movies and Video Guide*. NAL Penguin, 1988, 1989, 1990, 1991, 1992, 1993.

Marsh, Dave, and James Bernard. *The New Book of Rock Lists*. Fireside, 1994.

McDonald, Boyd. *Cruising the Movies*. Gay Presses of New York, 1985.

Marx, Kenneth S. *Star Stats: Who's Whose in Hollywood*. Price/Stern/Sloan, 1979.

Mellen, Joan. *Big Bad Wolves: Masculinity in the American Film.* Pantheon Books, 1977.
Monaco, James. *American Film Now.* New American Library, 1984.
Peary, Danny. *Guide for the Film Fanatic.* Simon and Schuster, 1986.
Phillips, Baxter. *Cut: The Unseen Cinema.* Bounty Books, 1975.
Pickard, Roy. *Who Played Who in the Movies.* Schocken Books, 1981.
Poundstone, William. *Biggest Secrets.* William Morrow, 1993.
Queenan, Joe. *If You're Talking to Me, Your Career Must Be in Trouble.* Hyperion, 1994.
Reed, Rex. *Big Screen, Little Screen.* Macmillan, 1971.
Robertson, Patrick. *Guiness Film Facts and Feats.* Sterling, 1994.
Russo, Vito. *The Celluloid Closet,* Harper and Row, 1981; rev. ed. 1987.
Rutledge, Leigh W. *The Gay Book of Lists.* Alyson Publications, 1987.
Sagin, Seth, and Philip Dray. *Hollywood Films of the Seventies.* Harper and Row, 1984.
Schatz, Thomas. *The Genius of the System: Hollywood Filmmaking in the Studio Era.* Pantheon Books, 1988.
Sinclair, Marianne. *Hollywood Lolitas.* Henry Holt, 1988.
Story, David. *America on the Rerun: Television Shows that Never Die.* Citadel Press, 1994.
Taki, and Jeffrey Bernard. *High Life—Low Life.* Jay Landesman, 1981.
Turan, Kenneth, and Stephen F. Zito. *Sinema.* Praeger, 1974.
Walker, Alexander. *It's Only a Movie, Ingrid: Encounters On and Off Screen.* Headline Book, 1988.
Wilkerson, Tichi, and Marcia Borie. *Hollywood Legends: The Golden Years of the Hollywood Reporter.* Tale Weaver, 1988.
Wood, Robin. *Hollywood: From Vietnam to Reagan.* Columbia University Press, 1986.

Newspapers, Periodicals

Celebrity Sleuth
Los Angeles Times
Movieline
Newsweek
People
Playboy
Playgirl
Premiere
San Francisco Chronicle
San Francisco Examiner
Time
Us
Vanity Fair

Television Programs

Barbara Walter's Interviews (ABC)
Hard Copy (syndicated)
Hollywood Babylon (VH-1)
Jonathan Ross Presents . . . (VH-1)